AF600605

THE UNIVERSAL DECLARATION OF HUMAN RIGHTS AND THE HOLOCAUST

THE UNIVERSAL DECLARATION OF HUMAN RIGHTS AND THE HOLOCAUST

AN ENDANGERED CONNECTION

JOHANNES MORSINK

Georgetown University Press / Washington, DC

Library of Congress Cataloging-in-Publication Data

Names: Morsink, Johannes, author.
Title: The Universal Declaration of Human Rights and the Holocaust : An Endangered Connection / Johannes Morsink.
Description: Washington, DC : Georgetown University Press, 2019. | Includes bibliographical references and index.
Identifiers: LCCN 2018003847 (print) | LCCN 2018033165 (ebook) | ISBN 9781626166301 (ebook) | ISBN 9781626166295 | ISBN 9781626166295 q(pbk. : qalk. paper) | ISBN 9781626166288 q(hardcover : qalk. paper) | ISBN 9781626166301 q(ebook)
Subjects: LCSH: United Nations. General Assembly. Universal Declaration of Human Rights. | Human rights. | Human rights movements. | Holocaust, Jewish (1939-1945)—Influence.
Classification: LCC K3238.31948 (ebook) | LCC K3238.31948 .M668 2019 (print)| DDC 341.4/8—dc23
LC record available at https://lccn.loc.gov/2018003847

∞ This book is printed on acid-free paper meeting the requirements of the American National Standard for Permanence in Paper for Printed Library Materials.

20 19 9 8 7 6 5 4 3 2 First printing

Printed in the United States of America.

Cover design by John Barnett.

To the memory of my parents, who,
during the Nazi occupation of the Netherlands,
in word and deed upheld the values this book defends.

CONTENTS

ACKNOWLEDGMENTS

Having as a professor made the library my home base on the Drew University campus, I am most indebted to Drew librarians for their help with yet another book on the Universal Declaration of Human Rights. Some of them need to be singled out because their expertise was repeatedly put to speedy use to help me write this book. I thank Rick Mikulski, who, as a historian and librarian overseeing Drew's collection of government documents, was an invaluable source for brainstorming about UN-related materials and for finding stuff we thought was lost or never existed. Similarly, I thank Jennifer Heise for help with both UN documentation and the reference section of this book. No library can have all the materials a scholar needs. So I need to thank Brian Tervo, head of Drew's Interlibrary Loan Office, who was most helpful in getting me items Drew did not have. I also thank Verna Holcomb in the Instructional Technology Center for helping me send off the manuscript in the required format. Of a totally different order are the thanks I owe my wife, Nancy, for creating an atmosphere at home that is conducive to researching and writing.

INTRODUCTION

The Universal Declaration as Postcard

In 1990 the headquarters of the Jewish police of the World War II ghetto in Lodz, Poland, was demolished, and a number of postcards were found. Gregory Fried bought one of these cards from a Polish dealer. It is a banal little thing, one side blank for a message and the other side split in half with the return address on the top left and the addressee on the right. It had a six-pfennige German stamp on it with a picture of Adolf Hitler above the words "Deutsches Reich." The return address was listed as A. Fajwlewciz, Litzmannstadt (Ghetto) Trödlerstrasse 15. (After Hitler and Joseph Stalin had divided Poland between them in 1939, the Germans changed the city's name from Lodz to Litzmannstadt, after a German general who had died in the area in World War I.) The postcard was addressed to a certain Hern J. Zuraw, the sender's brother who lived in the ghetto of Kraków, Poland, at Lwowska 5. Let's read it:

> Litzmannstadt, 24 December 1941
>
> My Dear Brother, Sister-in-law and Josiu! Your postcard, as well as the newspaper, I have received, for which I warmly thank you. Dear Mother is better, thank God. It makes me very happy that Josiu is working and earning so much money.

> I ask you please write me everything exactly. Also write me how Hella is doing with her health. Why doesn't Hella write me a few words? With us everything is as it was. We are, thank God, healthy; may God give you the same. Otherwise nothing special except many greetings and kisses, a special greeting and many kisses for Josiu. Also a warm greeting from dear Mother. Gucia and Abram please answer right away! (Fried 1998, 32)

Across the front of the postcard, the ghetto censor had stamped "*Inhalt Unszulässig*" (contents inadmissible). And Fried noticed that the words "as the newspaper, I have received" had been underlined with a blue pencil, as was the street part of the return address. As it reads on the surface, the card is an innocuous one. Just "a little chit-chat about people's health, polite inquiries about family activities, tid-bits of news—'nothing special.'" Ignoring the stamped message, the card looks "like something sent home from a summer vacation" (33). Of course, it is no such thing, and Fried decided to search out as much of the truth behind this card as he could. Who were Gucia and Abram, and why was their card never delivered? In a wonderful essay titled "*Inhalt Unszulässig*: Late Mail from Lodz—A Meditation on Time and Truth," Fried reports on what he found out about the Lodz ghetto in December 1941 and then turns one of the orthographic errors Gucia made in her imperfect German into a probing meditation on the relationships among modernity, the Holocaust, and postmodernity.

Using a variety of sources, Fried discovered that for the people in the Lodz ghetto in December 1941, instead of "everything" almost nothing "is/was as it was." In an area of only 1.6 square miles lived 144,000 Jews, crammed 5.8 persons to a room. Transports of Jews from German cities and the Prague and Vienna environs added to this number, while deportations to what many still thought of as "labor camps" further east were soon to reduce the total. Raul Hilberg reports that in the first five months of 1942, a third—that is, 55,000—of the inhabitants of the Lodz ghetto were shipped to the Chelmno death camp, which was located a little more than ten kilometers from the city (Fried 1998, 35).

The inhabitants were not to have any contact with the outside world, which, of course, precluded receiving newspapers. Fried therefore speculates that "the Jewish censors probably feared for their own sake that the German authorities would detect such a card, for it was the censors who had allowed the newspaper to get through in the first place. Better to remove the postcard from circulation entirely" (32). Hence the stamp "*Inhalt Unszulässig*." So the card was never sent to Kraków and became late mail for Fried and for us. The street part of the return address was marked with the same blue pencil because Gucia had written "Trödlerstrasse," which apparently did not exist, whereas Trödlergasse, meaning "Peddler's Alley," did exist. That's about it. All cards had to be written in German, and it is clear from the grammatical errors that German was not the native tongue of the Fajwlewicz family. For example, the Yiddish *zenen* shines through in the German "Wir senen [i.e., sind] G.z.D. Gesund." For the translated "With us everything is as it was," Gucia wrote, "Bei uns ist alles so wie es wahr." She had mistakenly used the German word *wahr*, which means "truth," where she should have used the past tense of "to be," which is *war*. The censors did not mark this mistake, but Fried turns the inadvertent insertion of the *h* and the conflation of "was" and "true" into a long meditation about whether it makes sense for us to search out the truth in and about the past, especially the Holocaust.

Chronicles of the ghetto show that in the week before the card was put in the mail, a tailor on his way to work had been shot by a sentry, and another man had been shot when trying to escape police custody. People were talking about these shootings and about the increased famine owing to the new arrivals from the west. In addition there were rumors about a speech that the megalomaniac chairman of the ghetto, Chaim Rumkowski, had given to the ghetto administrators. He said that he was sick and tired of the criminals, who "multiplie[d] like mushrooms after the rain . . . and [could] see no other way than to send this undesirable element out of the ghetto" (Fried 1998, 34). He had been ordered to thin out the population by 20,000 but had been able to talk the Germans down to half that much. Fortunately, he added, "on the basis of my authority and the ghetto's autonomy, I received permission to have the selection for deportation done by us alone" (35). So he announced the creation of a special committee of his "most trusted associates" to make the selections that would in the next five months add up to 50,000 and that in the end would kill all but 10,000 of the 190,000 that passed through the Lodz ghetto. Of that total, 120,000 were murdered in Chelmno and

Auschwitz and 60,000 in Lodz itself. We do not know how heavy receiving a newspaper from Kraków weighed with the police and so cannot be sure that the Fajwlewicz family was among this first wave of deportees. But Fried is surely right to think that the Fajwlewicz and Zuraw families "were almost certainly Polish Jews who had been confined to ghettos in Poland by the Third Reich and . . . [that they] almost certainly died along with millions of others, either killed at a death camp, or less directly murdered by starvation, suicide or disease" (24).

The postcard was picked up by the wind of circumstance and connected by Fried to the lava of hell that flowed out of this ghetto into the Nazi inferno called the Holocaust, with most of the Lodz "residents" going to the Chelmno camp located nearby. Fried spends most of his essay meditating in a Kierkegaardian fashion on the mistake Gucia made when she put that *h* into the German word *war*, which means "was" in English. She conflated the past / *war* with the truth / *wahr*. This conflation leads Fried to meditate on what he sees as the anti-foundationalism and frivolous play character of postmodern thinkers such as Jacques Derrida, Martin Heidegger, Michel Foucault, and Roland Barthes. It disturbs Fried to think that after the rupture of the Holocaust, all reading is seen by these authors as nothing more than interpretive play with an endless succession of different readings of the same text without an original standard of authorial truth or fact by which to judge the multiplicity of competing and conflicting interpretations. In the literature of postmodernism, the modern author as originator of a text has been supplanted by the reader's personal and subjective interpretations of the text. Fried is disturbed by this play reading taking place in the shadow of the Holocaust. For him the Holocaust is an incontrovertible fact of history on which he wants to help cast light with his research of this postcard from Lodz.

Since the 1948 Universal Declaration of Human Rights (UDHR) was written in this same shadow of the Holocaust, I sympathize with Fried's thesis. He takes the postcard seriously because he takes the Holocaust seriously. I feel the same way about my chosen text, the Universal Declaration of Human Rights. Fried titled his meditation "Time and Truth," for he does not want the passage of time to cloud the truth of what happened. This is not unlike the idea of "an endangered connection," which I use as the subtitle of this book. What goads

Fried into his meditation is not just personal curiosity about the truth behind this postcard—a curiosity he did satisfy to some extent. He uses his investigation of the truths behind the card to take issue with postmodern thinkers for whom the author of a text is no longer important and for whom there are no objective truths in the past or of the world generally. Fried disagrees with those who do not think there is that kind of factual and objective truth for us to search out.

On the surface we can easily recognize the threefold division of history into premodern, modern, and postmodern epochs; the Holocaust is seen as the final stage of the modern, just before the commencement of the postmodern. Fried (1998) quotes from Zygmunt Bauman's *Modernity and the Holocaust*: "If the pre-modern world was grounded in transcendent faith and unquestionable tradition for its guidance, and the modern world cast off these props in favor of a direction grounded in humanity's own proud rationality, then perhaps postmodernity announces a world where both faith and reason, both Jerusalem and Athens, have failed us, leaving us to freefall without foundation, center or certainty" (36). This free fall is what worries Fried.

The book I have written also is the result of a worry about this kind of free fall among certain contemporary historians and international legal scholars. My worry is that what I see as a causal motivational connection between the Holocaust and the Universal Declaration is endangered by these new historians and legal scholars. To preserve the connection between two pivotal events, I make the case that both historically and philosophically the adoption of the declaration and the certitude with which it was announced to the world are best explained by and traced back to the event of the Holocaust. Being serious about human rights and all they stand for means to me being serious about the Holocaust, and being serious about the Holocaust means we need to be serious about human rights. The connection goes both ways. I think of it as a cloud that happens to have a silver lining to which I want to draw my readers' attention.

For Fried the "post" in postmodernity is no longer indicative of a "shining future" in which we are guided by reason to an ever better world order. It instead indicates "afterward," an after-the-Holocaust world where uncertainty reigns and we grope our way among multiple readings of a text that has no sure foundation in an objective reality of historical facts. For postmodern thinkers the Holocaust signals the end of modernity in which the rational and executive efficiency of the "Final Solution" created a "rupture" in which "the temporal division of epochs according to the vantage point of modernity collapses and begins to erase itself" (Fried 1998, 36). Fried complains, "While Derrida seems acquainted with standards for moral condemnation and epistemic judgment, he reserves this knowledge for himself; he offers us nothing with which we *can* defend the truth as something *given*, as something impervious to 'abyssal' mythologization and perverse manipulation" (44; original italics). Fried himself, by contrast, "tried to uncover the truth of the circumstances of its [the postcard's] writing." He admits that that might be a bit naive but is distraught by the idea that the "postmodern critique of the conventional understanding of truth (. . . as a re-presentation of reality which corresponds to the facts) does not simply shed doubt on the methodologies for ascertaining the truth" but attacks the very idea of "absolute truth, of truth immune to dissolution, for 'Truth' is always an attempt to freeze the temporal play of meaning" (44). He sees the postmodern political gambit as "essentially anarchic" because it unhinges "all principles, all foundations, all Truths, and all absolutes" (41).

Fried's reconstruction of the conditions under which the postcard from Lodz was written is meant to serve as an antidote to this postmodern trend not to carry anything over from the modern period (which includes the Holocaust) to what supposedly comes after. I want to carry our text—the Universal Declaration of Human Rights—over from the modern Holocaust event as a set of moral truths discovered in that abomination and its aftermath and therefore worth preserving. In my own research on the Universal Declaration, I have also experienced this postcard effect of whittling away at basic truths and historical connections between, on the one hand, the abomination that was the Holocaust and, on the other hand, the birth of a universal code of ethics three years after the liberation of the camps. When Fried bought that postcard, he had the urge to trace the facts behind it. Similarly, in the early 1980s, when I first discovered the text of the Universal Declaration, I had the urge to research the conditions under which it was written. I went to the New York United Nations Library and Xeroxed sixty pounds of archival material that informs this pivotal text. This same material is today available in both digital and hard-copy form. With some notable exceptions, human rights historians and legal scholars have not been all that serious about the declaration, mostly I think because they fail to appreciate its connection with the Holocaust. They probably think that nothing good can or could come out of the Holocaust. While scholars make the usual scholarly references to the Universal Declaration, they have not pursued in what way the Holocaust and other Nazi crimes were the impetus or catalyst for the writing of this pivotal text.

The new historians I survey in chapters 1 and 2 indirectly question this linkage. While most of them endanger the connection by playing it down or ignoring it, some go out of their way to call the connection "a foundation myth" or simply "a myth." In part 2 of the book, I explore the philosophical fallout of that missed linkage.

"But the Holocaust is an event which appeals to us to 'Never Forget!'" says Fried. And he notes, "The exclamation point here is important: it gives an appeal the tenor of a command" (Fried 1998, 44). He is right. We too feel this duty in all the writings, films, workshops, museums, and Kristallnacht commemorations my readers are familiar with and know about. We must prove false the predictions of the death camp guards when they taunted their prisoners, saying they and not their prisoners would win the war, a fact none of these by then gassed victims would be able to verify. Asks Fried, "But what and how are we to remember if there is no truth and there are no facts, and the voices of those who survived as witnesses will succumb to silence all too soon?" How then are we to prove these guards wrong? The birth of the Universal Declaration out of that ghastly inferno is living proof of those guards' falsehoods. But also "the 'Never Forget!' implies that memory and, indeed, that knowledge and truth itself are fragile" (44). That too is true, and as I argue in the conclusion to this book, it makes it all the more important that nations and cities around the world are erecting museums to help us commemorate what happened, to whom it was done, by whom it was done, and for what reasons. I ask that we carry that commemoration over into our human rights activities.

To remember the Holocaust simply or only as the "rupture" of the metaphysics of presence, as postmodern thinkers seem to do, would in Fried's view be "pretty thin gruel" (45). I join him in denying that this kind of absolute rupture took place, and I affirm his observation that "commemoration asks that we seek to recover the lost voices of these dead, these authors of these countless lost texts, lost conversations, lost prayers; that we recover millions of 'someones' as persons, in all their human specificity, from the traces and scraps which they have left behind" (46). To all these millions of "someones," this book offers the billions of "everyones" who are addressed in the litany of "everyones" with which almost every article of the Universal Declaration starts.

Fried's own curiosity about life in the Lodz ghetto, Gucia's inadvertent insertion of that *h* into the German past tense *war*, and Fried's own desire to gainsay postmodernity's denial—because it is all a mere matter of interpretation—that there are any truths out there to be found led Fried to write the meditation on which I here reported. His meditation is the first essay in the volume *Postmodernism and the Holocaust*. I reported on it because I share his desire to gainsay postmodernism's denial that there are truths in texts and of texts to be found out, especially if those texts have to do with the Holocaust. The main goal of this book is therefore to restore this connection between the Holocaust and the Universal Declaration of Human Rights. Not so much against the writings of the postmodernists with whom Fried dialogues as against contemporary historians and postwar international legal experts with whom I differ on what truths are to be found in and behind the text of the declaration and what the overall meaning of this text is.

I have seven reasons for looking at the Universal Declaration as a lost postcard that needs to be reconnected to the Holocaust reality out of which it came. As I state them I give the reader a glimpse at the book's five chapters and conclusion.

First, even now—some seventy years after its 1948 adoption—the declaration is for many of us still a piece of late mail. It was not held up by any group of censors but by postwar historians and political/legal theorists who have not studied this pivotal text as a useful source for the postwar reconstruction of our world. While reconstruction is what the UDHR drafters intended their text to be used for, it is not what most historians and legal theorists take away from the document. I mean to change that equation. Throughout this book I use the following timeline for the development of human rights: idea → Holocaust +

UDHR text → system → movement. Chapter 1 talks about the first link of this chart and shows how recent literature on the idea of human rights fails to make the desired connection between the UDHR and the Holocaust. Researchers play down either the Holocaust or the declaration or both. The chapter shows that for most of the historians I name, the Universal Declaration is a piece of late mail that they have barely opened. In chapter 2 I single out Samuel Moyn because his dismissal of the connection is not inadvertent but willful, requiring a special refutation. In chapter 3 I myself read the mail and defend the 1948 adoption of the UDHR as *the* historic moment for our modern conception of human rights. Chapters 4 and 5 explain the philosophical impact of that historic moment on the later development of the international legal human rights system. In chapter 4 I offer an alternative to the reigning international positivism by defending the influence of the Universal Declaration on the current body of international human rights law. In chapter 5 I follow that up with the argument that human rights belong primarily to flesh and blood human beings such as those who died in the camps and that there are no territorial human rights that belong to collectivities as such. In the conclusion I discuss the impact of these two (historic and philosophic) moments on the human rights movement that makes up the last bin of the above flowchart.

The first three chapters are devoted to separating out the second link (Holocaust + UDHR text) from the other links in the chart and to restoring that link to what the UDHR drafters had in mind when they adopted the declaration in December 1948. Many new historians and legal theorists move too quickly from the *idea* of human rights to the later developed *system* and *movement*. The second link has dropped below their intellectual radar. In chapters 4 and 5, I add the charge that theorists of the later system years of the fifties and sixties and of movement years of the seventies have also failed to appreciate the connection I hold up in this book. For both these groups (historians and legal theorists), the declaration has been a piece of late mail from the Holocaust. They have not much studied the text of the declaration and have certainly not read it as mail delivered in the shadow of the Holocaust. Not just Fried's postmodern thinkers reject the idea of universal values and truths of the kind embedded in the declaration; Anglo-American political and legal philosophers have also never warmed up to the idea of a universal morality bequeathed to us by a text like the declaration adopted just three years after the camps closed. The thinkers with whom I disagree tend to pass by the gates of Auschwitz with averted theoretical gaze. I give examples of this averted gaze in all the chapters of this book.

The sad thing is that the Universal Declaration has lain on the floor of the academy, overlooked by the great works of political and legal philosophy or theory. Both Rawls in the Anglo-American world and Habermas on the European continent came to the idea of human rights late in their careers, and when they did come to it, they did not explore the connection between these human rights and their origin in the horrors of the Holocaust. These two thinkers operate with a procedural conception of justice and a coherence theory of truth that cannot accommodate (at the level of theorizing) the real world of the concentration camps or, for that matter, any of the gruesome massacres we have seen since. This defect has carried over into the followers of these giants in the political/legal theory field. What is needed to defend human rights morally and intellectually is an experience of radical evil (of the kind seen in the camps) that serves as a constant commemorative reference point to provide a philosophical anchor for a correspondence notion of truth found in the declaration. From horrific experiences like these, we learn the truths that become the foundation stones for political and legal theorizing that then informs domestic legislation. The truths of these experiences set limits to any procedures theorists and legislators may want to design.

Second, intellectually the Universal Declaration is far more like a postcard than like a piece of extended discourse. Its surface text, while full of practical and moral advice, contains no explicit, worked-out theories of philosophy, religion, or history. The practical advice it gives is backed only by mere hints of any kind of theory, which hints I explored in my earlier book *Inherent Human Rights: The Philosophical Roots of the Universal Declaration* (Morsink 2009). Perhaps the postcard character of the document is why so many theoreticians have ignored it for so long. In my first volume on the declaration (Morsink 1999b), I sought to reconstruct the document's authorial intentions based on a close reading of the *travaux préparatoires* the way Fried elicited the help of the chronicle written about the Lodz ghetto. But while often noted, that *Origins* volume often is not closely studied. Even now that these *travaux* are available both in hard copy (Schabas 2013) and in a searchable virtual one, the connection between the Holocaust and the declaration has not received the attention it should. There are strong hints of what the authors had in mind when they declared on December 10, 1948, that all people are born with equal and inalienable rights. Even a casual reader cannot fail to see in this immediate post-Holocaust language a continuation of Enlightenment modes of thought. It therefore cannot be that the Holocaust is the rupture that postmodern theorists say it represents. As I argue in chapter 3, "The 1940s Moment of Human Rights," there has got to be a link between the events that constitute attempts to erase the humanity from whole groups of human beings and a declaration that is shaped by the conscience of that same humanity. It is a connection between two kinds of universality, one a universal abomination and the other a universal morality, a point I further explore in the conclusion.

Third, just as Fried felt an obligation to commemorate the authors of the Lodz card, so this entire volume serves to commemorate both those who died in the camps and those who in the late 1940s drafted this 1948 code of universal morality as a response to their deaths. I take up that commemorative task most clearly in the conclusion of this book, setting the stage with the historic moment laid out in chapter 3. I follow up those history chapters of part 1 by showing in part 2 that the 1948 Universal Declaration went on to become the moral engine of a totally new area of international human rights with over a hundred legally binding treaties, many of which admit to being inspired by the moral code of the UDHR. For decades I have been drawn to the philosophical underpinnings of the UDHR, but I have only of late come to realize that before anything else the attention of the world community needs to be drawn to the very existence of this moral code so that (like that Lodz card that Fried researched) it is not lost to posterity owing to neglect. Throughout, but especially toward the end of chapter 4, I contend that the second link of our chart (idea → Holocaust + UDHR text → system → movement) is crucial for understanding all the other links, especially the last two. Unfortunately, this link is in danger of being overwhelmed by the other links in the chart because the new historians of part 1 move too quickly from one bin in this timeline to another, while the legal theorists discussed in part 2 remain stuck in their positivist sclerosis. By keeping an eye on the second link throughout and returning to it in the conclusion, I have sought to slow down these rapid-fire histories and these quick refusals of moral transcendence by international legal theorists.

Fourth, just like the Lodz card, which was written under conditions of severe censorship and therefore could contain only hints of things that could not be said, so the entire declaration was written under great time pressures and its last revisions overlapped with the onset of the Cold War. These pressures prevented the drafters from saying things that they at other times would have had no trouble saying. What they did not say is at times as important as what they did say, not just practically but also and especially from a philosophical point of view. Chapter 5 makes that point with the argument that the Universal Declaration has an unfortunate blind spot in it because it does not sufficiently protect the rights of members of minority groups. Many of the articles of the declaration are like fragments that cannot be fit together into one neat theory (though I tried to do that in my *Roots* book) but that fit together much better once we are aware of the conditions under which the document was written. In the fifth chapter, I suggest that we look at Article 27 of the International Covenant on Civil and Political Rights (ICCPR), the locus classicus of minority rights, as an amendment to the Universal Declaration. That amendment completes the philosophical framework of the declaration. I go on to demote a large segment of the third-generation rights with the argument that there are no such things as territorial human rights possessed by collectivities as such. I use the collectivist ontology of the common Article 1 of the ICCPR and International Covenant on Economic, Social, and Cultural Rights (ICESCR) as my case study. No matter how crucial to human development, a group of people as such is not a flesh and blood human being. It therefore cannot have genuine *human* rights.

Fifth, a postcard is usually sent to someone who knows the sender, to remind the recipient that the sender is thinking of him or her. The Lodz card was a piece of communication between family members. I see the declaration as a postcard from some members of the human family to all the rest of humankind, especially ordinary men and women of all walks of life in all cultures and corners of the world. It was with them in mind that the document was kept as brief and pithy as it is and why the politics of human rights must be carried on in their name. Shame on us if our scholarship clutters the landscape or clouds the message more than it already is.

Sixth, the Lodz card was written by someone whose native tongue was not German, which means that there are surface mistakes that luckily do not block our comprehension. In fact, they reveal things to us about the authors and senders. Similarly, while a few of the inner circle of drafters were philosophers and jurists by trade, most of them were not. Eleanor Roosevelt is a case in point, although she did function as a buffer between the two major antagonists in the Cold War, which was heating up toward the end of the UDHR deliberations. This means that any number of philosophical problems had to be dealt with on a level of practical and intuitive consensus rather than abstract argumentation. This may well be the reason why the document has become such a stunning practical success, for it was not driven or primarily written by intellectuals. It may also explain why it remained for so long under the radar of the scholarly establishment. While intellectually it is clearly incomplete and at some points probably mistaken, on an intuitive level it hangs together very well. What ties it together more than anything else is the fact that it was written in the shadow of the Holocaust. That event ran like a subtext throughout all the discussions, rose to the surface at some crucial points, and influenced many a vote. No delegation dared vote against the final version.

Seventh, like Fried, who—even after his investigations—could not really be sure who the two families were and what really happened to them, so I do not claim in any of my volumes on the Universal Declaration to have uncovered the meaning of this document for all time. Those other volumes and the chapters of the present one invite readers to join me in a continuing process of discovery as to what in our own time of chaos in world affairs the message from the Holocaust is for members of the human family the world over.

Part I

THE HISTORIC MOMENT

1

NEW HISTORIANS AND THE DECLARATION

When we look at the fast-growing field of human rights literature, it might be helpful to separate at least four (or perhaps five) possible fields of discussion, each with a different aim or emphasis and also quite different sources. Since the phenomenon of human rights is presently occurring but also has quite a history, all the authors writing on human rights are in some way bound to be historians, going way back to ancient times or narrowly focusing on our contemporary era. Even so, I find it helpful to approach the literature of human rights with this simple diagram or flowchart in mind: idea → UDHR text → system → movement.

The reader should take these arrows very loosely as both chronological and causal indicators. I think of the historical *idea* of human rights as preceding and causally (note the "loosely" above) leading to the *text* of the 1948 Universal Declaration of Human Rights. And I think of the UDHR text as being the inspiration for and in that way the cause of the legal human rights *system* that has enveloped our world and similarly as being the foundational text for the huge human rights *movement* we find operating today on all continents and in all countries.

I am not suggesting that all human rights authors and activists subscribe to this flow of events. But this diagram does underlie the arguments of this book. In various chapters I seek to explain or establish one or more of these arrows. My view is that when authors, as some do, shift back and forth between the various segments or discourses of this chart, they make it difficult for readers to evaluate the theses of their books or articles. I present a detailed case of this in chapter 2. Much of the present chapter is devoted to my use of this diagram as bins into which I suggest we drop various recent human rights publications. This exercise puts my views at odds with much of the recent literature on human rights in the sense that many human rights authors do not limit themselves to writing in just one category or bin of the chart. Many shift too quickly from bin to bin, paying insufficient attention to the causal arrows or—as we sometimes do in our sums—forgetting to carry anything over from one bin to the next.

The thesis of this first chapter is that the link between the event of the Holocaust and the UDHR text is frequently downplayed or ignored and, in my view, endangered. I argue that what I call the "new historians" (because they have spoken up recently) have downgraded the UDHR text far below the status it should have in our modern conception of human rights. The reason for this neglect is the lack of interest in the influence of the Holocaust on the writing of the UDHR. In the other three chapters of this book, I further explore the connection between the event of the Holocaust and the declaration. In what follows I put some authors and their articles or books into the chronological bins of this chart.

The Idea before the 1940s

In human rights literature, one can find a body of work that discusses primarily the history of the *idea* (or concept) of human rights. Some of these intellectual historians trace the idea of human rights way back to ancient times (Lauren 1998; Ishay 2004; Wolterstorff 2008), while others, like Moyn (2010) and Eckel (2014), believe it originated in the 1970s. Of the authors mentioned, Lauren's account of the "evolution" of the concept in the 1940s is the most complete. Yet, because he does not link the Holocaust explicitly and directly to the declaration's text, his otherwise excellent history weakens the unique role the Holocaust had in the birth of our modern conception of human rights. None of the writers who take the idea all the way back to the Greeks, Romans, or Christians and then connect that lineage to our own times do justice to the event of the Holocaust, which this book argues is the birthing ground for the contemporary notion of human rights. This is not to say that ancient philosophers like the Stoics had no thoughts about a universal ethic. It is only to say that the idea of human rights does not really have a smooth or incremental evolutionary history that finally blossomed after World War II or even later than that. Against this idea of a final blossoming, I maintain that the contemporary notion of human rights burst on our world on account of the Nazi horrors, which is a thesis I defend in detail in chapter 3, preparing the ground in chapters 1 and 2.

Some authors believe the *idea* has a long history but choose to lift up only one particular historical era for attention. While in *Bury the Chains* Adam Hochschild (2005) wrote about the British antislavery movement, Elizabeth Borgwardt (2005) expanded Franklin Roosevelt's Four Freedoms into *A New Deal for the World.* Lynn Hunt in her *Inventing Human Rights* (2007) has a similar era-focused approach when she argues that human rights were invented around the time of the French Revolution. This literature on the history of the *idea* of human rights is probably the largest of the four discourses I mentioned, for these historical explorations readily overlap with the other bins in the chart. Someone can write a history of water and either have or not have any additional interest in the chemical composition of water. In that way historians of the idea of human rights differ quite a bit in their explorations of the content of the *idea* of human rights, definitionally speaking. At that point the emphasis shifts from the history of the *idea* to the philosophy of the *concept* of human rights, and the author becomes a philosopher more than a historian. Both Nicholas Wolterstorff (2008), who traces the idea back to Judeo-Christian beginnings, and Lynn Hunt (2007), who sticks to the invention of the idea during the Enlightenment era, have a philosophical interest in the content of the idea of human rights. These authors do not just help us see the historical trajectory of the idea; they also share their views on what the content of the concept of a human right is. Their historical work therefore runs over into what in the second half of this volume I call the "Philosophic Moment" of human rights though I do not give either of them a role to play there.

One book of essays, *Revisiting the Origins of Human Rights* (Slotte and Halme-Tuomisaari 2015), has not just revisited the origins of our *idea* of human rights, but its editors in their introductory essay specifically focus on the timeline arrow between the first bin *idea* and the second one of the *UDHR text*. They point out that the open-endedness of the idea in its history fits poorly with what they call today's "textbook narrative," according to which human rights are "entities with an absolute, predefined essence." I do not question the editors' claim that their contributors give us an idea of human rights that is quite "open-ended and ambiguous . . . [and] . . . formed around an ideal of the universal human being as free and equal in particular" (1). But I do question that this idea "corrects" what they say is "the textbook narrative," in which human rights have an "essence" that sets the tone for us today. I agree that there was indeed a tightening of the idea of human rights in the 1940s, but not along the lines of a "predefined essence." The puzzle then is *why* there was this "tightening" (to call it that)—on which the editors and I agree—instead of *how* the history of the idea (as seen in these essays) corrects the contemporary "textbook narrative." I see no correction between what the contributing essays reveal is an open-ended idea and our own contemporary notion of human rights. Rather, I see a new start because of the intervention of the Holocaust into the history of the idea.

The editors wrap what I see as the main impulse behind our contemporary notion of human rights into a vague textbook narrative that I think happens to be correct but that is anchored in the outside Holocaust event instead of having evolved internally. If the content of the "textbook narrative" is properly specified, as it is in this book, then no correction was needed, because the tightening that took place and resulted in our contemporary notion of human rights is best explained by the event of the Holocaust, out of which cauldron came the text of the Universal Declaration. This Holocaust birth of that text constitutes the contemporary narrative of human rights, or so I argue.

I agree with the editors that there is an "internal coherence, logical continuity and comprehensiveness" to the contemporary notion of human rights, but I differ on what the source of these characteristics is. The editors do not tell us what produced these characteristics other than referring readers to some prominent law textbooks, like Henry J. Steiner and Philip Alston's very complete and often updated *International Human Rights in Context: Law, Politics, Morals*, which I myself used for some ten years in different editions (Slotte and Halme-Tuomisaari 2015, 3n3). Checking law textbooks, the editors got the "sneaking suspicion" that they "were effectively reading the same textbook narrative over and over again, as if it had been simply copied and pasted from one book to the next" (4). Might there not be a standard law textbook narrative about the origin of human rights because, as I argue in chapter 4, the Holocaust had a huge impact on the writing of the declaration and in that way informed our own contemporary notion of human rights?

What irks the editors of this revisitation volume is that a batch of scholars have wrapped the "textbook narrative as legitimating myth" (Slotte and Halme-Tuomisaari 2015, 10–16), a myth that is totally insensitive to the realities found on the ground by the contributors to their volume. Here the editors claim that the openness of the idea before the 1940s conflicts with the tightening of the concept after that date. These textbook and mythmaking theorists ignore "discussions of how reality is always mediated through language, thus resonating with 'hermeneutic naiveté,' the belief in 'immaculate perception'" (citing Gardner 2010, 10). The editors "paired" this mythical status of the contemporary notion with their own earlier suspicions and conclude that "the textbook narrative is a story with unknown origins and authorship that is frequently presented without references, yet with virtually unaltered details"; at this point the story has started "to resemble a myth" (11). I think the editors are tempted by this mythical origin of our contemporary notion of human rights because they themselves have no better explanation for "the internal coherence, logical continuity, and seeming comprehensiveness" of that notion. I ask whether instead of being hermeneutically naive these textbook authors may not have experienced the reality of the Holocaust through the mediation of human rights language.

The entire revisitation volume, editors and contributors alike, ignores the main reason why our own notion of human rights is tighter than the idea before 1948. This is especially evident in part 3 of the volume (titled "Institutional Practices and Relations of Rights: Towards the Universal Declaration of Human Rights") because none of the essays even in this part focus specifically on the drafting years (1946–48) of the UDHR. Yet these are the years our notion of human rights was made internally coherent and comprehensive beyond anything that came before. The results can be seen in the UDHR preamble and its thirty articles, unanimously adopted by the 1948 Third General Assembly of the United Nations.

If we separate the idea (in its historical sense) from the concept (in its philosophical sense), then in the first three chapters of this book I defend the late 1940s (specifically 1946–48) as the *historic moment* for human rights, and in the last two chapters I defend those same late 1940s years, running over into the 1950s and 1960s, as the *philosophic moment* for human rights. These two moments for human rights overlap because each is defined by the causal connection I defend between the Holocaust and the text of the Universal Declaration. Before I discuss the second bin of our chart (idea → UDHR text → system → movement), I need to explain that the Universal Declaration and its legacy make up just one of two tracks that came out of the cauldron that was the Holocaust.

The Holocaust Cauldron

That the Holocaust was a cauldron out of which came numerous horrors, some leading to numerous prosecutions—and not just the Nuremberg and Tokyo Trials—has recently been made clear by Dan Plesch in his revealing book *Human Rights after Hitler* (2017). Plesch records in detail the work done by the United Nations War Crimes Commission (UNWCC) in the years 1943–48. By the time the commission folded owing to lack of support by the United Kingdom and the US State Department, it had aided in the indictments of "more than thirty-six thousand individuals and units" (5). "The records," says Plesch, "overturn one of the most important accepted truths concerning the Holocaust: that despite the heroic efforts of escapees from Nazi-occupied Europe, the Allies never officially accepted the reality of the Holocaust and therefore never condemned it until the camps were liberated after the war" (6). In an early chapter, Plesch shows how "contrary to conventional understanding, the Allies did in fact repeatedly and in detail condemn what we now call the Holocaust, as well as other crimes committed by the Nazis" (4). In his fifth chapter, Plesch describes indictments "for anti-Jewish persecution" that "appear to have been unknown to scholars for the last seventy years" (112). The soldiers indicted were mostly members of the Wehrmacht (armed forces), the Schutzstaffel (SS), the Sicherheitsdienst (the Security and Intelligence Service), and the Geheime Staatspolizei, or Gestapo. The indictments were "against low- and mid-level participants in the extermination of the Jews because their actions were such an important part of Nazi crimes and because the general assumption is that there was very little attempt by the victorious Allies to take legal action against those who exterminated the Jews" (113). Plesch's table 5.1 gives us a list of indictments for anti-Jewish crimes submitted to the UNWCC. It lists 3,999 for Belgium, 55 for Czechoslovakia (52 versus Germany and 3 versus Hungary), 14 for Denmark, 93 for France (91 versus Germany and 2 versus Italy), 16 for Greece (4 versus Bulgaria and 12 versus Germany), 4 for Luxembourg, 110 for the Netherlands, 9 for Norway, 372 for Poland, 24 for the United Kingdom (21 versus Germany and 1 each for Italy and Japan), 5 for the United States (4 versus Germany and 1 versus Japan), and 42 for Yugoslavia (30 versus Germany, 7 versus Hungary, and 2 versus Italy). These anti-Jewish indictments are part of a far larger and more general horror show.

The UN War Crimes Commission operated as an international clearinghouse for the prosecution of mostly German, Italian, and Japanese war criminals. The seventeen member nations of the UNWCC presented to the commission dossiers and charge files that summarized the cases they wanted to bring. Between 1944 and 1948, the UNWCC approved more than 36,000 individuals and units for prosecution. "If the cases were approved, the individuals and units were listed as accused and the nations concerned sought to apprehend them and bring them to trial in national courts" (46). One of Plesch's tables shows the nationality and the numbers of persons charged by the governments that were UNWCC member nations and therefore listed by the commission: Albanian, 38; Bulgarian, 422; German, 34,270; Hungarian, 69; Italian, 1,204; Japanese, 363; Romanian, 4. Different tables break down the numbers of prosecuted people into Germans, Italians, and Japanese by countries that filed the charges and conducted the prosecution. Following is a list of nations that prosecuted German persons with the number in parentheses; some of the trials, including most US ones, were held in the respective German occupation zones: Belgium (4,592), Canada (30, plus through the UK), China (1), Czechoslovakia (1,543), Denmark (159), France (12,546), Greece (339), India (through the UK), Luxembourg (90), Netherlands (2,423), New Zealand (through the UK), Norway (209), Poland (7,805), the United Kingdom (1,709), the United States (828), Yugoslavia (1,926), UNWCC (70) (table 4.2). Additionally, as seen from these numbers, Ethiopia (10), France (85), Greece (191), the United Kingdom (188), the United States (3), and Yugoslavia (809) charged many Italian persons (table 4.3), and Australia (94), France (3), the United Kingdom (120), and the United States (223) charged Japanese persons (table 4.4). All this activity took place before the fall of 1948, when the UNWCC stopped operating because of a lack of funds (mostly withheld by the US), and much of it commenced long before the end of the war (see Plesch 2017, chap. 5). In his essay "The Two Different Ways of Looking at Nazi Murder," Christopher Browning reports Christian Gerlach's calculation "that altogether in World War II between six and eight million non-Jewish noncombatants died alongside six million Jews at the hands of Germans and their allies and supporters" (Browning 2016, 58). That adds up to between 12 and 14 million Nazi-caused deaths.

I ask my readers to imagine all these murders and all this collecting of evidence, filing of charges, and conducting of trials in many different countries and place their impressions into the cauldron of figure 1.1, which shows my new bifurcated chart, the top layer of which traces the legacy of the Nuremberg trials. Then I ask that they mix into this same cauldron the inevitable raising of social and Holocaust consciousness in the nations where these murders and trials took place, and they will gain an understanding of the birth of the chart's lower track, on which I placed the most important noncriminal human rights texts. As Plesch makes clear, the phrase "human rights" can refer to a system that monitors violations of international criminal law, but it can equally well refer to the moral and legal norms that govern the noncriminal civil, social, economic, and cultural spheres of nations. Violations of human rights can therefore be seen as violations of international criminal codes, as abundantly shown by Plesch's newly revealed data and portrayed on the upper level of our chart. And they can also be seen as violations of noncriminal international moral and legal norms codified in the texts

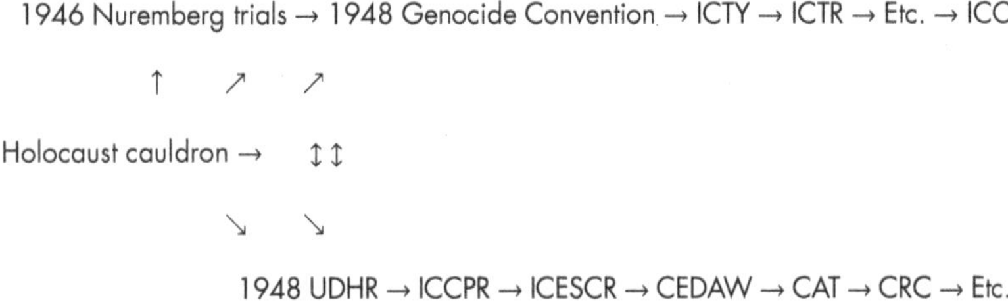

FIGURE 1.1: Two-track flowchart. ICTY = International Criminal Tribunal for the Former Yugoslavia; ICTR = International Criminal Tribunal for Rwanda; ICC = International Criminal Court; UDHR = Universal Declaration of Human Rights; ICCPR = International Covenant on Civil and Political Rights; ICESCR = International Covenant on Economic, Social, and Cultural Rights; CEDAW = Convention on the Elimination of All Forms of Discrimination Against Women; CAT = Convention Against Torture and Other Cruel, Inhuman, or Degrading Treatment or Punishment; CRC = Convention on the Rights of the Child.

I list on the lower level of the chart. Plesch points out that the combined efforts "from political parties and religious organizations, from governments exiled to London from Europe, from China and the pre-independence government of India, and from a few Anglo-American officials contributed to the creation of the International Military Tribunal (IMT) that tried the Nazi leadership at Nuremberg, the Universal Declaration of Human Rights and the Genocide Convention" (48). For obvious reasons I have designated the last two items—the Universal Declaration and the Genocide Convention—coming out of this whirlwind of diplomatic and juridical activity as the lead texts of the bottom and upper track, respectively.

Since the two systems have a common origin in World War II (before which the sovereign immunity model held sway), it makes sense to think of this system as a bifurcated one that split at the time of its birth into two parts, sort of like twins. I put in so many arrows to indicate that both in reality and in the realm of ideas, the Holocaust was indeed a cauldron spewing out events and texts that eventually coalesced into two separate tracks, an upper-level system of international criminal tribunals and a lower-level system of international human rights law. If I had gone further back in time, I would have needed to list the 1907 Hague Convention on how not to wage war and the 1928 Pact of Paris forbidding aggressive wars as legal texts underlying the Charter of the Nuremberg Tribunal. Also, the eighteenth-century American and French Bills of Rights would have served as precedents for the UDHR. But my focus is on what the cauldron of the Holocaust produced in our own time.

Each track has a lead text forged by the Holocaust. In chapter 4, "The Moral Engine of the System," I defend the present system of international legal human rights as a hybrid of moral rights possessed by individuals and legal obligations mostly ascribed to states. That explanation lies behind the "moral/legal" designation used in this section. The arrows of this new chart indicate influences back and forth between the items. Clearly, the Holocaust led both to the Nuremberg trials and the Genocide Convention, the former of which became the template for the international criminal tribunals that make up the top track. And just as clearly the Holocaust shaped the text of the Universal Declaration, which then gave moral birth to far more human rights treaties than I list on the bottom track. The double vertical arrows indicate that the drafting of these two pivotal texts overlapped, as I discuss in chapter 3. For a fascinating look into the birth complications on the upper-level track out of the Holocaust (which foreshadows the lower-level birth as well), the reader cannot do better than read Phillipe Sands's superb book *East West Street: On the Origins of "Genocide" and "Crimes against Humanity"* (2016). After their twin births and common start in life, each of these two layers of the system straightened itself out, with the top one becoming the Nuremberg criminal legacy and the bottom one becoming the UDHR moral/legal legacy. I now want to make a plea for us not to confuse these two tracks and to keep them separate from each other.

On Not Criminalizing the Idea of Human Rights

The drafters of the 1948 Universal Declaration were all members of a visionary generation that saw the end of World War II as an opportunity to make the world totally anew. From that vision grew the multilayered system that we to a large extent still have. As I mention these components, I will not count an extra one having to do with the worldwide environmental threat, which was added to the "human rights project" by way of UDHR Article 28: "Everyone is entitled to a social and international order in which the rights and freedoms set forth in this Declaration can be fully realized." Since the threat to the world environment with its resulting damage to human rights was not part of the intellectual worldview in the 1940s, I do not count this threat as part of the 1940s visionary perspective, though it most certainly has become a part of our own worldview.

That leaves us with four components to the vision of renewal as seen in the 1940s. First, the visionaries wanted to create a new international *political* world and gave it a good start with the 1945 creation of the new United Nations, which replaced the old League of Nations. Second, they wanted to create a new international *economic* reality, which they did by negotiating the charters for the International Monetary Fund, the World Bank, and the International Trade Organization, which in 1994 became the World Trade Organization (WTO). Third, since the Axis Powers had flouted the rules of war, the 1940s visionaries thought that the Nazi and Japanese leaders should be held accountable at criminal trials that would set the principles of international *criminal law* on a new course. They did this by first conducting the 1946 Nuremberg trials and soon thereafter the Tokyo trials (together with numerous domestic secondary trials) and also by writing and then adopting on December 9 the 1948 Genocide Convention, which in embryo was closely connected to Nuremberg and its legacy. Also, because Hitler had used Poland's supposed mistreatment of its German citizens as a reason for invading that country, the Minority Rights Treaties, which had been part of the League of Nations, were thought to have been a clear failure. As a result, these visionaries wanted, fourth, to create a new *moral and legal* international order that would reach beyond the criminal aspects of the war that had just ended and the failed League of Nations treaties. The visionaries started this moral renewal when on December 10, 1948 (one day after the Genocide Convention), they adopted the Universal Declaration of Human Rights.

All four of these attempts at reshaping the world order have led to complicated sets of international rules and regulations, each one of them becoming a system unto itself. They all have some enforcement mechanism: the International Court of Justice (ICJ) for the world political order; the dispute settlement panels of the WTO for the world economic order; the International Criminal Court (ICC) and various regional and local criminal tribunals for the new criminal order; and the regional European, Latin American, and African Human Rights Courts—together with the many expert committees that monitor human rights conventions—for the new moral/legal order. While many authors use the language of "human rights" to refer to just any one of these attempts to reshape our world, for ease of reference I propose that we call these four attempts collectively the 1940s "human rights project," which encompasses numerous institutions, norms, and people that either create or seek to implement these norms on a domestic or international scale. Clearly, one book cannot do justice to this vast enterprise. Only one of these four attempts at renewal (the moral/legal order) is the real subject of this book. So I bite off only a quarter of the project.

The moral/legal and criminal systems or layers have much in common, but we should not criminalize the entire system by conflating or confusing these two tracks or systems. Some authors do that when they almost interchangeably refer to either track. The title of Dan Plesch's book contributes to this trend; the main title is the undifferentiated and ambiguous *Human Rights after Hitler*, while the subtitle tells the readers the book really is about *The Lost History of Prosecuting Axis War Criminals*. The main title is misleading because the book has next to nothing to say about the lower-level noncriminal layer of figure 1.1, which in chapter 3 I show to also be about human rights after Hitler.

This trend toward criminalizing all that came out of the cauldron diminishes the status of the bottom track. In these conflations or collusions, the moral/legal human rights system bequeathed to us by the Universal Declaration of Human Rights is downplayed or ignored while the criminal system is made to look as if it is the only real "system" there is. As in domestic legal systems, so there is in international human rights law a bifurcation that splits criminal from civil proceedings as reflected in the two forks of figure 1.1. One scholar notes that international criminal law

> is different from human rights law but the impulses behind human rights law animate international criminal law as well. The common

> premise of the two bodies of law is that individuals should be protected from abuse at the hand of the state. International criminal law imposes liability on individuals, such as soldiers or leaders, while human rights law, as is typical for international law, is directed at states. Thus a soldier violates international criminal law by killing a prisoner of war, while a state violates international human rights law when its government orders that detainees be tortured. (Posner 2014, 52)

After she has set aside the sovereign "immunity model" that reigned before World War II, Kathryn Sikkink also divides the post–World War II human rights system into two parts (or tracks, as I call them): one with "state [civil] accountability," which holds states as such accountable for violations of the (lower-track) human rights treaties they ratify, and one with (upper-track) "individual criminal accountability," which aims to stop leaders of and within states from committing "core crimes," like "torture, summary execution, and genocide, as well as war crimes and crimes against humanity" (Sikkink 2011, 17–18). Though she speaks of two parts, her subtitle fuses them into one with the announcement that her book shows *How Human Rights Prosecutions Are Changing World Politics*, as if there is not also that other civil track. The rights just mentioned form a core set of what are referred to as "physical integrity rights." I have incorporated both these civil and criminal modes of culpability as separate but complementary layers in my bifurcated chart and object to any conflation of the two.

I have three reasons for listing the criminal layer above the moral/legal one. The first is that the 1946 Nuremberg trials were finished when the 1948 UDHR was adopted. The second is that the Genocide Convention was adopted the day before the declaration was and that the former is a treaty while the latter is a "mere" declaration. Third, I put the criminal track on top because it gets top billing in the media and often in academic discussions. For instance, the death of Slobodan Milošević, the jailed president of Serbia who had been charged before the International Criminal Tribunal for the Former Yugoslavia (ICTY), made headline news. Similarly, when on March 24, 2016, Radovan Karadžić, the mastermind of the Srebrenica genocide, was "convicted of genocide, war crimes, and crimes against humanity," the

New York Times carried a large photo of the memorial at Srebrenica on the front page and spelled out in great detail what the charges and the guilty verdict entailed. Then, a few days later, it carried another article that detailed the life of this "Most Delusional War Criminal." All the notorious cases we have heard about—from Adolf Eichmann and Augusto Pinochet to Charles Taylor and Cambodia's Duch—fit into this top tier of international criminal law. It represents a new order of crimes that are counted as international and not just domestic. They include crimes against humanity that arouse the interest of the world community and that are tried (among other crimes) in the International Criminal Court, which was set up as a permanent court with statutes to pursue these crimes.

Sikkink calculated that internationally by 2009 there had been more than 400 criminal prosecutions of individuals who violated what she called the "core crimes" (Sikkink 2011, fig. 1.1). These numbers make me worry about the "criminalization" of our concept of "human rights." Sikkink's 2017 book *Evidence for Hope: Making Human Rights Work in the 21st Century* gives a more balanced view with the inclusion of tables on children's deaths and malnutrition and on women's self-actualization (150–51, figs. 5.7 and 5.8). It is not that I do not believe in criminal prosecutions; I simply want to safeguard and strengthen the bottom track of the bifurcated chart. The crimes adjudicated before criminal tribunals often involve massive and gross human rights violations, which feed into the popularized idea of human rights and in turn help the movement expand. The downside is that these criminal trials associate the idea of human rights with the *criminal behavior of nations' leaders* and take away attention from violations by nations, where human rights groups fight on the ground in mundane and peaceful settings to raise the minimum wage or hold police accountable for deaths on their watch.

Defending the Separation of the Tracks

My authority for wanting to keep these two layers of the system somewhat separate from each other comes in part from the *travaux préparatoires* of the declaration. As the bifurcated chart shows, the Nuremberg trials were over and done with when the Universal Declaration was being drafted and adopted in the fall of 1948. The declaration's drafters held three positions as to what to do about the just finished Nuremberg trials (and still ongoing Tokyo trials): strongly support their judgments, strongly disavow them, or steer a middle course. The drafters chose the third option. As I wrote in my *Origins* account, "The problem was that some delegations thought that at least some of the Nuremberg charges were not firmly grounded in pre-existent law, which in their eyes made the judgements questionable from a strictly legal point of view" (Morsink 1999b, 52). The term "international" in UDHR Article 11(2) ("No one shall be held guilty of any penal offence on account of any act or omission which did not constitute a penal offence, under national or international law, at the time it was committed") is the tip of quite a debate (17). The other provisions of Article 11 (innocence until proven guilty and "all the guarantees necessary for his defense") were easily agreed to because the Nazis had constantly violated all these safeguards.

At the start of the second session of the Human Rights Commission, the Belgian and Filipino delegations submitted this joint text for adoption: "Nothing in this Article shall prejudice the trial and punishment of any person for the commission of any act which, at the time is was committed, was criminal according to the general principles of law recognized by civilized nations" (Morsink 1999b, 54). This phraseology was taken from Article 38 of the Statute of the International Court of Justice, which is the world court that oversees enforcement of the United Nations Charter. The article is generally considered to be the basic source for public international law. The second session adopted this joint amendment. But it ran into trouble in the third session as a result of the strong opposition from the USSR delegation, which wanted to see "civilized nations" replaced by "democratic countries." The USSR objected to the ICJ distinction between civilized and uncivilized nations, thereby injecting Cold War terminology into the debate (55–56). The Belgians, French, British, and Americans were all opposed to weakening this reference to Article 38 of the ICJ Statute.

Referring to Resolution 95(I), the Egyptian delegate, Omar Loufti, pointed out that the UN General Assembly "had [already] proposed that in light of the Nuremberg trials, the International Penal Code of Law should be revised to cover war criminals" (Morsink 1999b, 56). We see the results of this revision in the creation of a separate international criminal track as a legacy of the Nuremberg trials. Loufti's implication was that the UDHR drafters did not need to upgrade the international legal system. They could just write their declaration as they wanted. Although Loufti still stressed that the word "international" should be interpreted in accordance with the provision of Article 38 of the ICJ Statute, the Belgian delegation withdrew its amendment (56). Avoiding both extremes of overtly supporting or overtly holding back, the Third Social, Humanitarian, and Cultural Affairs Committee of the General Assembly kept the text as we have it. (This committee is an arm of the General Assembly and functions as a conduit for other organs [like the Human Rights Commission] that have social, humanitarian, and cultural issues to place before the assembly.) Because it wanted to see more distance between the declaration's text and the Nuremberg judgments, the Cuban delegation supported this amendment: "Every accused person has the right to be judged by tribunals established prior to the offence with which he is charged" (57). This amendment was rejected eighteen votes to eight, with seventeen abstentions.

After the present text with the words "international law" in it was adopted, the delegations of Mexico, Venezuela, and Cuba "explained that they had favoured the adoption of Article 9 [11] in its amended form on the understanding that the term 'international law,' appearing in paragraph 2 of that article, should be interpreted as meaning positive international law" (Morsink 1999b, 57). Applying this comment to the entire UDHR text and not just to Article 11, I take it to mean that these delegations did not want to see the Universal Declaration lifted up above international law as an authoritative moral code not anchored in the positive legal enactments of nations. Those who wanted to give more support to the Nuremberg process worried, as did the Belgian delegate Count Carton de Wiart, that the adopted text "might be used as a basis for the argument that such trials as the Nuremberg Trials had been illegal. He agreed with those who held that those trials had been based on the laws of the human conscience which were higher than national laws" (57). He was joined by Alexander Contoumas, the Greek delegate, who suggested that the rapporteur "mention specifically in his reports the doubts in that regard expressed during the general debate on article 9 [11]" (271). In other words, the validity of the Nuremberg trials and the role human conscience had played in them, they agreed, were not to cast doubts on the idea of non-retroactivity in criminal law generally.

The Soviet delegation had no such worries. To it, the adopted text fit perfectly with the Nuremberg judgments. Alexei Pavlov, the USSR delegate, told his Belgian colleague to have no fear because "the crimes of those brought before the Nuremberg Tribunal had constituted a glaring violation of all the laws of war; they had in effect, been crimes under international law. There was no cause to fear that the adoption of paragraph 2 of Article 9[11] in Paris—a city which but a few years ago had itself been under Hitlerite occupation—would be considered by anyone an amnesty for those crimes" (Morsink 1999b, 58). His colleague, Ljuba Radevanovic from Yugoslavia, was less positivistic: "The *nulla poena sine lege* was almost universal in national law; in international law, on the other hand the responsibility was different." Furthermore, "the General Assembly had adopted a resolution codifying the legal findings of the Nuremberg decisions" (58). Article 11(2), with some additions not connected to this discussion, was adopted by nineteen votes for, six against, and nineteen abstentions. I interpret this large number of abstentions as delegates wanting to see more or less distance from the Nuremberg trials. The UDHR drafters clearly wanted to keep a healthy distance from the Nuremberg process and outcome. This supports my wanting to keep the two tracks of our flowchart separated from each other.

Examples of Conflation

Let me now show how some well-known books help confuse the human rights landscape by writing as if there is mostly only one system, usually the criminal one.

The Nuremberg charges of "crimes against humanity" were further deepened and solidified by the two Geneva Conventions of 1947 and 1949. Readers may be familiar with Article 3, common to both conventions, since it played a role in some US cases coming out of the Guantánamo Bay detention camp. Some international tribunals, such as those in Cambodia, Sierra Leone, and East Timor, are not simply UN Security Council creations but hybrids of the UN in cooperation with member states. The crimes committed in these countries have long aroused the interest of the world community, which is why the ICC was set up as a permanent court with statutes to pursue these kinds of crimes. Sikkink (2011) gives us two pie charts: one for domestically conducted criminal prosecutions, which shows 55 percent have taken place in the Americas, 25 percent in Europe, 13 percent in Africa, 1 percent in the Middle East and North Africa, and 6 percent in Asia (22, fig. 1.2), and one for the regional distribution of foreign and international criminal prosecutions, which shows that 51 percent took place in Europe, 17 percent in Africa, 10 percent in the Middle East and North Africa, 5 percent in Asia, and 17 percent in the Americas (23, fig. 1.3). These charts show that the 400 prosecutions named are indeed spread around the world, supporting Sikkink's claim that these prosecutions indicate a worldwide trend. This trend is precisely why I want to draw attention to the bottom, noncriminal or civil track of our bifurcated chart. Both tracks are supported by a huge public interest. The fact that some scholars have argued that a parallel International Human Rights Court is needed to function as a civil match to the ICC indicates how different the lower level of the bifurcated system is from the upper criminal level, which gets most of the media and scholarly attention. I devote most of chapters 4 and 5 to this lower-level system.

Sikkink contributes to the criminalization of the idea of human rights when she suggests that the failure of noncriminal state accountability attempts on the lower level led to later upper-level criminal prosecutions. She writes, "The Holocaust revealed the dramatic failures of the sovereign immunity model and led states to construct the [lower-level] human rights regime, with its state accountability model. But while naming and shaming and the state accountability model had some successes, they were often inadequate in dealing with the most repressive states" (Sikkink 2011, 254). This failure of the state accountability model on the lower level of our chart then led to the development of the individual criminal accountability model that takes place on the upper level in criminal prosecutions of leaders of the "most repressive states." I do not think that the idea of "state accountability" was a general failure; thus, I argue that Sikkink moves too quickly to the upper-level criminal accountability. Although they are based on or deal with different texts, both levels of the chart in some way deal with human rights. Therefore, there must be interplay between the two levels of our bifurcated chart, and that interplay is most visible when the phrase "human rights violations" is used in criminal charges and when people in the movement agitate for prosecutions.

But I do not think that the failure or ineffectiveness of the civil state level led in any straightforward way to the development of the other upper-level criminal one, as Sikkink seems to suggest. Both layers of our chart had a more or less independent birth in the same cauldron of the Holocaust. From the start both charts have had their own successes and their own failures. Sikkink lists the following texts as grounds for the criminal prosecutions of her "justice cascade": the 1948 Genocide Convention, the 1949 Geneva Conventions, the 1980 Apartheid Convention, the 1987 Convention against Torture, the 1996 Inter-American Convention on Forced Disappearances, and the 1998 Rome Statute (Sikkink 2011, 97, fig. 4.1). Only the Convention against Torture overlaps with the list of key human rights conventions that Posner (2014) lists and that are part of the moral legacy of the UDHR displayed on the lower level of our chart (to which in chapter 4 I add some 125 texts and counting). To say that the moral level's failures called for or caused the development of the criminal level unnecessarily criminalizes the shared concept of human rights.

The history of the city of Nuremberg reflects the overlap between the two parts of the layered system. Nuremberg was the city where Hitler's National Socialist Party headquarters and famous parade grounds were located. Not wanting to be saddled by the negative reputation of hosting the Nuremberg trials, the city has since turned itself into a model human rights city with an alley of pillars, each carved with one of the articles of the Universal Declaration in a different language of the world. The former Nazi headquarters were turned into a human rights and Holocaust museum, and the attic above the courtroom where the Nazi leaders stood trial was also turned into a museum space. To celebrate the sixtieth anniversary of the UDHR, the courtroom was used in November 1998 for a conference on Das Recht das uns zu Menschen Macht (Rights that make us human), a theme that perfectly represented what the Universal Declaration is all about. One of the points I make in the conclusion of this book is that it would be good if more of the world's Holocaust museums would embrace the connection between commemorating the Holocaust and calling for the implementation of the UDHR, as this German city and now an increasing number of Holocaust and Genocide Study Centers are doing. Nevertheless, I plead for maintaining a bifurcated system in which each track is kept separate from the other. The criminalization of international human rights as a concept does not help the moral movement that has at least one foot—the UDHR—outside the positive legal international human rights system.

My reader can now see why I have difficulty placing certain recent human rights books in one of the bins of our simple diagram: idea → UDHR text → system → movement. Books that give a great deal of attention to the Nuremberg trials and their legacy fit better on the upper-level criminal part of the bifurcated chart than on the lower-level moral/legal level. Because international criminal cases receive so much public attention, the danger exists that the lower level of our bifurcated chart will be usurped by or "criminalized" in a shift of attention to the upper criminal level of the chart. The split that happened right after World War II is in danger of being ignored. *The Endtimes of Human Rights* by Stephen Hopgood is one of the best recent human rights volumes, but since his focus is on the upper-level criminal chart (1946 Nuremberg trials → 1948 Genocide Convention → ICTY → International Criminal Tribunal for Rwanda [ICTR] → Etc. → ICC), I have trouble placing it in one of the bins of the simpler chart with which I started this volume. The phrase "human rights" in Hopgood's title is left ambiguous between the two levels of the bifurcated chart. Because of this ambiguity, Hopgood's book contributes to the "criminalization" of the concept of human rights that I oppose.

Hopgood begins by noting that there are two forms of "human rights" at work in the world today: one written with lowercase letters (human rights) and one written with capitals (Human Rights). The lowercase term refers to "local and transnational networks of activists who bring publicity to abuses they and their communities face" (Hopgood 2013, viii). These activists seek to raise awareness and put pressure on governments and UN organs to ameliorate the abuses. They are motivated by "compassion, solidarity, freedom, brotherhood, sisterhood, justice, religion, grace, charity, kin, ethnicity, nationalism, pity, love or equality" (viii). This type of local "banding together" of a community will not spell the end of the human rights that Hopgood's title announces. Ultimately, much of Hopgood's book is a story about what in our simple diagram we call the human rights *movement*, and since Hopgood starts with the creation of the International Committee of the Red Cross (ICRC), this movement comes at the beginning, and not at the end, of the human rights story he tells.

The other form of Human Rights, with capitals, refers for Hopgood to the "global structure of laws, courts, norms, and organizations that raise money, write reports, run international campaigns, open local offices, lobby governments, and claim to speak with singular authority in the name of humanity as a whole" (Hopgood 2013, ix). While the lowercase "human rights" clearly is about a section of the human rights movement (in this case anchored in the author's East Timor experience), the capitalized version of "Human Rights" at first glance seems to be about the lower level of the bifurcated diagram, in which case it would seem to be about the UDHR and its legacy of international human rights law. But that would be a misreading of Hopgood's book. For his story is about the upper-level criminal part of the bifurcated chart. Hopgood's thesis is that the failure of the elite (criminal) Human Rights system brings the human rights movement on the ground down with it.

At the heart of the disconnect between the lowercase "human rights" and capital "Human Rights" levels of the same phenomenon lies a failure of the secular humanist ideology, which Hopgood traces to a nineteenth-century episode in the history of the *idea* of human rights. This failure started with the creation of the ICRC, which Hopgood recounts in his first chapter. This humanism "was a secular replacement for the Christian god," which "nineteenth century Europeans elevated . . . into a set of social practices and institutions, most prominently the International Committee of the Red Cross" (Hopgood 2013, x). From this fascinating start, Hopgood draws the doubtful lesson that "it is only as a strategy for coping with what Nietzsche called 'the death of god' in the West that we can begin to understand the real social function of humanitarianism and human rights in the twentieth century" (x). Hopgood does not indicate whether in this citation we are to read "human rights" as lowercase or capitalized, but the context suggests that he is thinking about capitalized Human Rights here. Though he admits that the laws and activities of the ICRC "were grounded by a culture of transcendent moral sentiment with strong Christian components," in the rest of his book he tends to stress the "universal, secular, and absolute norms of this humanist ideology" that is driving Human Rights and is in trouble (3, 45, 118, 155, 174). I have an amendment and an objection to Hopgood's way of linking his two levels of human rights talk.

The amendment is that the *system* (lowercase, as in our simple first diagram) or the *System* (on both tracks of the bifurcated chart) was not nearly as soaked in overtly secular ways of thought as Hopgood portrays its later twentieth-century history to be. In my *The Universal Declaration of Human Rights and the Challenge of Religion* (Morsink 2017), I present the UDHR as the caboose of the lower-level *system* that is closer to Hopgood's lowercase human rights than to his capitalized criminal Human Rights. My thesis is that lower-level human rights, for Hopgood in font and for me in the simple chart (that later split in two), resulted from a genuine cooperation of all the world's major religions and Marxist delegations, which thought it inappropriate to ground any UN document, capitalized or not, in religious thought. Hopgood (2013) presents the nineteenth-century bourgeois Europeans as "responding to the erosion of religious authority by creating authorities of their own from the cultural resources that lay scattered around them and which they then globalized via the infrastructure that the imperial civilizing project bequeathed them" (Hopgood 2013, x). The creation of "the system" was a question of the "white man's burden," which is also what worried the American Anthropological Association when it addressed its concerns to the Human Rights Commission during the drafting of the UDHR, but which the Human Rights Commission found a way around (Morsink 1999b, introduction).

Hopgood basically starts his story with the Holocaust and then links that event primarily to the adoption of the Genocide Convention and not, as we do in our lower-level chart, to the adoption of the Universal Declaration. This genocide text and the atrocities it bans dominate his "Holocaust Metanarrative" chapter. This means that the connection between the Holocaust and the Universal Declaration is played down. Given that there are two foundational texts and two "systems" at play in the world today, each with its own flowchart, "the endtimes" of Human Rights (capitalized) receives greater billing than it should have. Hopgood reminds us that UN Secretary-General Kofi Annan "explicitly tied the Holocaust to the UDHR (rather than 'civilization') in a speech at the first-ever UN Conference on Anti-Semitism in 2004" (Hopgood 2013, 55). Shortly thereafter the General Assembly passed a resolution that "drew explicit links between the Holocaust, the UDHR, and the Genocide Convention . . . designating January 27 (the day Auschwitz was liberated) as an international day of commemoration of the victims of the Holocaust, encouraging governments to set up national education programs and requiring the secretary general to establish a United Nations Holocaust outreach program" (55). In the rest of his metanarrative, the Genocide Convention, linked as it is to the Nuremberg trials and their legacy, outflanks the UDHR as the text of most interest.

Hopgood notes that the "Holocaust destroyed the idea that a civilized conscience could prevent atrocity or that European modernity was inherently progressive, but [that] even so the efforts made to counter it with human rights law kept Europe front and center" (Hopgood 2013, 61). I argue in the next two chapters that Europe was *not* front and center at the very early moral stages of the development of human rights law. The historic moment for human rights (1946–48) came before the 1951 adoption of the European Convention. While it is true that the conscience of humanity was caught absent when Hitler committed his horrors, that same conscience did rise up and pull out of the flames both the Genocide Convention and one day later the UDHR, each of which have in different ways profoundly shaped our post–World War II world. One of the reasons Hopgood thinks we have pretty much reached the end times of Human Rights as a bone fide movement is that the secular humanistic ideology of early nongovernmental organizations (NGOs) like the ICRC is starting to crumble and with it the foundations of the Human Rights system to which it gave rise. To him this calls for a universalization of the Holocaust experience into a broader moral lesson, and I share this view. This view should have made him put more stress on the lower-level moral/legal fork of the chart.

To raise the alarm further, Hopgood cites Mark Goodale's puzzling question, Why should "liberal (or neoliberal) legal and political theory . . . continue to prove so foundational [for human rights] when this political choice is no longer necessary?" (Hopgood 2013, 64). The implication, which Goodale explicitly states, is that "the constellation of Western liberal legal and political theories that formed the foundation for the 1948 Universal Declaration of Human Rights—and most of the follow-up instruments—remains the dominant intellectual resource within the international human rights system" (Goodale 2009, 10). Goodale gives his readers no evidence for his claim that the UDHR and its legal offspring are the brainchild of liberal political theorists. This was not the case. The declaration's origin and philosophical foundation is far more universal and existential than that. For that reason we do not yet face the end times of human rights, lowercase, or for that matter, capitalized. From the day of its adoption too much religion was involved in the UDHR and its legal offspring to ascribe its success primarily to "liberal (or neoliberal)" thinking (Morsink 2017).

I need to discuss two more authors who make the Nuremberg trials and their legacy a centerpiece of their human rights history. While these authors have their own purposes, I do think they have given insufficient attention to the connection I seek to lift up. In her award-winning *A New Deal for the World: America's Vision for Human Rights*, Elizabeth Borgwardt (2005) stresses the 1942 Atlantic Charter telegram by Franklin Roosevelt and Winston Churchill as the incubator for three charters that she believes shaped America's vision for the postwar world: the Bretton Woods Charter, the United Nations Charter, and the Nuremberg Charter. Borgwardt is interested in the new political order the 1940s visionaries wanted to create, but none of these charters have a key place in my own story, which focuses on the moral/legal world order these same visionaries sought to create. There are, of course, obvious overlaps between the political and moral world orders; all of them are part of the larger human rights project begun after World War II. Borgwardt's *New Deal* is one of the four (political, moral, criminal, and economic) attempted ways to reshape our world that I mentioned at the start of this subsection.

Throughout her book Borgwardt uses Roosevelt's Four Freedoms theme as a unifying factor in these charters. With exquisite research she weaves these Four Freedoms for a postwar world into a tapestry about America's vision for human rights in that world. It is all the more surprising that the Universal Declaration—which refers in its second recital to Roosevelt's proclamation of "the advent of a world in which human beings shall enjoy freedom of speech and belief and freedom of fear and want" and which was first of all a moral message to the world—plays no big role in Borgwardt's study. President Franklin Roosevelt had proclaimed these Four Freedoms in his January 1941 message to Congress just before he and Churchill alluded to them in the sixth principle of their August 1941 Atlantic Charter telegram. There they expressed the hope that "with the final destruction of the Nazi tyranny . . . [a peace will prevail] which will afford assurance that all men in all the lands may live out their lives in freedom from fear and want" (Borgwardt 2005, 304). Roosevelt had added the words "all men in all the lands" to the final draft, which begs for alignment with the drafting of a list of moral rights that his wife, Eleanor, oversaw some five years later.

Borgwardt ignores the direct link between the Holocaust and the UDHR when she notes that in the aftermath of Nuremberg "in 1948 the Universal Declaration of Human Rights emerged from a contentious drafting process to serve as a kind of Atlantic Charter of the human rights movement" (264). Like the US Declaration of Independence, the UDHR is presented as a "toothless" declaration but at the same time as a good "way-station on the path toward more detailed and binding provisions on human rights," which she then proceeds to recount (Borgwardt 2005, 264–65, 362n37). Just as was Hopgood's, Borgwardt's main discussion of the Holocaust comes in the context of Nuremberg. Although the connection between the Holocaust and the Nuremberg trials is clear and was mediated by the Genocide Convention, the connection between the Holocaust and the Universal Declaration needs more attention, especially since Borgwardt's Four Freedoms theme emphasizes FDR's social and economic agenda for the postwar world, which the second half of the Universal Declaration spells out in great detail.

Borgwardt often calls for support from another good *political* human rights story told by Kirsten Sellars in her *The Rise and Rise of Human Rights* (2002). The main players in Sellars's story are government ministers, diplomats, United Nations elite, and human rights activists, with the former usually, but not always, prevailing over the latter. After Sellars has given a fairly accurate report on some of the drafting issues involving the UDHR preamble and Article 1, she ignores the rest of the *travaux préparatoires* in her overall conclusion that "the declaration is nevertheless cast in distinctly American idiom. Every stage of the process was indelibly stained with their effort, from the creation of the institutional framework structure to the appointment of Eleanor Roosevelt [as chair], to the labour of State Department officials," who guided Eleanor's every move and ended up pleased that almost all the votes went their way (Sellars 2002, 23). This analysis misrepresents what happened. Eleanor (as she is affectionately called even in scholarly essays) was not appointed but elected to be the chairperson of the Human Rights Commission, and the form and content of the UDHR is not primarily the result of a two-power cooperation between the United States and Great Britain. These powers did not, as Sellars would have us think, outflank the very substantial contribution of the French delegation headed by René Cassin (16). Cassin was not the "father" of the declaration by any means, but I rank his contribution above that of any particular UK or US delegate. Precisely because Eleanor Roosevelt was chair of the proceedings, she could not shape the outcome nearly as much as her own State Department would have liked. For fear of being found partisan, she could not push the US point of view as her advisers wanted. She was too fair a chair not to see the Soviet point of view on numerous issues. After Sellars has recounted the San Francisco and UDHR rise of human rights, she takes her readers straightway to chapters on the Nuremberg and Tokyo war crimes trials and then to chapters on the legacy of these trials in the regional tribunals sitting in the Hague. I believe Sellars's story of the rise of human rights in the post–World War II world unnecessarily contributes to the criminalization of the idea of international human rights.

The UDHR Text and Its Moral and Legal Legacy

Having made my case against the criminalization of the idea of human rights, I want to return to the simple chart (idea → UDHR text → system → movement) and start over again with just the lower track of our bifurcated chart. Also—having introduced the event of the

Holocaust—we should now go back and take another look at the second link of that simple initial diagram.

The Holocaust and the UDHR Text

There is a huge difference between the drafters of the declaration using the historical precedents of the *idea* of human rights (such as those of the Enlightenment) and their being goaded into drafting their UDHR text by the ghastly events of the Holocaust. I wrote this book because I believe that any number of authors writing on the subject of human rights ignore this Holocaust link in the birth of the 1940s contemporary *idea* and *concept* of human rights. For example, the editors of the earlier discussed revisitation volume think there are two versions of the textbook narrative: one that imagines the source of human rights in some past era in which rights were prominent, especially the Enlightenment era of Immanuel Kant, John Locke, and the American founding fathers, and another version that they call the "big bang theory." I have inserted the step numbers in this big bang version, which

> [i] emphasizes a vacuum of rights initiatives in the inter-war period, and [ii] highlights global abhorrence awakened by the Holocaust as the decisive factor behind the newly sprung universal consciousness of mankind. This in turn resulted in [iii] worldwide mobilization to ensure that similar atrocities would never occur again, thus [iv] laying the foundations for rapid geographic spread and empirical growth of the post-UDHR contemporary human rights phenomenon, eventually [v] elevating human rights into the "idea of our time." (Slotte and Halme-Tuomisaari 2015, 6)

In these steps the editors rapidly move across most of our timeline, from (i) the *idea* before the 1940s to (ii) the late 1940s *Holocaust* (minus text) to (iii) the 1960s *system*, ending with the 1970s *movement* in (iv) and (v). By omitting the UDHR text they fail to detect the tightening of the notion, for the Holocaust by itself did not tighten the notion. It did so by influencing and inspiring the world community to adopt the preamble and thirty articles of the 1948 declaration.

I admit to being a contributor to this big bang version and agree with what the editors say about the other "imagined antiquity" version. They say that in that version the authors—though probably not the contributors to their own volume—often "disregard material reality and context by selecting any activity that has been formulated with *rights* vocabulary, although not *human* rights language, or which otherwise emerges as emancipatory with preferably trans- or international tendencies as predecessors for the post-UDHR human rights phenomenon, without elaborating the connection between the two" (Slotte and Halme-Tuomisaari 2015, 9–10). That is exactly my own criticism of many writers on human rights who go too quickly from the *idea* before the 1940s to the other bins of the chart, as the editors themselves also did in their description of the big bang. They ignore the Holocaust's impact on the UDHR text and, by way of that text, on the ensuing system and movement.

When the editors of the revisitation volume tell us that "the history of the contemporary human rights phenomenon has *never* been organized around a distinct, absolute and unchanged conception" (Slotte and Halme-Tuomisaari 2015, 19; original italics), I agree and disagree. I agree that none of the rights in the UDHR are absolute because each one of them needs to be read in light of the correlative duties spelled out in Article 29. I also agree that when one of these abstractly stated rights is lowered into local or regional contexts its concrete meaning can and often does change, since basic foods, shelter, and education change from locale to locale. But I do not agree that the notion of human rights that we get when reading the Universal Declaration of Human Rights is not a distinct notion. It is, and nothing like it had ever before been enunciated. The distinctness of these rights does not lie in just one abstract characteristic they share. It lies in their inherence in the human person, in their universality, in their UN-sponsored Holocaust origin, and in their applicability the world over, a feature I think of as their transcendence over local, domestic, and regional political boundaries. While the editors ascribe this last feature to the mythic character of the notion, I trace it instead to the "inalienability" of these rights that the UDHR drafters gleaned more from what the Nazis did than from their familiarity with intellectual history (11).

Think of Aristotle's theory of the four causes. He thought that a statue had four causes: a formal one, which was the idea that the sculptor had in his head; a material one, which was the block of marble in front of him; an efficient cause, which was the energy expended and put out by the sculptor chiseling away; and a final cause, which was the finished product standing in the Parthenon or wherever. Analogously, we might think of the historical *idea* of human rights as the formal cause of the Universal Declaration that was in the drafters' minds and that they may or may not have gleaned from times past, of the events of the Holocaust as the efficient cause that propelled them into action, and of the survey by John Humphrey (the first UN director of human rights) of extant world constitutions that contained options from which the drafters might pick their rights as the declaration's material cause. Looking at things this way, we can think of the 1948 UDHR text as the final cause lifted up for all the world to see.

In any case, there is a difference between the *idea* of human rights feeding into the text of the declaration as our diagram shows and the moral energy coming from the Holocaust that goaded the drafters into action. Historians of the idea tend to stress the formal cause of human rights at the expense of the efficient cause. But without a good source of energy, nothing happens. The editors of the revisitation book ignore this efficient cause (the Holocaust) when they observe that "the textbook narrative is a story with unknown origins" that has started "to resemble a myth" (Slotte and Halme-Tuomisaari 2015, 11). Whatever the content of the textbook notion of human rights is, to present it as having "unknown origins" is tantamount to deleting the middle years of 1946–48 from the decade of the 1940s. These are the years the Universal Declaration was written as a direct result of the experiences of the Holocaust and the war that ended in 1945.

Since there can be several causes for any one event or thing, I suggest we put the Holocaust into our one-track diagram as shown in figure 1.2. According to figure 1.2, there was an intervention into the supposedly smooth flow from the historical idea of human rights to the UDHR text and from there to the system and the movement of human rights that followed. That intervention was the occurrence of the Holocaust, which in my thinking makes the second link more complex than it is in the view of many human rights authors. This intervention by

Holocaust

↓↓

idea → UDHR text → system → movement

FIGURE 1.2: Amplified flowchart

the Holocaust into the intellectual history of rights discourses produced many of the characteristics (internal coherence, logical continuity, comprehensiveness) the editors of the revisitation volume ascribe to the textbook notion of human rights. I myself have, for example, defended the idea of the inherence of human rights in the human person, which gives enormous coherence and logical continuity to our contemporary notion of human rights (Morsink 2009). My complaint against the bulk of the literature is that it plays down or mostly ignores the complexity of this second link of our one-track diagram.

Most authors move too easily from the idea to the system or to the movement and then back again as their theses demand. In chapter 3 I argue that this complex link (of *Holocaust* + *UDHR text*) constitutes the 1940s historic moment of human rights, while in chapters 4 and 5 I make the point that this historic moment has had philosophic import. Even when general histories acknowledge the complexity of this link, they often tend to lift up just one half of it, as Lauren (1998) lifts up the UDHR or Hopgood (2013) lifts up the Holocaust part, and not the whole of the link, as I think they should. I admit to having helped create the complexity of this second link of the one-track chart. My first book on the declaration (Morsink 1999b) contained a chapter titled "World War II as Catalyst," the second book (Morsink 2009) had a chapter called "Obeying the Conscience of Mankind," and the first section of the third book (Morsink 2017) had as title "Holocaust Origins." In all three places, I explore and give evidence for what the subtitle to the present volume claims is an endangered connection. I summarize what I say in these places in chapter 3 of this volume.

The point of the present book is that in recent scholarship this linkage has been ignored, played down, or even objected to. The neglect of this link is surprising because, in the United Nations Archives, we have available to us a very detailed account of the origin of the declaration text. I used those archives to first write a crib-to-finish biography of the document, then to explore the philosophy of this pivotal text, and after that to explore the declaration's relationship with the phenomenon of religion.

These UN archives contain the minutes of the hundreds of meetings and votes over a period of more than two years in different layers of the UN bureaucracy. In these *travaux préparatoires*, we also find important supporting documents from the UN Secretariat's Division of Human Rights and hundreds of documents submitted by participating delegations and interested parties over the two-and-a-half-year drafting period. For some years this archival material has been available among the research guides on the United Nations website, which is a most useful way of accessing drafting documents for scholars who pretty much know what documents they want to see (United Nations, n.d.). The documents are retrievable by year (1946/1947/1948) and by individual title and meeting, listed under a given year and divided by individually dated sessions (of the commission and of its Drafting Subcommittee). In each case document information is preceded by a most helpful list of supporting documents relevant to the dated and numbered meetings that followed. More recently Cambridge University Press (Schabas 2013) published these same archival materials in a print and online set. Here I recommend the reader first go to the up-front table of documents or to the subject index to decide which of the more than 3,000 pages he or she wants to access instead of scrolling through the entire set until a point of interest is found. Scholars now have easy access to the material that I Xeroxed in the early 1980s and used to build this second link of the flowchart, first in a biography, then in an essay on philosophical foundations, and most recently to give an account of the document's secular, nonreligious character. It seems that these three books are the only ones in English that take advantage of the full scope of the UDHR *travaux préparatoires*. Others have made use of only the most accessible parts of these archives available in depository libraries around the world, but because they have not used the full scope of these archives, they leave out crucial details.

Two earlier studies in French are an exception to this partial coverage: one by Philippe de la Chapelle (1967), who does an exhaustive job, and one by Albert Verdoodt (1963), who gives the link cursory treatment. The fact that these two volumes were never translated into English severely limited access in the English-speaking world to what the UN archives tell us about the writing and adoption of the declaration. Scholars had to travel to New York or Geneva to consult the complete archives before they were made digitally available on the UN website. Not having the time or ability to consult these archives themselves, scholars produced literature on the Universal Declaration that came to have a distinct smell of inbreeding. Scholars repeatedly used and exchanged the same citations and archival references, often without going to the UN archives themselves, robbing themselves of a chance to add to or to change the prevailing opinion on an article or item or on the whole intent of the document. Probably the first book-length account in English by an outsider of what transpired in the UN when the declaration was adopted was the 1950 edition of Nehemiah Robinson's *The Universal Declaration of Human Rights: Its Origin, Significance, Application, and Interpretation.* Unfortunately, Robinson's account is very brief and mostly limited to the debates in the 1948 Third Committee, leaving out many of the early drafting stages and challenges the drafters faced along the way. There is far more to the birth of the Universal Declaration than what the Third Committee debates—available in all UN depository libraries—tell us. Scholars who have used Robinson as their guide to the adoption of the declaration are therefore handicapped by Robinson's limited use of the UN archival materials.

This incomplete and limited use of the UN archives has led to some contemporary discussions of the declaration's formation and significance that lack the depth and nuance the subject deserves. In her 2001 book *A World Made New*, Mary Ann Glendon describes the role Eleanor Roosevelt played in the drafting of the declaration, to which she added and includes biographical details about other important drafters. The subtitle of her book, *Eleanor Roosevelt and the Universal Declaration of Human Rights*, correctly states Glendon's focus, which is first on Eleanor Roosevelt and secondarily on the UDHR. Glendon nicely summarizes the scholarly information on Eleanor's role in that process and gives us sketches of other important personages, like Peng-chun Chang from China, René Cassin from France, Charles Malik from Lebanon, Hansa Mehta from India, Hernán Santa Cruz from Chile, and Alexei Pavlov from the Soviet Union. She lets her readers feel the excitement these visionaries experienced in those heady early days of the United Nations. Unfortunately, she seems not to have gone to the UN Archives themselves in either New York or Geneva. Her notes indicate a limitation to just those UN Archives that she found in the personal files of Charles Malik, a key member of the drafting team and chairperson of the Third Committee. While she accurately sketches the international tensions that at times threatened to engulf the drafters as they feverishly finished their job, Glendon's limited use of the archives led her to oversimplify the story she tells. Her use in chapter 10 of Cassin's portico structure for the declaration does not fit the *travaux préparatoires*, and her prominent use in chapter 5 of the UN Educational, Scientific, and Cultural Organization (UNESCO) survey misrepresents how the UDHR drafters did their job.

In her fifth chapter ("A Philosophical Investigation"), Glendon implies (but does not openly say) that Eleanor's commission approved or even initiated a survey that UNESCO had made in 1947 of "the philosophical bases of human rights." UNESCO had sent a questionnaire to 150 philosophers around the world, and the 70 replies received had been studied and summarized with the inclusion of a tentative list of rights drawn up by a UNESCO committee of experts. The minutes of a December 1947 meeting of Eleanor's commission show that the members of that commission were not at all pleased with the initiative UNESCO had taken. In a letter to Mrs. Roosevelt a few days after this closed-door meeting of complaints (E/CN.4/78), J. L. Havet, the UNESCO representative to the commission, explained in detail what UNESCO's plan for 1947 had been and what it was going to be into 1948. At the time UNESCO had not released the report on which Glendon based her chapter 5 and about which the commission members in this December 3 meeting complained. Columbia University Press published the UNESCO findings in 1949, that is, a year after the declaration was adopted. The report was reissued by Greenwood Press in 1973. Over Eleanor's own and the Secretariat's objections, the commission Eleanor chaired decided "by eight votes to four with one abstention, not to reproduce the UNESCO report for distribution to all the Members of the United Nations" (E/CN.4/SR.26/16).

The majority of Eleanor's colleagues displayed no interest in what the UNESCO philosophers thought about the underlying principles of the bill they were working on. They did not want any more of the UNESCO material leaked to the press (as had happened in Brussels), and they kept the UNESCO investigations at arm's length from their own deliberations.

Glendon's account misses the rebuke that Eleanor's fellow drafters gave her and those who had drawn up the UNESCO questionnaire. Glendon's emphasis on the UNESCO survey puts the Holocaust effect on the UDHR drafters in the shadow. Her chapter 5 illumines the external philosophic climate that was not published until at least a year later and had little or no connection to the declaration's internal struggle for the shape it was to receive. The UNESCO committee's desire to be helpful (which Glendon also mentions in chapter 12) was experienced by the UDHR drafters as interference and was not appreciated. After having administered the rebuke, the UDHR drafters continued to debate the declaration text for another year without ever taking note of these interesting but external philosophical ruminations. In his 1949 introduction to the UNESCO edited survey, Jacques Maritain made the observation that there "is a kind of plant-like formation and growth of moral knowledge and moral feeling, in itself independent of philosophical systems and the rational justifications they propound, even though there is a secondary interaction between them" (Maritain 1973, 12). This might explain how common ground could be found among all the different ideologies involved in the UNESCO survey and also in the drafting of the UDHR. This happens to be my own view of the relationship between the growth of morality and its later justifications (Morsink 2017, conclusion).

After chapter 5's UNESCO disconnect, Glendon creates a second disconnect in chapter 10 between her presentation of René Cassin's portico interpretation of the declaration's structure and the discussions that took place about that structure in the Style and Arrangement Subcommittee that was set up by the Third Committee. The portico idea is a helpful way of looking at the UDHR text as a whole, but students of the declaration should know that the majority of the UDHR drafters did not subscribe to the portico idea. These drafters were more comfortable with accepting the order of the thirty articles as they had organically grown over a process of more than two years (Morsink 1999b, section 6.5).

These critical comments on other authors' lack of sufficient familiarity with the *travaux préparatoires* indicate that Daniel Cohen's claim to present a "more ambivalent picture" of the UDHR drafting process than what I gave in my *Origins* book is also misplaced (Cohen 2012, 59). He gives Verdoodt and Robinson as sources for what he presents as the "more ambivalent picture" of these UN debates, as if it is not entirely clear that the Holocaust was the main cause. Cohen ignores the fact that what he presents as additional causal factors (such as Enlightenment precedents) make their appearance in chapter 8 of my *Origins* book. As his source for these "corrections," Cohen mentions the books by Verdoodt and Robinson. These two authors make more limited use of the *travaux* than I did. While they wrote long before I did, I do not see how an earlier, more-limited use of the same historic data can serve as a correction to a more thorough though later use of the exact same data. The problem with these mistakes is that they feed on each other. For instance, Aryeh Neier uses Glendon's portico idea in his own chapter on the declaration (Neier 2012, 59).

The Human Rights System as a UDHR Legacy

Let us take stock of where we are in putting books in the various bins of our initial flow chart: idea → Holocaust + UDHR text → system → movement. So far I have first put some mostly historical studies into the *idea* bin. Then—because the Holocaust cauldron came first in time and is the pivotal event in this book—I skipped the UDHR text link and pleaded for not criminalizing the lower-level moral/legal system of international human rights law by confusing it with its upper-level criminal cousin, the cauldron having produced two tracks and not just one. Because I had skipped the UDHR text link, in this section I backtracked and put some books in that second *UDHR text* bin, enlarging it by making its connection with the Holocaust more obvious than most historians make it out to be. Before I move on to discuss the human rights movement, which is also part of the UDHR legacy, I feel I do still owe the reader some more general comments on the moral/legal system (UDHR → ICCPR → ICESCR → CEDAW → CRC →

Etc.) that in the previous section I separated from its criminal cousin. Though I discuss some key philosophical details of this part of the legacy in chapters 4 and 5, I make some general comments here.

Hundreds and possibly thousands of books and articles have been written about this huge system of international human rights law. While the real payoff lies in the flourishing of human beings, if we go by just the number of books published on the international human rights system that took shape in the decades of the 1950s through 1980s (and is still growing), there can be no doubt that this system is a resounding success. In chapter 4 I list some 125 international legal texts that fit into the lower half of our bifurcated chart. Unfortunately, the thousands of reports and books involved in maintaining this legal or civil system often do not make for interesting reading for the nonexpert. Ineke Boerefijn's *The Reporting Procedure under the Covenant on Civil and Political Rights: Practice and Procedure on the Human Rights Committee* (1999), Brigit Toebes's *The Right to Health as a Human Right in International Law* (1999), and Magdalena Sepúlveda's *The Nature of the Obligations under the International Covenant on Economic and Cultural Rights* (2003) are just three volumes I am familiar with that were published in the School of Human Rights Research Series by Intersentia/Hart. I forgo listing more human rights series by other publishers or thousands more monographs thrown up by simple Google searches asking for information about a certain international human right listed in the UDHR. These books, related papers, and reviews are often very analytical and narrowly focused on a particular aspect of this huge moral/legal system and thus not all that interesting for the general reader. But for those who want to know the fine historical and legal details of a certain part of this system, this literature is indispensable.

Once in a while, though, a provocative book on the civil human rights system shakes things up. Eric Posner's *The Twilight of Human Rights Law* did just that in 2014. As his title suggests, Posner thinks that the international civil human rights system is dying and should be allowed to fade. We disagree on both scores. Posner tells his readers that there are some 300 specific human rights proclaimed in the lower level of our bifurcated chart (Posner 2014, 92). That happened because one right or article in the UDHR, which he admits is the start of this system (Posner 2014, table 1.1), turns into multiple rights when it is translated into the international legalese of one or more human rights conventions, only a few of which I identified by acronym on the lower track of the chart. In chapter 4's discussion of this system, I identify many more of these so-called human rights instruments. Because the system is getting so big and bloated, I compare it to an elephant. But like real elephants, the system still has plenty of moral feeling, which I claim it draws from the UDHR often mentioned in the preambles of international legal texts.

Of this still-growing system of human rights law, Posner lists only nine major treaties. I give them as he lists them with the number of ratifying states as of January 2013 in parentheses after the acronym: in 1965 the International Convention on the Elimination of All Forms of Racial Discrimination (ICERD, 176); in 1966 the International Covenant on Civil and Political Rights (ICCPR, 167); in 1966 the International Covenant on Economic, Social, and Cultural Rights (ICESCR, 160); in 1979 the Convention on the Elimination of All Forms of Discrimination Against Women (CEDAW, 187); in 1984 the Convention Against Torture and Other Cruel, Inhuman, or Degrading Treatment or Punishment (CAT, 153); in 1989 the Convention on the Rights of the Child (CRC, 193); in 1990 the International Convention on the Protection of All Migrant Workers and Members of Their Families (ICRMW, 46); in 2006 the Convention on the Rights of Persons with Disabilities (CRPD, 132); and also in 2006 the International Convention for the Protection of All Persons from Enforced Disappearance (ICPPED, 39). Posner believes this system of international human rights law and its institutions of enforcement are in their "twilight years" because they have "failed to accomplish [their] objectives" (Posner 2014, 7). He wants "to wipe the slate clean and start over with an approach to promoting well-being in foreign countries that is empirical rather than ideological," as the human rights approach supposedly is (8). I respond to what Posner sees as the system's failures.

One is that extrajudicial killings, torture (with its extracted confessions), arbitrary detentions, slavery, and all forms of suppressing dissent seem to continue unabated in the world, despite a "two-hundred-fold" increase in the use of the phrase "human rights" in English books since 1940 (Posner 2014, 6). To this point Dinah Shelton, who reviewed

Posner's book for the *American Journal of International Law*, responded that many of these violations often also violate the domestic laws of the countries in which they occur, as was the case with Posner's opening example of the disappearance of Amarildo De Souza, a bricklayer from Brazil. Posner might have, Shelton says, titled his book *The Twilight of the Rule of Law* in general, instead of just human rights law (Shelton 2015, 229).

The increase in the use of the term "human rights" happened during the same years that the previously mentioned system of human rights instruments was created. That leads Posner to observe that "there is little evidence that human rights treaties, on the whole, have improved the well-being of people, or even resulted in respect for the rights in those treaties. The major goal of this book is to explain why" (Posner 2014, 7). These treaties are failures because their language is too vague and indeterminate, which "raise[s] numerous interpretive difficulties" (34). For instance, the texts of UDHR Article 23 (on work) and Article 7 of the ICESCR (on conditions of work) raise questions about fair or decent wages, about reasonable limitation of working hours, and about what is too high of an unemployment rate. So Posner asks how one would "ascertain whether a government has satisfied or failed to satisfy the right to work" (35). As he sees it, "The problem is not so much that states violate treaty terms but that the treaties do not create any meaningful obligations. This is so because they are vague; they conflict with each other; and they conflict with other rules of international law. . . . Thus, a state that attempts to comply in good faith with the treaties would find itself thrown back on its own judgment as to how to advance the common good" (86). Posner does not think that the UN Office of the High Commissioner of Human Rights, or the Human Rights Council, or the main monitoring committees, or the more than a dozen thematic mandates, or the dozen special rapporteurs who travel the world are of any real help in telling countries what the norms in the system demand of them when the language of a treaty itself is (as Posner holds) to them not clear enough. I think this proposition is untenable.

Much of the language of the civil human rights system came straight out of the Universal Declaration, which is a clear enough text and has without difficulty been translated into more languages than has the Bible. Its translation into legal human rights treaties has not suffered more than similar translations that turn domestic constitutional phrases into legal statutes and juridical decisions. The implementation process of these obligations that starts after a state has ratified any of the conventions is a complex one with interactions between (1) the Treaty Monitoring Committee (made up of experts on the rights the treaty covers), which receives periodic reports from (2) the states that ratified that treaty. The states are often helped by (3) domestic NGOs that are often advised by (4) international NGOs that have members in many different states that ratified the same and other conventions. Since the ratifying states involved do these reports after intervals and since the treaty body after each such report publishes its "concluding observations" on the improvement (or not) of that state's behavior, when it works, this process yields helpful "best practices" for implementing the supposedly abstract and vague international norms. Scholars have taken Posner to task for ignoring all these intricacies and iterations.

Under the title "Human Rights Experimentalism," Gráinne de Búrca aims her description of this process at Posner's belief that there can be "little confidence that the treaties have improved human lives" (de Búrca 2017, 298). She admits that human rights law is not "the magic bullet" some think it is but spells out the conditions that need to hold if ratifications are to have an effect on people's lives. The two main conditions she cites are the presence of a strong civil society in which NGOs can thrive and the existence of democratic regimes. The Netherlands, New Zealand, and Finland are all democracies with strong civil societies. Jasper Krommendijk's finding regarding the effect of CEDAW in those countries should therefore not surprise us. Pace Posner, de Búrca notes that Krommendijk found "that 'the concluding observations' of the human rights treaty bodies are not the result of a compliance pull from the committee or treaty body itself, but rather are attributable to the mobilization and lobbying of NGOs and the attention given in domestic parliaments to the 'concluding observations'" (de Búrca 2017, 300n101). Similarly, de Búrca reports on Nevena Vučković Šahović's study of ratifications of the CRC in twelve Organization for Economic Co-operation and Development (OECD) countries, which found that often a "strong partnership" grew up between the relevant NGOs and the monitoring CRC committee.

Much weaker but still notable improvements were found in nondemocratic Fiji, Morocco, and Kyrgyzstan.

To this effect of domestic NGO activity, we need to add the influence of transnational networks, for that is where we will find the desired cross-fertilization between countries, where what works in one nation may (or may not) be seen to be helpful in others. De Búrca tells us that the Child Rights International Network (CRIN) counts as many as 2,100 organizations in 150 countries in addition to the NGO Group for the CRC (now known as Child Rights Connect), "which is a network of eighty national and international organizations that works to facilitate CRC implementation" (de Búrca 2017, 292–93). The case study of Albania at the end of de Búrca's study shows, she says, "that the process of ratification and operationalization of human rights treaties may come to have a positive impact on human rights standards within states. It demonstrates how the process is neither wholly domestic, nor wholly international, and how it depends on the interaction of a series of different actors and institutions over time" (309). In the case of Albania, it took twenty-one years to go from ratification in 1993 to the universal periodic review of 2014, during which time Albania experienced increased political liberalization. Before this 2014 periodic review conducted by the Human Rights Council, Albania reported in 2012 to the CRC committee. That CRC committee received no fewer than four "shadow reports" written by domestic and international NGOs that supplemented what the Albanian government told the committee it had done since the previous report it submitted in 2005.

What makes the international (civil) human rights system so huge is that its main treaties are at times ratified by close to 150 states with very different cultures, legal systems, religions, and economies. No one norm fits all contexts, Posner argues. As the Albania case shows, scholars correctly believe that some states ratify these treaties because they are pushed to do so by various sections of the human rights movement, which is the last bin in our flowchart and also a legacy of the UDHR. The last arrow of our chart should therefore be redrawn to go both ways: idea → Holocaust + UDHR text → system ↔ movement. Domestic and international human rights organizations operating in almost every country on earth help make the system at least somewhat effective, and the system brings relevant parts of the movement into being when the movement's members turn themselves into watchdogs over that part of the normative system. Sometimes these members bring about an entirely new treaty, as happened with the one that banned landmines. And often they unsuccessfully push for a certain ratification, as happened with CEDAW in the United States.

The empirical research on the effectiveness of ratifications goes both ways. In the same year that Posner published his dire prediction, Christopher J. Fariss argued in the *American Political Science Review* that "respect for human rights has improved over time and that the relationship between human rights respect and ratification of the UN Convention Against Torture is positive, which contradicts findings from existing research" (Fariss 2014, 297). Fariss's findings depend on a distinction between holding human rights standards that are used in reports on violations constant and making them variable because over time reporters increase a state's standard of accountability, and that increase should be tabulated in the research model. Once this turning of the accountability screws is considered, Fariss believes the "results suggest that human rights protectors are more likely to ratify the treaty, [and] that the treaty may in fact have some causal effect on human rights protection, or possibly both. Overall, these findings suggest that the [CAT] treaty is not merely cover for human rights abusers" (313), as Posner's account would have us think.

Posner does not believe that countries ratify treaties or change their social systems because of a domestic need to do so. He writes, "If domestic pressure can force a government to respect human rights, then it will do so regardless of whether the government enters into a human rights treaty" (Posner 2014, 83). In Posner's view, a treaty adds nothing to domestic electoral institutions. Scholars like de Búrca and Fariss do not agree. They believe that NGOs do make a difference at home and abroad. Shelton reminds us, "Nelson Mandela's first trip after his release from Robben Island prison was to Geneva to thank the World Council of Churches for their contributions to ending apartheid in South Africa, which is viewed almost unanimously as an improvement in the well-being of the people of South Africa, despite continued poverty in the country" (Shelton 2015, 232).

I attribute Posner's negative view of the efficacy of human rights law to a lack of appreciation of the impact the Holocaust had first on the writing and adoption of the Universal Declaration and then, by way of impregnation, on the rest of the system. Hitler engaged in internationally illegal, aggressive wars for which the Nazi leaders were condemned in Nuremberg. But that aggression goes back at least to 1933, when Hitler abrogated his own citizens' civil and political rights. Writes Posner, "One interpretation of all this is that if Germany had somehow been forced to respect the rights of its own citizens, the Nazis would never have gained power and turned Germany against its neighbours. The Universal Declaration of Human Rights, and the human rights treaties that followed it, reflect this line of thinking" (Posner 2014, 124). They sure do. And the Holocaust should have had an entry in the index of a book exploring the twilight of the system that came out of that abomination. Posner goes on to explain: "But the causal mechanism that connects respect for human rights and aversion to war is obscure. Human rights treaties do not forbid countries to go to war" (124). Both of these claims are true, but they miss the connection between the Holocaust and the Universal Declaration, in which revulsion against the former caused the latter to be shaped and adopted. The aversion or revulsion that informed the drafting of the UDHR has more to do with the manner of warfare Hitler engaged in than with the idea of war itself.

Posner claims, "*People don't care (much) about the human rights of foreigners*" (Posner 2014, 104; original italics). If true, this would take away most of the reason for the 1948 adoption of the Universal Declaration, which then would undercut the ensuing system on which, I argue, the UDHR had and has an enormous influence. Posner's comment destroys the connection between the Holocaust and the declaration, for that connection is based on the idea of the unity of the human family awakened anew in the UDHR drafters when they were confronted with the horrors of the camps and that led them to the supposition that we are each other's brothers and sisters. This caring about the rights of strangers depends very much on the situation. The UDHR drafters tell us in Article 1 that we have "reason and conscience" that should make us want to treat "one another in a spirit of brotherhood." I cite Posner again: "Most people in the world pay little attention to international human rights law, and do not try to make their voices heard" (115). This belies the enormous growth of the human rights movement in the last quarter century. Shelton too disputes this claim:

> From Tiananmen Square to the Khmer Rouge trials in Cambodia, where victims by the thousands have sought to testify, to the one hundred thousand-plus persons who file complaints each year at the European Court of Human Rights in Strasbourg, to the more than ten thousand rural indigenous Maya who showed up in Guatemala to participate in an onsite visit by a UN special rapporteur, to those who combated apartheid for decades at great cost to themselves and their families, the facts on the ground suggest that most people everywhere (apart from those in power) care about human rights and increasingly know about and raise their voices to demand human rights and fundamental freedoms. (Shelton 2015, 234)

These are large numbers from a variety of situations. The human rights movement has many ordinary people in it. It is not dead and not about to flounder.

The Human Rights Movement as a UDHR Legacy

Before I conclude this chapter I still need to discuss the last bin of our diagram: idea → Holocaust + UDHR text → system ↔ movement. Like the legal human rights system, the human rights movement embodies and concretizes the moral legacy of the declaration. Let me stipulate that the human rights movement is made up of NGOs either seeking to nudge states and their citizens into adherence to human rights treaties (both civil and criminal) that these states have ratified or seeking to foster respect for human rights regardless of any appeal to ratified treaties. Although NGOs and human rights organizations (HROs) are not formally required to define themselves as seeking to implement one or several articles of the UDHR, most scholars write as if this is the case, for in practice it seems nearly true. Since the phrase "human rights" was not much used before the 1940s, we cannot really say that there was a "*human* rights" movement before that time. But it is clear that the people in Adam Hochschild's 2005 book *Bury the Chains*, which recounts the story of the British anti-slavery movement and those who worked for the ICRC, with which Hopgood begins his 2013 book, had what we today call a "human rights" agenda. The antislavery movement and the ICRC prepared the way for our human rights project. I therefore propose that we call these earlier organizations the "precursors" of the modern human rights movement, the seeds for the movement itself being the thirty articles of the UDHR. Whether or not they say so overtly, many modern HROs were inspired by one or several of the articles of the UDHR. William Korey tells the early part of that story in his 1998 *NGOs and the Universal Declaration of Human Rights: A Curious Grapevine*. Two decades later the United Nations has registered thousands of HROs as qualified lobbyists for human rights within its monitoring system of legal international human rights. The relationship between these thousands of NGOs or HROs and the text of the UDHR is an area that invites further investigation.

Jonathan Reader, a colleague of mine, suggested I read up on what sociologists David Snow and Robert Benford have called a "master frame" for "social movement organizations" (SMOs), the idea being that the presence of such a master frame helps explain the success of these SMOs. The authors see "social movement organizations and their actors as actively engaged in the production and maintenance of meaning for constituents, antagonists and bystanders or observers" (Snow and Benford 1992, 136). That is precisely what the 1948 UDHR drafters saw themselves as doing: producing meaning for their constituents. Generally, a frame "refers to an interpretive schemata that simplifies and condenses 'the world out there' by selectively punctuating and encoding objects, situations, events, experiences, and sequences of actions within one's present and past environment. . . . Master frames form the same specific functions as movement-specific collective action frames, but they do so on a larger scale. . . . [They] provide a grammar that punctuates and syntactically connects patterns or happenings in the world" (137–38). As a human rights scholar—using the Universal Declaration of Human Rights as my master frame—that is exactly how I interpret and connect various local, regional, or international human rights events occurring around the world at any one time. This is the first of ten propositions the authors defend: "Associated with the emergence of a cycle of protests is the development or construction of an innovative master frame" (143). Snow and Benford do not focus all that much on what to me seems a crucial factor in the success of some SMOs, that is, the role of the anchoring text that provides the ideational content and scope for the movement. They speak of "ideational content" but link that content only vaguely to a widely known text that movement chapters can readily access and repeat.

The authors use the peace and the civil rights movements as their main examples. The former is anchored in "Randall Forsberg's proposal for a freeze on the development, testing, and deployment of nuclear weapons . . . as an innovative master frame that stimulated a dramatic upswing in peace movement activity throughout the first half of the [1980] decade" (Snow and Benford 1992, 143). The master frame for the civil rights movement, "as initially espoused by Martin Luther King, Jr., and his associates, accented the principle of equal rights and opportunities regardless of ascribed characteristics and articulated it with the goal of integration through nonviolent means" (145). The tactics of bus boycotts and lunch counter sit-ins "were congruent with the master frame espoused by King and other civil rights leaders and thus followed directly from the movement's nonviolent philosophy" (146). The authors didn't but might have picked Dr. King's "Letter from Birmingham Jail" as embodying the master frame for that movement.

If they had also used the human rights movement to make their case, in my view they would have had to pick the Universal Declaration of Human Rights as the place where the master frame was articulated. The role the declaration has played and is still playing in the human rights movement fits the idea of a master frame very well. Usually the ideational content of a master frame is anchored both in historical circumstances (the nuclear arms race, the burning of black churches, the Holocaust) and in a master text, speech, essay, or declaration that was produced in response to those empirical circumstances. In the case of the Universal Declaration, the historical events of the Holocaust have made its text the most important guide for the worldwide human rights movement.

Evidently, the master text of a movement can spin off subsidiary texts that elucidate and embellish elements of the master frame, which is what I will argue happened in the decades of the 1960s and 1970s, when numerous legal "progenitors" of the UDHR master frame were drawn up. These translations of the UDHR into international legalese do not happen without social and political activity by members of the human rights movement, which is why a moment ago I placed a double arrow between the last two bins. Aryeh Neier, who spent a couple of decades as the executive director first of the American Civil Liberties Union (ACLU) and then of Human Rights Watch, subscribes to this double arrow. His 2012 book, *The International Human Rights Movement: A History*, includes a very thorough exposition of the complex relationship between the international human rights *system* ↔ *movement* of our diagram. He observes, "The fact that monitoring has proven so effective has contributed significantly to the emergence and development of the international human rights movement and is the principal factor that has made it an international force. In essence, therefore, it has been the role of international human rights law in making possible the mobilization of global public opinion that is its main contribution" (Neier 2012, 114). That is our third arrow going forward. He then adds, "The international human rights system is unique in depending for compliance with its requirements above all on monitoring by a citizens' movement" (115). That is the third arrow going back to the system. Then the arrow goes forward again: "Were it not for international [human rights] law setting standards against which the conduct of governments can be measured monitoring would not be effective" (115), and there would be no movement.

Neier does not mention the idea of a master frame, but a "great many of the millions of persons worldwide who consider themselves human rights activists feel a kinship and seek ties to others within the movement" (Neier 2012, 9). Neier thinks that "there is little or no prospect that this movement will fade away or decline significantly when it achieves a particular goal, as happened, for example, to the feminist movement for nearly half a century after it won women's suffrage. The contemporary human rights movement responds to victories and defeats by shifting focus from time to time, but it shows signs that it will remain an enduring force in world affairs" (Neier 2012, 7). Snow and Benford might explain this phenomenon with their proposition #7: "The shape of a [later] cycle of protest is in part a function of the mobilizing potency of the anchoring frame" (Snow and Benford 1992, 145). The UDHR text demonstrates its "mobilizing potency" as different cycles of human rights protest make use of its different articles. Neier does not tell us what he thinks the signs of longevity of the movement are. It could be the fact that the moral and ideational master frame of the human rights movement enunciates more than thirty of what he calls "aspects of humanity" (Neier 2012, 57).

It is disappointing to see Neier cast aside so many of those vital aspects of humanity even though they are clearly enunciated in the Universal Declaration as the movement's master frame. Says he, "Civil and political rights mean the same thing everywhere. Freedom of speech, freedom of assembly, freedom of religion, the right to be treated equally and fairly, and the right not to be tortured do not depend upon economic contexts. On the other hand, it is inevitable that social and economic rights have to be applied differently in different circumstances" (Neier 2012, 86) and therefore cannot be counted as core human rights that are the same everywhere. In an October 2016 panel discussion at the City College of New York, the panelists were asked whether the right to a college education was a human right. None of the panelists answered in terms of UDHR Article 16. However, one of them (Gay McDougall) took the opportunity to argue that the time has come for the human rights movement in the United States to put boots on the ground and make the case for US ratification and implementation of the 1966 Economic, Social, and Cultural Covenant. Neier demurred because he thought these matters were not a fit subject for human rights. This even though the mother text of the movement devotes a good deal of space to these very rights. McDougall rightly pointed out that the problem of justiciability, which was one of Neier's objections, has been faced head-on by Europeans and countries like South Africa and India. Also pace Neier, researchers Brinks and Gauri found that "the impact of courts is positive and very much pro-poor in India and South Africa and slightly negative in Indonesia and Brazil. Overall, [we found] that the results of litigation are more positive for the poor than the conventional wisdom would lead us to expect" (Brink and Gauri 2014, 375).

Neier's latent legal positivism reveals itself when he omits the term "human" in the title of his third chapter: "What Are Rights?" "Rights," he says, "are ethical norms with a legal content that requires that they should be honored and enforced by public institutions" (Neier 2012, 56). At the time of their being put down in the text of the UDHR, these moral norms had as of yet no legal content, but they were moral rights nevertheless. Since it took the community of nations till 1967 to give legal content to the norms stated in the 1948 UDHR, are we to suppose that in 1948 these norms were not yet "rights" and the document is wrongly named? What for Neier is the source of this requirement of honor and enforceability? Neier's Hohfeldian analysis starts with the public duties of enforceability that yield what human rights there might or might not be. Starting at the other end, the UDHR drafters began with a good twenty articles of inalienable moral rights that all individuals have, ending with just one short article (the twenty-ninth) on everyone's duties. Because the Holocaust had put them on edge, the UDHR drafters were willing to work out the legal details later. That was done in 1967, when the two international covenants—the ICCPR and the ICESCR, discussed as part of the human rights system—were adopted.

It is not that Neier ignores the Holocaust; for him it just did not lead to the discovery of moral (human) rights the way it did for many UDHR drafters. He writes, "The human rights provisions were incorporated in the text of the [UN] Charter in June 1945, just a few weeks following the first publication in May 1945 of photographs of the Nazi concentration camps and death camps. The crimes that were recorded in those photos demonstrated the connection between gross abuses and human rights and a cataclysmic international conflict" (Neier 2012, 96). Neier does not connect these photos straightway to the Holocaust as the driving force behind the Universal Declaration. His denigration of moral rights as such leads him to consider the "symbolic significance" (99) of the declaration over the real existence of moral rights inalienable to the human person. But then he also explains that "the most important contribution of the Universal Declaration was its assertion that [human?] rights are universal. They are not attributes of nationality or citizenship. Rather, they are an intrinsic part of what it is to be human" (99). I take this to mean that all the rights listed in the Universal Declaration are intrinsic or inalienable, not just Neier's own shorter list of mostly civil, physical security, and political rights.

Although it frequently crosses the boundaries between the bins in our diagram, Samuel Moyn's book *The Last Utopia* also fits best in the movement bin of our diagram. The story Professor Moyn tells is quite straightforward. He wrote this book "out of intense interest in—even admiration for—the contemporary human rights movement, the most inspiring mass utopianism Westerners have had before them in recent decades" (Moyn 2010, 9). He presents his book as a much needed "alternative history of human rights" to the "textbook narrative" we met with at the start of this chapter (but he doesn't use the phrase). His account focuses on human rights as a popular social movement that took off in the 1970s owing to a "confluence" of factors in different regions of the world, especially Eastern Europe and the cone of Latin America. The birth of this movement came as a surprise with sources that were "unseen and underground" but that then suddenly appeared as "a shocking groundswell that has to be explained" (Moyn 2010, 42). "Human rights," Moyn holds, "were the creation of later and unanticipated events [in the 1970s] that upended previous assumptions" (41) on which other human rights historians have relied and by which they have been misled. His key charge is that "almost unanimously contemporary historians have adopted a celebratory attitude toward the emergence and progress of human rights, providing recent enthusiasms with uplifting backstories, and differing primarily about whether to locate the true breakthrough with the Greeks or the Jews, medieval Christians or early modern philosophers, democratic revolutionaries or anti-racist visionaries" (5). Through their teleological thinking, these misled historians have "recast world history as raw material for the progressive ascent of international human rights . . . [not] conceding that earlier history left open diverse paths toward the future, rather than paving a single road toward current ways of thinking and acting" (5). Historians like Ishay, Lauren, and Wolterstorff—but not the contributors to the revisitation volume—whose work I placed in the idea bin of the chart, were according to Moyn wrongheaded in their "quixotic search for deep roots" (312) of human rights.

While I may not agree with how these other authors treat a particular historical thinker as a precursor to human rights, I do not follow Moyn in his wholesale condemnation of this quest for deep roots. I myself, for example, have sought to give legitimacy to the concept of inherent rights by linking the UDHR drafters' use of the words "inalienable" and "born with" to various Enlightenment predecessors. According to Moyn, this kind of historical thinking makes the mistake of downplaying the discontinuities and contingencies that make up most of history. There is no point, he thinks, in looking for intellectual connections between thinkers of different eras. Previous conceptions of rights and our own conception of human rights are "radically different" and have nothing in common. History is full of surprises, and the sudden birth of the popular human rights movement in the 1970s is one of them. I locate the intervention of history into the idea at the time of the Holocaust and not in the 1970s.

Moyn's own work presents "a much more recent timeline" than the ones used by these searchers for deep historical sources. "Rather than attributing their sources to Greek philosophy and monotheistic religion, European natural law and early modern revolutions, horror against American slavery and Adolf Hitler's Jew-killing, [Moyn's alternative history] shows that human rights have distinctive origins of a much more recent date" (Moyn 2010, 7). Moyn here dismisses the entire history of Western thought and politics, including the Holocaust, as not relevant to our understanding of the conception of human rights that guides the movement in the 1970s and further into the twenty-first century. In a recent essay on Giuseppe Mazzini, Moyn admits to "perhaps having gone too far" (Moyn 2015b, 119). Without any justification, the 2010 passage cited before this admission sweeps aside the first three bins and all three arrows of our flowchart, leaving the 1970s in total isolation to fend for itself as the birthing ground for contemporary human rights both as concept and as movement. As Moyn sees it, intellectual historians who dwell on deep sources for today's human rights concept forget that "few things that are powerful today turn out on inspection to be longstanding and inevitable. And the human rights movement certainly is not one of them" (9). They fail to see that "the drama of human rights, then, is that they emerged in the 1970s seemingly from nowhere" (3). What are intellectual historians to do if they are not allowed to explore possible connections between *ideas* from different eras? Must intellectual history be reduced to just the material conditions of history that help explain the sudden rise of the human rights *movement* as such and get rid of the realm of ideas, including those laid out in the master text of the movement, altogether?

The main piece of quantitative evidence provided for the sudden birth of the movement in the 1970s is a chart on page 235 of the 2010 *Utopia* book showing a spike in the *New York Times* usage of the phrase "human rights"; the term appears "nearly five times as often in 1977 as in any prior year in that publication's history" (Moyn 2010, 4). To research her own 2005 book, *A New Deal for the World*, Elizabeth Borgwardt also checked out the *New York Times Index* and found that

> for 1936 it contains no "human rights" heading at all. The term makes a tentative appearance with two articles in 1937, one on property rights and one on labor rights. By 1946 the term is listed as a separate heading, but the reader is referred to "civil rights," where there are approximately 150 articles we would recognize as addressing human rights–related topics. In 1956, the human rights heading is no longer cross-referenced to civil rights, but rather to a whole new conceptual universe, "freedom and human rights," under which heading there are over 600 articles. (Borgwardt 2005, 55)

With the help of these data (and much else), Borgwardt locates the moment for human rights not in the 1970s, as does Moyn, but in the 1940s as I also do. David Rodick reviewed Moyn's book for the *Review of Metaphysics*, a high-quality philosophy journal. Rodick was also puzzled by Moyn's argument from the *Times Index*, which to him made the year 1977 show up as "truly a blip on the screen." This left Rodick to wonder "if human rights might suffer a 'disappearance,' much like that which Foucault predicted for man in *The Order of Things*." He concluded that "Moyn offers an interesting narrative, but is not convincing enough [for] this reviewer to dismiss the search for deep origins as quixotic" (Rodick 2011, 177). I share Rodick's sentiment and will, for instance, continue to link Thomas Aquinas's talk of natural human inclinations to contemporary groundings of human rights in species-wide human capabilities or basic human interests.

My argument in this chapter has been that many new historians have sometimes rather cursorily passed over the late 1940s as pivotal for what I think the overall human rights story is. Passing over the historic significance of the UDHR drafting years of 1946–48, their histories endanger the link I see between the event of the Holocaust and the text of the declaration. But I do not argue that this endangerment is caused intentionally on their part. While the authors I have mentioned are neglectful of and inattentive to the connection between the Holocaust and the Universal Declaration, I do not think that this neglect is by design or on purpose. Their books have their own theses that do not require them to focus on the late 1940s, which is when I claim the connection I highlight was forged. The neglect is therefore an inadvertent side effect of the other purposes their books are meant to serve. Even so, I call them out on this oversight because I believe that neglecting or ignoring the crucial relationship between the Holocaust and the declaration robs each part of the equation of the moral power it gets from being yoked with the other. Without this connection the Holocaust has no moral power at all, and that huge cloud loses the sliver of silver lining it has. And the declaration, like all other historic declarations with their own verbal energy, loses the enormous moral power it gets when connected to its birthing ground, which was the Nazi horrors, especially those perpetrated during the Holocaust.

However, this unintentionality cannot be ascribed to Samuel Moyn. For he has gone out of his way to deny the connection this book seeks to affirm, even calling it "false" and "untrue." For sorting purposes I put his book *The Last Utopia* in our last movement bin, but his outright and active denial of the connection separates him from the other historians. I therefore discuss his views in a separate chapter to which I turn next. Any reader who has had enough of my critical views of other scholars and wants to know what the evidence is for the connection I defend should go straight to chapter 3 without losing the main threat of this book.

2

MOYN'S DISMISSAL OF THE CONNECTION

Throughout his body of work, Samuel Moyn pushes the 1940s and especially the Holocaust into the background of the human rights story he tells. The very years that I want to lift up—1946 through 1948—make for a gap in Moyn's timeline. He never specifically tells us which of the years in "the 1940s" interest him most. While he roams freely throughout the decade, he only sporadically enters the years on which I focus because, as I see it, that is when the human rights *movement* received its founding text or master frame, a moment one would expect Moyn to celebrate but which he studiously avoids. He prefers the context of the times, as he interprets it, over the declaration's text as it was debated and adopted inside the halls of the United Nations. He tells his readers, "The now well understood drafting of the Universal Declaration, the usual focus, cannot be separated from far larger historical forces that doomed it to irrelevance in its time" (Moyn 2010, 46), that time being the years I mentioned. There probably is a sense in which this comment is true, but placing an *X* (e.g., the UDHR) in context presupposes that one knows what that *X* is, which in Moyn's case I question. My view is that what was done inside the UN drafting chambers in the years 1946–48 had a remarkable integrity of its own, one that was not dictated by context or "larger historical forces" other than the Nazi horrors that I inserted in the timeline in the preceding chapter and for which I will give details in the next. I suspect that some of Moyn's general put-downs of the generic 1940s as the moment for human rights are actually aimed at the connection here defended.

The Gap in Moyn's Timeline

It is not that Moyn does not operate with a framework of his own. He seems to put little stock in conceptions of human rights current before the times he writes about. In the follow-up book to his better-known *Utopia*, he offers us a "typology of three stages in the conceptual evolution of human rights starting in the early 1940s. Brutally simplifying one might label them the welfarist, anticolonial and humanitarian paradigms in which the coin of human rights was minted and minted again" (Moyn 2014, 87). As Moyn sees it, the welfarist consensus of the 1940s bypassed the principle of self-determination announced to the world in the 1942 Atlantic Charter declared by Roosevelt and Churchill. The abortion of this charter's promises for national independence of all peoples meant that the human rights itemized in the declaration were seen by millions of people living in the colonies as a substitute for the real thing and as a consolation prize. Looked at this way, the work involved in drafting the UDHR was irrelevant and marginal to the big questions of the world as seen by most non-Western peoples who wanted liberty for themselves as whole peoples. The principle of collective self-determination announced in the Atlantic Charter was violated and ignored by the United Nations when the colonial peoples did not immediately get their freedom. So the millions in the colonies saw the third generation of human rights that is not mentioned in the Universal Declaration (see chapters 3 and 5) die in the narrow birth of the two earlier generations that did find their way into the declaration.

In the prologue to his *Utopia* book, Moyn writes, "In 1948, in the aftermath of World War II, a Universal Declaration of Human Rights was proclaimed. But it was less the annunciation of a new age than a funeral wreath laid on the grave of wartime hopes" (Moyn 2010, 2). Again, in the 1940s "human rights turned out to be a substitute for what many around the world wanted, a collective entitlement to self-determination. For the subjects of empire were not wrong to view human rights as a kind of consolation prize" (45). I am not sure what "many around the world" and what "subjects of empire" thought, but I am sure that nothing could conflict more with the mood of optimism that prevailed throughout most of the declaration's drafting sessions, including many non-Western delegates. Drafters from all over the world in no way saw the rights they were proclaiming as "stillborn principles" (2). Even the communist delegations that often spoke for the colonial peoples participated actively in the process of drafting the UDHR. They abstained in the end not because there were no collectivist rights but because the social and economic ones were not strong enough. The commission of which Eleanor Roosevelt was elected chair is the only one mandated in the UN Charter, and she and her cohorts in no way looked at their task as "an afterthought" in UN business (82). As Moyn sees it, the fact that the right to collective self-determination was ignored led to the "irrelevance" and "marginalization" of the two previous generations of civil/political rights and of social/economic human rights. These two generations simply had nothing to say to the pressing problems of the world as seen from a Westphalian perspective by the millions living under foreign rule who, according to Moyn, wanted rights for themselves as individuals but far more so for their collectivities as whole peoples. In part 2 of this book, I defend the idea that there are no genuine human rights with a collectivist ontology and that the UDHR drafters were therefore right to be careful about the question Moyn raises. Here I object to the idea of the marginalization of the first two generations as a mere "consolation prize" at the time they were included in the declaration.

After the initial stillbirth in the 1940s, Moyn sees the second stage of contemporary human rights history in the decades of the 1950s and 1960s, when numerous nation-states were liberated and freed as colonies of metropolitan powers and joined the United Nations. Moyn admits that these wars of independence were not really human rights fights, except that conceptually this period did bring the third generation of human rights to the attention of the world. As a result the membership of the United Nations rose from 56 in 1948 to more than 150 in 1970. That then led to the third humanitarian stage of human rights in the decade of the 1970s, which is when Moyn thinks modern human rights were really born. Writing more recently, he thinks that human rights are still irrelevant in our world and that the movement needs to come down from the heights of moral purity, dirty its hands, and adopt more politically oriented and party-like agendas for change (Moyn 2014, epilogue).

Moyn's description of human rights in their first 1940s stage does not do justice to the years 1946–48. I take exception to two of the points he makes: that they displayed only a "pretense of unity" (Moyn 2010, 73) and that scholars operate with a "myth that human rights were a direct response to the Holocaust" (83). The Universal Declaration does not have a mere "pretended unity"; it is a genuine collective response to the Holocaust. I do not think that in the 1970s human rights "came to mean something radically different" than they did in the 1940s, not if we count the three years I highlight. I cite a passage in which Moyn passed over the years 1946–48 as if they never happened: "The announcement of the Truman doctrine in March of 1947 with its call for a decisive choice between 'two ways of life' meant that the passage of the Universal Declaration must have seemed too much of a pretense of unity at a crossroads for humanity to really matter" (73). Moyn believes that "there is perhaps no better testament to the fact that human rights died through birth than that they could prompt no more general campaign of thinkers to defend them or even define them" in those years of the 1940s (75). On the contrary, we can and should count the hundreds of international delegates, supporting staffs, and attendant NGOs involved in the UDHR drafting process as thinking campaigners for human rights.

Moyn credits Moses Moskowitz with saying that human rights "died in the process of being born" (Moyn 2010, 47; Moskowitz 1976, 82). But he does not tell his readers that Moskowitz added, "Commitment to the promotion of human rights and fundamental freedoms for all recommended itself [in 1948] as the most compelling form in which to register and illuminate the world's response to the Nazi Holocaust and its determination to prevent the recurrence of similar catastrophes" (Moskowitz 1976, 82). The dying of human rights for Moskowitz had especially to do with the quick deterioration of international relations during the Cold War, which was the reason the UN adopted two instead of just one covenant, as the UDHR drafters had envisioned. This next line from Moskowitz applies only to the two later covenants and not to the UDHR, which was finished in the rough by the time the 1948 Berlin Airlift was put in place and the Cold War took off: "After the basic human rights texts [of the covenants] were drafted it became increasingly difficult to maintain the fiction of nations united in a common cause by allowing the widest range of ambiguity to words in order to accommodate divergent views and interests" (Moskowitz 1976, 83). This lack of uniform meaning was clearly present during the negotiations for and after the adoption of the two international covenants that are part of the human rights system of the 1960s. There was a strong push to have only one covenant, but that failed. When it comes to the *Holocaust + UDHR text* link of chapter 1's flowchart, Moskowitz agrees that after the Holocaust "the only way in which the world could redeem itself was to affirm the inviolability of the human person" (83). Moskowitz shares our view that in spite of the UN's ingrained Westphalianism "the emphasis on the promotion of human rights legitimized the United Nations' claim to moral stewardship of the post-war world" (83). The disappointments brought on by the Cold War soon *after* the adoption of the UDHR cannot be taken to mean that the rights in that document died in the act of their birth. Moskowitz's disappointment stemmed from the Cold War fights that led to two abstract covenants instead of just one. He clearly did not belittle the connection between human rights and the Holocaust.

In his race through history, Moyn overlooks the window of opportunity presented by the Holocaust. The birth of human rights in the 1946–48 moment was a traumatic one, and it took these rights some decades to have their effect on the world, but born they were. Reading the declaration, one does not get the impression that the text is based on a "fiction of ideological consensus" (Moyn 2010, 79). Ideology was minimal and produced a remarkable list of rights, most of which were agreed on—to cite Moskowitz (1976) again—as "the world's response to the Nazi Holocaust and its determination to prevent the recurrence of similar catastrophes." Just as there was nothing "fictional" about the processes of constitution making at the Federal Convention in Philadelphia and at the Assemblée Constituante in Paris from 1789 to 1791, so there is nothing fictional about the debates in the United Nations that led to the proclamation of the Universal Declaration of Human Rights "as a common standard of achievement for all peoples and all nations." It is absurd to say, as Moyn does, that it is a "gross error to assume that the language of human rights, let alone, the law of human rights, matter[ed] in the beginning" (Moyn 2010, 81). Obviously both the language and the law it later shaped mattered a great deal from the very start. Moyn is speaking about human rights in the 1940s when he writes that "never at any point were they primarily understood as breaking fundamentally with the world of states that the UN brought together" (Moyn 2010, 45). This does not fit how the UDHR drafters viewed their task. Holding up their list of rights as "a common standard of achievement for all peoples and all nations" to follow, they clearly broke with the reigning surface Westphalianism of the UN organization in the 1940s. This book means to show just how fundamental that break was.

Marco Duranti, a former student of Moyn, has looked at the references to Nazi practices that I cite in my *Origins* book, some of which I repeat in the next evidentiary chapter. He notes how I describe the invocation by the UDHR drafters of "*the evils of the Nazi regime*'s racial theories, discriminatory laws, arbitrary judicial theories, euthanasia program, medical experiments, use of slave labor and torture, and trafficking of women and children" (Duranti 2012, 164). Those were the evil practices the UDHR drafters mentioned when they wanted to give a rationale for a certain article or clause to be included in the declaration. Duranti rightly points out that "an expansive definition of 'the Holocaust' might encompass these phenomena, each of which was arguably a precursor to or homologous with the attempted *annihilation of European Jewry*, though the International Military Tribunal in Nuremberg referred to them as 'crimes against humanity' that pertained to all Nazi victims" (164). I have italicized the two senses in which Duranti uses "the Holocaust" and in which the term has come to be used in Holocaust and human rights studies. The first sense of "the Holocaust" as "the evils of the Nazi regime" is what Duranti calls the expanded definition. This definition includes all kinds of evil practices of the Nazis, and it is the one I mostly used in my *Origins* book. The narrower definition refers to "the annihilation of European Jewry." Duranti adds, and I agree, that today "any mainstream usage of the term 'the Holocaust', however, necessarily, denotes the physical destruction of over five million Jews during the war" (164). I gave sixty pages of evidence for there being a causal connection between these

Nazi evils and the declaration in *Origins*, and unlike most scholars, Duranti took a look at. In my next chapter, I use select quotes from that larger body of evidence, which still calls for more investigation.

Duranti is right when he says that in the *Origins* account, I "repeatedly elide the difference between 'the Holocaust' and 'the horrors of the war'" (Duranti 2012, 164). I agree. I wrote my earlier account in the 1980s, when the expanded definition was already current. I might even then have used the narrower definition, but I did not. In the present book, I mostly (but not exclusively) use the narrower term because I see the connection endangered and want to fortify it. The strengthening of the endangered connection is helped by the fact that in Holocaust memory studies today the two senses of "Holocaust" often overlap. Many people who use the expanded definition include in it "the annihilation of European Jewry." In the present study I reverse the overlap in that I use the term "Holocaust" to also include Nazi horrors generally. This view has recently received confirmation from Dan Plesch's 2017 book detailing, pace Moyn and much contemporary scholarship, how the "Allies condemned the Holocaust" (chap. 3) in the mid- and late 1940s and held thousands of criminal trials against mostly German "foot soldiers of atrocity" (chap. 5) that began before the war ended and were stopped around the time the declaration was finished.

The second sense of "the Holocaust" refers specifically to the annihilation of European Jewry. Moskowitz seems to have had this sense in mind when he pointed out that "Nazism was . . . the embodiment in a new form of an ancient urge to purify the world by annihilating categories of people condemned as agents of corruption and incarnations of evil, conjured up by the powers that be" (Moskowitz 1976, 83). This narrower sense sees the Holocaust "as a discrete phenomenon" aimed at the destruction of the Jews in Germany and occupied territories. Duranti comments that during the debates on the Universal Declaration, "UN delegates do not appear to have ever represented Germany's genocidal campaign against the Jews as qualitatively distinct from the horrors perpetrated by the Nazi regime" (Duranti 2012, 168). The word "ever" seems far too strong here. It conflicts with the UNWCC report I introduce in chapter 3 as evidence for the connection between the Holocaust and the UDHR that I am defending. The writing, reception, and discussion of that report suggest that some or many of the UDHR drafters (who glanced at or read the UNWCC report) may have conflated the two senses of "Holocaust" when they used the expanded definition in the debates on the declaration. They may or may not have been thinking of Jewish victims specifically. Duranti cites René Cassin and Salomon Grumbach, two French delegates, who did refer to the Holocaust as a discrete phenomenon, although only one of these references concerned the UDHR. Duranti concludes, "We cannot assume that indignation about the Holocaust was the chief catalyst for the postwar development of these norms, much less the primary factor shaping their content" (168). Clearly Duranti has the second discrete-event meaning of "Holocaust" in mind when he makes this sweeping observation, and just as clearly, as we look at the Holocaust cauldron, we now can say with more confidence than I had in 1999 that the Holocaust as a discrete event was included in the Nazi horrors and thus a catalyst for many of the rights in the declaration and hence for the new postwar norms. For example, the entanglement of cultural genocide and UDHR minority rights discussions on which I report in chapter 3 supports my contention that even in the late 1940s the two senses of "Holocaust" are hard to separate.

Since it is notoriously difficult to know what people are thinking when they use a term and since awareness of the Holocaust as the annihilation of the Jews has increased enormously with the increase of Holocaust study programs and centers around the world, I believe I am on safe ground with the title of this book. I seek to rehabilitate the connection between the Holocaust (in both senses of that term) and the declaration. The more my readers conflate the two senses, the deeper the connection will be. The increase of specific Holocaust memories and increased awareness in our own day will give extra depth to the connection I seek to rehabilitate with the result that other generations will take human rights more seriously than they might have had they encountered only the expanded definition. Israeli historian Yehuda Bauer contends in "A Past That Will Not Go Away" that "the Holocaust has become a cultural code—the paradigmatic symbol of evil in Western civilization" (Bauer 1998, 22). That is how I use the term in the title of this book.

Just as the French Revolution has come to stand for its own era, so the Holocaust has come to stand for the evils of World War II.

"There is," notes Bauer, "the dim understanding that the Nazi rebellion against civilization and the murder of the Jews that resulted from it form a universal threat to every person everywhere" (14), a threat, I add, the UDHR drafters sought to combat with their declaration. Of the two reactions to the Holocaust—either universalizing it by using the expanded definition or insisting on its total uniqueness and incomparability to any other evil past or present—I have adopted the first alternative. My reason is that today the two uses are starting to merge in that more and more people have a definite "Holocaust consciousness" and know, as Bauer puts it, that "there is simply no way of comprehending the Holocaust unless one realizes who the Jews were and are, and why they became the chosen victim of an ideology that wanted to rebel against what we call 'Western civilization' utilizing the most modern achievements of technology and science to do so" (Bauer 1998, 20). I wager that most of the readers of this book work with both definitions simultaneously. As Bauer puts it, "the Holocaust is a combination of the uniqueness and the universal; it is the uniqueness, and the fact that it happened to a certain people, at a certain time, for distinct reasons, that makes it so real, so threatening, so universal. Hence the fact that the Holocaust has become a cultural code; hence the fascination with the Holocaust; hence its universal aspects" (22). Hence the *Universal* Declaration of Human Rights.

In most of his references to the Holocaust, Moyn stresses the narrow subjective awareness of the killing of Jews at the expense of the broader expanded reference to Nazi atrocities generally, though those atrocities would also include the killing of the Jews. I see Moyn switching from the narrow sense to the expanded definition of "Holocaust" in this single passage: "In real time, across weeks of debate around the Universal Declaration in the UN General Assembly, the genocide of the Jews went unnoticed, in spite of the frequent invocation of other dimensions of Nazi barbarity to justify specific items for protection, or to describe the consequences of leaving human dignity without defense" (Moyn 2010, 82). He puts his case starkly: "Contrary to conventional assumptions, there was no widespread Holocaust consciousness in the postwar era, so human rights could not have been a response to it. More important, no international rights movement emerged at the time" (7). Because the human rights movement, in Moyn's narrative, did not take shape till 1970s, the real historic moment for human rights cannot have been in the 1940s, when there was no real Holocaust consciousness yet. Moyn thinks that because historians have misread the UDHR, "the now deeply ingrained assumption that the entire aftermath of World War II and not least the Universal Declaration just must have been a response to the Jewish Genocide is wrong" (89). The words "just" and "must have been" overstate his case and have been superseded by new research. Moyn's argument does not allow for an overlap of the objective definition that does apply with a subjective awareness that we know some of the drafters must also have had. "From the early 1940s," writes Moyn, "human rights was not yet a concept linked primarily with atrocity and certainly not with the supranational protection of individuals which only a few advocated" (88). That cannot be true, for the expanded definition is nothing but a list of atrocities that match the UDHR list of rights as I explained them in previous publications. Against the background of the narrow sense Plesch uses in his chapters 3 ("Allies Condemned the Holocaust") and 5 ("Foot Soldiers of Atrocity") and the fusion of the two senses of "Holocaust" by Duranti and Bauer, I submit that we regard the drafting years (1946–48) as *the* historic moment for human rights because of their connection to the Holocaust in both its senses.

At the start of his book *Christian Human Rights*, Moyn (2015a) lists four "conventional opinions about human rights in the 1940s" with which he disagrees. The first is that "institutions such as the United Nations, which allowed for the birth of the Universal Declaration, deserve the most scrutiny" (12). While Moyn focuses on the "broader view of the scene as a whole," I have focused my energy on the drafting years of the declaration (1946–48), in part because those years produced what arguably became the most important sociopolitical text of the twentieth century and because it was produced by official delegates of a consort of fifty-six nations that wanted to inject a transnational morality into the new political world order they were creating. I maintain that this large-scale official international effort was successful and therefore outranks in importance the personal opinions of the theologians and jurists Moyn cites to paint the surrounding landscape. The second "conventional opinion" Moyn rejects is that "historians have followed the general public in treating human rights as a response to the Holocaust. Yet few who said they cared about human dignity and rights in the 1940s said so because of the Jewish fate, and the pope [Pius XII] is a good example of this broader truth" (13). Here we have an overlap of the two definitions: the first has an objective referent and the second involves the subjective interest in the fate of the Jews. Regarding the first use, I cannot speak for other historians, but I will say that my own wanting to link the Holocaust (objective referent) to the text of the Universal Declaration came from years of studying the *travaux préparatoires.* Regarding the subjective referent, we are not told who "the few" are and do not know what specifically Pope Pius XII was thinking when he made reference to "human dignity and rights" in his 1942 Christmas message.

Moyn dismisses this "conventional opinion" of the Holocaust's causing a 1940s human rights interest because "this notion fails to do justice to the fact that the sole abstentions to the Universal Declaration in the United Nations General Assembly reflected the sway of organized Christianity's greatest enemies, old and new: Islam and communism" (Moyn 2015a, 14). Some time ago I showed that these abstentions, which also included South Africa, came as a result of two and a half years of negotiations and some close votes. On at least one occasion, even the communists forgot to abstain, and at the final vote on December 10, ten of the eleven Muslim nations voted *for,* and not against, adoption of the declaration, a fact Moyn fails to mention. The only Muslim nation that voted consistently against each of the drafts was Saudi Arabia. Also, Yugoslavia and the Soviet Union had just had a falling out, which caused turmoil in the communist camp and influenced the details of those abstentions (Morsink 1999b, chap. 1). Moyn is reading Cold War politics back into the UN drafting chambers, a point I address in a moment.

In the sixth chapter of his book *Human Rights and the Uses of History,* Moyn provocatively asks: "How did human rights and the Holocaust get entangled?" (Moyn 2014, 87). That the war ended in 1945 and photos of the camps were shown around the hall in San Francisco just before the UN Charter vote was taken does not arouse any curiosity about the adoption of a universal code of ethics only three years later by the same organization. Ordinary folk may think that post hoc means propter hoc, but Moyn believes historians of human rights should know better. "High profile observers—Michael Ignatieff for example—see human rights as an old ideal that finally came into its own as a response to the Holocaust, which might be the most universally repeated myth about their origins" (Moyn 2010, 6).

Moyn sets out to destroy that myth, noting in a later book that "If the historiographical goal is to celebrate an international or supranational response to the Holocaust as such in the 1940s, the most vivid example" he can think of is "Eastern European antifascism" (Moyn 2014, 90), not the two-year-long debate about a global morality for the postwar world. He believes that "for practically no one and for few Jews was the Holocaust, to the extent its enormity was understood at all, the rationale for suprastate law or atrocity prevention directly" (90). He speculates that "mass death, genocidal or not" was not on anyone's mind in the 1940s and therefore could not have been the rationale for any kind of "supratstate law or atrocity prevention" (90) such as we find in the declaration. He rightly feels a need to catch himself, so he adds, "If so, it is not surprising that in the United Nations records it seems that no one—the one possible exception is the likely author of the line about barbarous acts, French Jew Rene Cassin, had what is now known as the Holocaust of European Jewry in mind as the core meaning of the idea. At least no diplomats of any nationality mentioned the Holocaust during the yearlong debate around the Universal Declaration" (90). The strong, repeated, and successful participation of the World Jewish Congress in the drafting of the declaration over a period of *more than two years* belies these claims (see Morsink 1999b, chaps. 1 and 2).

For me the Universal Declaration sits on a three-legged motivational stool. First there was a strong desire to respond to the horrors of World War II. The UDHR drafters tell us straight out that "the conscience of mankind" was "outraged" by the "barbarous acts" of the Nazis. This leg of the stool is the main load bearer and unifier of the process that in the end kept delegates attending meetings and putting up with Eleanor's cajoling whenever they dallied. It was this shared desire to respond to the war's devastation that caused the UN Economic and Social Council (ECOSOC) to give the Human Rights Commission the mandate of producing on short order an "international bill of rights." All the UN documents of the time, including the communications between

ECOSOC and the commission, show Moyn to be clearly off base with his suggestion that "the general consensus about itemization of rights suggests that little was at stake in the proceedings, in spite of a few interesting debates over details" (Moyn 2010, 63). On the contrary, a great deal was at stake, and the representatives of the fifty-six nations knew it, which is why they attended the hundreds of meetings. The wonder of it all is that there was enough abhorrence at what the Nazis had done and enough goodwill that they were able and willing to rise to the occasion and fulfill their mandate. Moyn's observation that "if the Universal Declaration was a response to an experience, it was essentially to an experience of depression and war, not one of atrocity and genocide" (Moyn 2014, 92) reverses the first and second legs of the motivational stool. The first leg is the shared abhorrence of the Nazi barbarities, including that of the camps.

The second leg of the motivational stool consists of John Humphrey's data and his Latin American connections. These helped the participating nations discover that they shared various socialist inclinations that the majority thought should be included in the mandated international bill. Their overlapping interest in welfarism was not what brought these nations together in the first place. And the birth of "human rights" in the 1940s as an alternative to Hitler's tyranny was not a "subsidiary" factor to "more widely circulating promises for some sort of social democracy," which is how Moyn sees the motivational alignment (Moyn 2010, 44, 90). I reverse this order and place the welfarist goal within the larger desire and mandate to respond to the "barbarous practices" of the Nazis.

The third leg of the UDHR's motivational stool emerges as a limiting factor when close to the end of the process the Cold War started to have an effect, with the result that no agreement could be reached on a legally binding covenant (for which there would not have been enough time in any case) and only a morally binding declaration was produced. I argue later that thanks to the work of Eleanor Roosevelt, this Cold War leg of the stool did not undercut the integrity of the declaration as a universal moral text. Pace Moyn, I maintain that her presence kept the influence of the Cold War at bay for some crucial months in the spring and summer of 1948. I also argue that what he says was a debilitating disagreement about types of welfarism enhanced the UDHR because it can be shown to be the product of genuine compromises between different ways of looking at welfarism (Morsink 1999b, chap. 5). The human rights in the declaration are not, as Moyn has it, "a vague synonym for some sort of social democracy . . . [that] did not address the genuinely pressing question of which kind of social democracy to bring about: a version of welfarist capitalism or full-blown socialism" (Moyn 2014, 44–45). The rights listed in the declaration are not a "vague synonym"; they are the real thing.

Responses to Alternative Readings

If the Holocaust—in both senses of the word—was *not* the main and unifying factor in the adoption of the Universal Declaration, then naysayers like Moyn and his cohorts owe us some suggestions as to what might have been the unifying factor and main cause instead. In what follows I discuss some of the alternative rationales Moyn himself suggests, none of which give even the expanded definition of the Holocaust as evil Nazi practices a modest role to play, let alone making it the load-bearing leg of the motivational stool.

Domestic or Universal Labor Rights?

While Gregory Claeys's aspirational view of human rights (Claeys 2015, 218–35) differs from my own inherence view, his emphasis on the fact that many socialists, especially in the nineteenth century, operated with a full slate of rights—social and economic as well as civil and political—fits well with what we find in the 1948 declaration. There is therefore no novelty in the inclusion in the UDHR of the rights to property (Art. 17), to social security (Art. 22), to work under good conditions and labor union activity (Art. 23), or to an adequate standard of living and medical and social services (Art. 25). Claeys shows us that the ground was prepared for the inclusion of these rights by a long history of socialist and progressive activity. He does not discuss their inclusion in the UDHR, and I therefore pick up where he leaves off, with the proviso that we have different ontologies in mind.

In April 1946, at the very first organizational meeting for the Commission of Human Rights, which was to draft the declaration, Henri

Laugier, the assistant UN secretary-general in charge of social affairs, told those present, "You will have to show that the political rights are the first condition of liberty but that today the progress of scientific and industrial civilization has created economic organizations which are inflicting on politically free men intolerable servitude and that, therefore, in the future the declaration of the rights of man must be extended to the economic and social fields" (E/HR/6/2). The visionaries of the late 1940s did exactly that when two years after Laugier spoke they included social, economic, and cultural rights in the Universal Declaration. Theirs was to be a new declaration for a new age that would face up to the excesses of the industrialization of the world and seek to merge the moral human rights track with the economic Bretton Woods track, which had been eclipsed by the security consciousness that prevailed in the writing of the UN Charter. The inclusion in the declaration of these so-called newer rights on equal footing with the civil and political rights did not happen without tough discussions and negotiations involving not only the phrasing of clauses in various articles listing these rights but also the entirety of Articles 22 and 28.

Henri Laugier was a French medical professor who left Vichy France to find exile in Montreal. While there he befriended John Humphrey, who at the time was a socialist law professor at McGill University with a keen interest in Latin American affairs. Laugier appointed Humphrey to be the first director of the Human Rights Division in the UN Secretariat. As human rights director, Humphrey was assigned the task of doing backup research for the Human Rights Commission, which had just been established, but he did far more than that when he produced the first rough draft of a declaration of rights based on a survey of the rights included in the world's extant constitutions. This survey provided the commission with a set of data that told them at a glance that, for instance, twenty-seven countries at that time gave their citizens the constitutional right to an education. Using the results of this survey and early lists of human rights submitted to the commission by Panama, Chile, and Cuba (and a bit later the US), Humphrey wrote his rough draft to include a list of no fewer than ten social, economic, and cultural rights. After these had been trimmed back and condensed by the French delegate René Cassin, they worked their way through the other five or six drafting stages in the UN bureaucracy, ending up as Articles 17 and 22 through 28 of the Universal Declaration. At the end of the last section, I disputed Moyn's point that this welfarist consensus was the main motivational stool for the declaration, but I do not deny that it was a leg of that stool. Moyn also correctly noted that it was mostly Latin American states that pushed for these rights. But I dispute his claim that this consensus amounted to nothing more than domestic overlaps between constitutional provisions and that it had no supra- or international element built into it. Moyn oversimplifies when he notes that "these [Latin American] constitutions reflected long since globalized European practices in the first place" (Moyn 2014, 66), as if there were no internationalization of these rights involved.

The *travaux préparatoires* do not support Moyn's claim that "the inclusion of the social and economic rights in the mid-1940s . . . were [nothing but] earlier products of citizenship struggles and ha[d] still barely affected the international order" (Moyn 2010, 81–82). Moyn thinks these rights were not yet seen as part of anything supranational. On the contrary, the UDHR drafters saw these rights as newer ones that required more attention so they would not be shortchanged in comparison with older civil and political rights. UDHR Article 22 elicited a lot of discussion. After numerous go-arounds, it was adopted as a bridge article to lift up these rights to the same internationalization as the first generation of human rights (Morsink 1999b, chaps. 5–6; Morsink 2009, chap. 5). When Moyn says that few people in the 1940s who talked human rights "had in mind the creation of supranational sorts of authority on which human rights are now based" (Moyn 2014, 138), he forgets that in the case of second-generation social and economic rights, such a supranational organization already existed in the International Labor Organization (ILO), which had come out of the First World War. Representatives of the ILO participated throughout the proceedings. Also, the very idea of creating an *international* bill is itself a supra idea. What is so impressive about the presence of these social and economic rights is that this time the communists—who, Moyn rightly notes, used to follow Marx in attacking "states and rights alike in recognition of their umbilical linkage" (Moyn 2014, 40)—participated in cutting that linkage when they helped draft an "*inter*national bill of rights."

Moyn claims that "the language of rights could not determine the choice between a welfarist and a communist scheme" and that that fact "marginaliz[ed] human rights as a new ideological paradigm at this moment" (Moyn 2010, 73). He bases his claim on what he believes were the *external* intellectual currents at the time, arguing that Christian personalism (discussed later) beat out communism and socialism in the ideological battles of those years. But the *internal* United Nations history does not support this view. It is true that in the fall of 1947 (when UDHR drafting had not yet reached the Third Committee stage), the Third Committee was seized by a disagreement between socialist and communist nations about the need and scope for welfare rights in the international bill of rights being drawn up. The controversy was created by a memorandum (E/372) sent by the World Federation of Trade Unions (WFTU) asking ECOSOC, the parent body of the Human Rights Commission, for "guarantees for the exercise and development of trade union rights" (UNOR ECOSOC, Fourth Session, Annex 31). ECOSOC did not make that guarantee but instead in Resolution 52 (IV) transmitted the relevant documents to the ILO and to the Commission of Human Rights for consideration. As a result, several meetings of the Third Committee (which in the fall of 1948 was to discuss the UDHR) were in the fall of 1947 dominated by ECOSOC asking advice from the ILO instead of taking up the matter itself.

Communist delegations argued against ILO consultation because in their eyes it was not a "real" labor organization as it had in it representatives from government, labor, and management. Socialist representatives accepted this "tri-partite" ILO approach and approved of the consultation. In addition, representatives from the International Federation of Christian Labor Organizations spoke up and defended the "inalienable" right of workers to join associations of their choosing. Socialist delegations by and large supported the principles enunciated by the ILO in its 1944 Philadelphia Declaration, while communist ones instead wanted to see more just labor rights. Yugoslavia, for instance, argued that "the principle of trade union association, and any other safeguards—such as minimum wages, equal pay for equal work, for man and woman, abolition of racial discrimination in economic and social activities, full employment, effective struggle against unemployment, especially in a period of crisis, and compulsory social insurance" were "rights inherent in the human person" and should provide "the basis for a minimum well-being within the reach of all the workers of the world" (UNOR Third Committee, 1947, Annex 23, 1607). Anyone who reads the UDHR after perusing these 1947 discussions is surprised to see how many labor rights did end up in the declaration. It so happened that the ILO did provide a supra-element for these rights and lifted them up beyond their domestic confines.

In his book *The Sovereignty of Human Rights*, Patrick Macklem (2015) included a chapter on labor rights titled "International Law at Work," in which he discusses two models for the relationship between domestic labor rights and their internationalization or universalization. The first model is that of the old ILO of 1919, which was set up to confront "the risk of revolutionary agitation and contagion created by the Bolshevist threat" (Macklem 2015, 79). This ILO was "a response to concern by States that domestic protection of labor rights would increase the price of production and create competitive disadvantages as against States that chose not to legislate to protect the interests of workers" (79). As Macklem sees it, there is a means-end relationship here in which the internationalization of labor rights is seen as a means to the protection of domestic labor interests. The other model creates the inverse relationship between the domestic and the international. This model took hold of the ILO when it adopted the Philadelphia Declaration of 1944, which said that "all human beings, irrespective of race, creed or sex have the right to pursue both their material well-being and their spiritual development in conditions of freedom and dignity, of economic security and equal opportunity" (84). Writes Macklem, "On this [1944] approach, domestic procedural rights to form a union, bargain collectively, and strike, are necessary to secure freedom of association for all workers, and domestic substantive rights, such as a right to a minimum wage and maximum hours, are linked to other universal norms, such as freedom and equality" (88). It is this model with its supranational emphasis that the ILO brought into the declaration's drafting sessions, helping improve the text at various crucial points. Chapters 5 ("The Socialist Shape of Work-Related Rights") and 6 ("Social Security, Education, and Culture") of my *Origins* book (Morsink 1999b) give a great many details and tallies showing that Moyn's supposition of a welfarist fight between communists and socialists holding back the cause of human rights is not correct.

In the epilogue to his 2014 *Human Rights and the Uses of History*, Moyn lists five theses that to him indicate how human rights should reengage, just as the progressives did, with the power politics of our own day. His fifth thesis makes it seem as if the UDHR does not have in it a second half devoted to social, economic, and cultural rights: "*A politics of human rights will move away from framing norms individualistically and will cease to privilege political and civil liberties*" (Moyn 2014, 145; original italics). There is not now and certainly was not in the 1940s this kind of privileging of civil and political rights in the international arena. All along, the master frame for the human rights movement has had in it ample social, economic, and cultural rights; they were never dropped from the slate, and there is no need to reintroduce them. The whole of the master text needs to be lifted up instead of denigrated. Ever since the founding of the ILO in 1919, their subsequent internationalization and incorporation in the UDHR, and their later translation into the legal obligations of the ICESCR and of numerous ILO conventions, these rights have engaged with the power politics of their day. Their texts have been used by thousands of NGOs and HROs in their fights for the welfare rights of millions of individuals the world over, not least because they are so prominent in the UDHR. Moyn's fifth thesis does apply to the United States, which has not ratified the ICESCR and where the rights to food, housing, and health care go unmet for millions. A great deal of credit for the inclusive character of the UDHR goes to the socialist delegations from Latin America whose contributions I recorded in an earlier work (Morsink 1999b, chap. 5).

Was There a Cold War Freezer?

I am inclined to accuse Moyn of the very same mistake that he says other historians constantly make: reading future events (like the growth of the movement) into their discussion of the past (like fighting the British slave trade), as if the past is always and inevitably pregnant with the future. Before I do that, I need to set the stage.

The year 1946—and thus the year right before the deliberations about the declaration started in earnest—was pivotal in the development of the Cold War. Relations between the superpowers had become badly frayed. Western powers felt betrayed when Stalin presented first Roosevelt at Yalta and then Truman at Potsdam with a fait accompli in Eastern Europe, and the Russians were angry because France and Britain were going to get huge reconstruction loans to rebuild their countries while Soviet requests for similar aid was first lost and then tied to good behavior. On February 6 Stalin announced in the Bolshoi Theater his plan for the next five years. He said that he needed to include the development of heavy armament because of what he called the "capitalist encirclement" of the Russian people. Churchill answered him on his visit to the United States the next month. On a platform in Fulton, Missouri, Churchill declared that "from Stettin in the Baltic to Trieste in the Adriatic, an iron curtain has descended across the continent." Truman was with Churchill on the podium and had read the speech in advance. Partly because of Churchill's strong language, the British request for a huge loan passed Congress without trouble. Almost two and a half years later, on June 11, 1948, Alexei Pavlov, the Soviet representative to the third session of the Human Rights Commission, which was drafting the declaration, came back to Churchill's speech. In a discussion on the right to an education, Pavlov pointed to the hate-filled Nazi educational system. Then he added that "there were certain circles in New York where one could see the development of a new racial theory, which alleged the superiority of the Anglo-Saxon race. The origins of that theory could be traced to Mr. Churchill's speech at Fulton" (E/CN.4/SR.69/3).

The international tensions at the end of 1946 were so great that many American and other diplomats and policymakers feared a third world war was imminent. The Cold War tensions kept building while the declaration was being drafted and completed between January 1947 and December 1948. They reached their pitch in the summer and fall of 1948, which is when the Allied Powers were forced to feed and supply the city of Berlin by air because the Russians (who controlled the area around this "international" city) constantly interrupted and blocked the overland route. In the midst of these mounting international tensions, the Third Committee and the UN General Assembly of 1948 went over the draft declaration produced by the Human Rights Commission. One can well imagine, therefore, how easily at any point during this two-year drafting process these procedures might have been derailed and undercut or greatly compromised either by the actual events of the Cold War or by the rhetoric that accompanied that war. Moyn conjectures that "the deep freeze of the Cold War affecting human rights, far from being their death-knell, only extended the original mortification of their birth" in 1948 (Moyn 2010, 81). While the proximity of the dates makes these speculations tempting, they are not correct.

In teleological fashion Moyn seems to have read the severity of the Cold War not just back into the 1940s generally, when they did indeed begin. He also reads those Cold War tensions back into the very meetings in which the Universal Declaration was drafted (in 1946–48) but in which, as I show in the following discussion, they did not have the impact he claims they had. This means that the ideological bipolarity Moyn believes held the proceedings hostage until after the Cold War did not really occur. From Moyn's perspective, "the search for the origins of human rights is a by-product of the end of the Cold War—more specifically the temporary age of the bipolar standoff of the past and the multipolar struggle of the future" (Moyn 2014, xiv). In the 1940s "the pressing problem as most people understood it was not how to move beyond the state, but what sort of new state to create. And in this situation the [UD] fiction of a moral consensus provided no help" (139). He continues, "In the 1940s, human rights were bypassed because they offered the mere fiction of a moral consensus that plainly did not match the need for [the] political choice" demanded by Cold War antagonisms (140–41). In his *Utopia* book, he writes, "The fact that the [European] convention's negotiations extended later than that of the Universal Declaration meant that the fiction of ideological consensus about basic values could no longer be maintained, and by 1950 European human rights consecrated the basic values of the Western side in Cold War politics" (Moyn 2010, 79). Here I see Moyn reading the bipolarity of the Cold War—which did play a significant role in the drafting of the European Convention—back into the making of the UDHR.

My response is that the declaration was never put into any kind of Cold War freezer. From the beginning we see a multicultural and even multipolar world at work during its drafting, even or especially in the fall of 1948. In the General Assembly debates of that fall, Brazilian delegate Austregésilo de Athayde noted that the declaration "did not reflect the particular point of view of any one people or any group of peoples. Neither was it the expression of any one political doctrine or philosophical system. It was the result of an intellectual and moral cooperation of a large number of nations; that explained its value and interest and also conferred upon it great authority" (UN DOC [1948] GAOR, 878). The writing of the declaration did not, as Moyn thinks, get caught up in a choice between two "social models": the mostly liberal Christian welfarist and the communist welfarist model of entitlements (Moyn 2010, 73). Chilean representative Hernán Santa Cruz acknowledged this difference in social systems, but he did not think that those differences led to a bipolar standoff. Speaking in the Third Committee just before the General Assembly debates, he told his colleagues "It had been necessary to reconcile the different ideologies of the Soviet Union and other Eastern European countries and of other Members of the UN, the difference between the economic and social rights recognized by Christian Western civilization and those recognized by the Oriental civilization; the varying legal systems of Latin and Anglo Saxon countries" (UN DOC Third Committee [1948] 49). The Cold War contest of meanings did not hold human rights hostage until the human rights movement emerged in the 1970s with "its post–Cold War dreams" (Moyn 2014, xx), nor was "a profound redefinition in a new ideological climate" needed (Moyn 2010, 48).

Moyn overlooks the fact that immediately after the war there was a window of opportunity for a supra-state or global morality to take hold. Its immediate context was the Holocaust and its drafting hero was Eleanor Roosevelt. Her leadership through hundreds of meetings was far more than skin deep and helps explain the passion with which she approached her task of leading the UN Human Rights Commission that drafted the UDHR. On May 15, 1948, when she left her New York apartment to go to one of those meetings, she encountered "a drunk or ill or asleep [man], very thin and very poor looking." While others hurried by, she made sure he was breathing and reported his presence to the police. She writes in her column that "the next day, at Lake Success, as we argued about human rights at a committee meeting, I wondered how many human rights that poor man had" (Roosevelt

1999, 137). Claiming inexperience in international affairs, Eleanor had been reluctant to accept President Truman's appointment as a US representative to the United Nations. She accepted because she wanted the chance to help strengthen the United Nations, which she considered her husband's "most significant legacy to the world." She did a great job defending the Western position on the problem of refugees and was made the US representative to the Third Social, Humanitarian, and Cultural Affairs Committee. In this capacity she was appointed to serve on the Nuclear Committee, which was to make recommendations for the structure of the Human Rights Commission, which the Charter had mandated ECOSOC create. She was elected to chair that planning committee by acclamation, an honor repeated at the first session of the Commission on Human Rights in January 1947. She was still chair of that commission when the General Assembly adopted the declaration two years later, on December 10, 1948.

Truman's appointment of Eleanor was fortuitous because she was one of the few diplomats in Truman's circle who was respected and listened to by the Russians. Since she was also the widow of a revered US president and for many years had a national agenda of her own, she was also highly regarded in her own country and thus in her own person became a talking bridge between the two superpowers. Her regular newspaper column, *My Day*, was carried by seventy-five to ninety newspapers in the country. Eleanor did not share the militarism that had come to dominate the inner circle of Truman's advisers, and the Russians knew this. For example, on September 21, 1946, like others, she worried that "an atomic world is unthinkable," adding that the Russians should know that while Americans did "not want to be a tail to their kite, we do want to cooperate with them in order to give Russia and ourselves greater security" (Roosevelt 1999, 75). She had been polite to Churchill when he had stayed at Hyde Park after his Iron Curtain speech of March 1946. But she felt that Churchill had prematurely divided the world and that the Cold War antagonists had "not worked together enough really to feel that we understand each other. We still question whether our different political and economic systems can exist side by side in the world. We are still loath to give up the old power and attempt to build a new kind of power and security in the world," one based on mutual respect and understanding (cited in Lash 1972, 85). It is no coincidence that Lash's chapter on Eleanor as a "reluctant cold warrior" comes after he has told us about her role in drafting "A Magna Carta for Mankind," for she worked on the latter before she became the former.

The first session of the commission Eleanor chaired met in January and February 1947. No draft was produced, but delegations used the session to express their basic views on what was to be done. On February 18 *Look* magazine published an article by Eleanor titled "The Russians Are Tough." She tells readers that she "never had any personal bitterness against any of the people in the Eastern European group," which included and was controlled by the Russians. "I have had, nevertheless, to argue at some length with them because we could not agree on fundamental problems," she added (Roosevelt 1999, 191). She found that "it takes patience and equal firmness and equal conviction to work with the Russians. One must be alert, since if they cannot win success for their point of view one way, they are still going to try to win in any other way that seems to them possible" (191). This was borne out by the numerous meetings of both the commission and its drafting subsidiary that followed, during which Eleanor's demeanor toward the Russians showed the goodwill she had toward them. She ended the *Look* article with the observation that Russians "are not familiar with the customs and thinking of other peoples. This makes them somewhat insecure and, I think, leads them at times to take an exaggerated, self-assertive stand which other people may think somewhat rude. I think it is only an attempt to make the rest of the world see that they are proud of their own way of doing things" (191). Later that fall communists published their Cominform manifesto, which openly divided the world into two warring camps: the American imperialist camp and the Soviet democratic camp. For many American diplomats, a September 22, 1947, speech by Andrei Zhadanov, Stalin's heir apparent, confirmed expert views that "a spirit of innate aggressiveness shaped Soviet foreign policy" (Yergin 1977, 35). According to Lash, Eleanor had not liked the Cominform's "warmongering document," but she wrote publicly in the *New York Times* that the "two political systems had to work together, [for] growing apart is not going to help us" (Lash 1972, 103n46). The second session of the Human Rights Commission met in January and early February 1948 in Geneva, Switzerland.

General Carlos Romulo was the delegate of the Philippines to this session and a member of the Working Group on the declaration. In this capacity he met daily with Alexandre Bogomolov, the USSR delegate, whom he describes as "courteous and conscientious about his work with the Commission" (Romulo 1986, 71). He writes, "Probably the best working relations I experienced with delegates from the U.S.S.R. was during the three months we spent in Geneva drafting the Universal Doctrine of Human Rights" (71). The reason seems to have been that Bogomolov "did not seem to have a parochial view of what we were doing, but indeed a global view, which was rare for a delegate of Soviet Russia" (71).

During these months of the second session, a GI asked Eleanor how to get along with the Russians. She responded with four quick points: Have convictions. Be friendly. Stick to your beliefs. And work as hard as they do (Lash 1972, 83). This experience of cooperation in Geneva helps explain Eleanor's muted reaction to what happened right after this session ended. She was as shocked as anyone else by the February 1948 communist coup in Czechoslovakia and by the supposed suicide of its foreign minister, Jan Masaryk, shortly thereafter. Still, her response was not a militaristic one. In a letter to Truman, she put blame on both sides in the Cold War ("I am sure that we have not been blameless and probably the Russians think that we have done some things against them") and suggested that a peace mission be sent to Stalin to talk things over. Secretary George Marshall responded within a week and told her the mission was not a good idea, as "mere words get us nowhere at this time" (Lash 1972, 105).

Given how tense the world outside the UN drafting chambers was, it is remarkable how calm and orderly the proceedings inside were. There were almost never rhetorical excesses. Eleanor was a competent parliamentarian whose personal integrity kept the chair at the center of authority. Her rulings were almost never questioned, and when they were (usually by the delegate from the USSR), they were upheld. She was very good at blunting various time-consuming objections with the calm observation that "we are already doing what you want done" (E/CN.4/AC.1/SR.76-7). A reporter for the *New York Times* wired home from Geneva that "the proceedings sometimes turn into a long vitriolic attack on the U.S. when she is not present. . . . These attacks, however, generally degenerate into flurries in the face of her calm and undisturbed replies" (Lash 1972, 39). She was almost never absent, and these attacks were minor ones. In the spring and summer of 1948, when the hearings before the House Committee on Un-American Activities (which sought to eliminate communists from American public life) were at their most intense, Eleanor disputed the idea "that no one who declares himself a communist can be a good citizen of a democracy. I have known a number of theoretical Communists," she wrote, "who certainly were not going around with guns" (Roosevelt 1999, 135). Some called her naive for making this distinction between theoretical and practical communists, but there can be no doubt that this kind of attitude helped keep the declaration on track. Without the moral authority and energy of her person at the center of the process, the commission might well have become stuck and produced nothing but reams of paper. Charles Malik, the delegate from Lebanon, was a very influential core member of the drafting team. Years after the adoption of the declaration, he looked back and reflected that he "didn't see how they could have accomplished what they did without her presence" (cited in Mower 1979, 58).

No Cold War deep freeze kept the UDHR drafters from developing a code for a global morality. What did happen was that delegates from the fifty-six nations had no time to agree on the terms of a legally binding convention and were not ready to nail down various measures of implementation. But these incomplete measures did not prevent them from going beyond the UN Westphalian framework to develop the human rights seeds in the Charter into a complete and widely accepted bill of inherent and inalienable human rights.

Christian Personalism or Benign Secularism

I have argued that the main rationale for the writing and adoption of the Universal Declaration was a shared abhorrence of the Holocaust. The 1940s ideology of human rights is in this one respect a "reactionary" one in that it condemns the great evils of the age and seeks to create a moral-political world order that will not let such abominations happen again. To begin that process of condemnation, the drafters needed a way of stepping outside their Westphalian framework.

Though Moyn does not think the UDHR drafters succeeded, he does speculate that they had three possible platforms to help them take this crucial step: a liberal democratic one, an authoritarian/totalitarian one, and a conservative Christian one. As he sees it, these three ideologies waged a fierce battle for the meaning of "human rights," with Christian conservatism winning out and creating the first European homeland for human rights immediately after the war. In the 1930s and 1940s, this mostly Catholic Christian conservatism went by the name of personalism. Moyn believes that "as the communitarian third way that it promised between individualism and communism [it] survived its reactionary (and occasional leftist) connotations to be linked tightly to Cold War conservatism" (Moyn 2015a, 73). "Briefly, it was the disappearance of Christian reaction and fascism that set the stage for the preeminent role Christianity could play in the postwar framing of human rights; but that role also deeply affected the meaning of those rights as a third-way, personalist, and communitarian alternative to liberal atomism and material communism alike" (Moyn 2010, 74). According to Moyn, Christian personalism more than the Nazi menace provided the drafters with whatever unity they had. He believes the UDHR rechristened the individualist liberal "rights of man" it inherited from the eighteenth-century revolutions as "human rights." The drafters were also very familiar with the totalitarian choices of fascism and communism, which they also had good reason to suspect might not be respectful of the autonomy of the human personality, subsuming it under the aegis of the state. Neither of these totalitarianisms could have the final say in this battle about meanings, because the one had just been defeated in the war and the other one controlled only six of the fifty-six nations involved in the UDHR drafting. I do not reject Moyn's citations from Christian leaders in the 1940s, because they speak of a tension between materialism and the life of the spirit. That tension most certainly existed. Instead I dispute the purposes to which Moyn puts them, for they do not preclude all the world's major religions from having supported a nonreligious moral code for the moral reconstruction after the war (Morsink 2017, part 1).

It puzzles me why Moyn thinks that Christian conservatism beat out 1789 liberalism in this fight about the meaning of human rights in the 1940s. He does not engage with the UN *travaux préparatoires*, which any researcher of the meaning of human rights in the 1940s should take into account. My view is that both the narrow and expanded definitions of the Holocaust (discussed previously) forestalled the kind of "competition over the meaning of human rights" that Moyn envisions took place (Moyn 2010, 51). After he has demoted Eleanor as an overly strict "schoolmistress," he argues, "The general consensus about the itemization of rights suggests that little was at stake in the proceedings, in spite of a few interesting debates about details" (63). Aside from there being far more than a few of such details, one would think that both the drafters and the ordinary people they addressed knew what it was to define something by way of example. The declaration contains a wide range examples of what the drafters thought a human right is, and as I show in the next chapter, not a few of them got the depth of their meaning from their connection with the Holocaust. This connection universalizes and generalizes the rights involved. "Never again" translates into "everywhere." The short of it is that modern human rights have no regional homeland, Christian European or otherwise. The 1940s birth of human rights was a supranational and cosmopolitan event.

When the Cold War really got going, Moyn's Christian personalist or "communitarian third way" was no longer viable as an ideology that could defeat the benign secularism of human rights enshrined in both the UDHR and the European Convention on Human Rights (ECHR). While Danny Nicol has argued that "the record of the negotiations fails to show consensus in favour of a 'minimalist' interpretation of the ECHR" (Nicol 2005, 171), Wolfram Kaiser adds injury to this insult with his observation that "by the time the Cold War reached its height in 1948–9, all [even successful] Christian democratic parties had effectively given up the idea of Europe as a 'third force' positioned between the superpowers" or "in world politics" (Kaiser 2007, 167, 177). Additionally, as I argued previously, we should not read Cold War antagonisms into the drafting years of the UDHR until the very end and then only with great care.

I can only very briefly comment on a few of the interesting persons and personalities that populate Moyn's story. Some fall clearly outside the 1946–48 years that are my focus, others touch those years only incidentally, and some actually were involved in drafting the declaration but did not set the tone. I mention them in this order. Moyn cites Pius XI and his successor, Pius XII, as personalist popes who shaped the meaning of human rights in the 1930s and 1940s. He quotes Pius XI's March 1937 antifascist encyclical *Mit Brennender Sorge*: "Man as a person possesses rights that he holds from God and which must remain with respect to the collectivity, beyond the reach of anything that would tend to deny them" (Moyn 2015a, 75). He also cites Pius XII's 1941 desire to "safeguard the inviolable sphere of the rights of the human person and to facilitate the fulfillment of his duties" as a way of encapsulating the public authority of the state (76–77). In this vague way, the "human person" of personalism is placed against the "individual human being" of the liberal rights ideology as if they are mutually exclusive. The use of the phrase "the human person" in these encyclicals is meant to support Moyn's claim that "recovering the centrality of personalism through the 1930s and 1940s should deeply unsettle prevailing opinion about what the concept of human rights really meant in its founding moment" of the 1940s (67). I doubt that and am not unsettled by it. Pius XI's antifascist encyclical includes this classic statement of the Catholic natural law doctrine:

> Such is the rush of present-day life that it severs from the divine foundation of Revelation, not only morality, but also the theoretical and practical rights. We are especially referring to what is called natural law, written by the Creator's hand on the tablet of the heart (Rom ii.14) and which reason, not blinded by sin or passion, can easily read. It is in the light of the commands of this natural law, that all positive law, whoever is the lawgiver, can be gauged in its moral content, and hence in the authority it wields over conscience. Human laws in flagrant contradiction with the natural law are vitiated with a taint which no force, no power can mend. (Pius XI 1937b, para. 30)

Many legislators, reformers, and revolutionaries—including Dr. Martin Luther King Jr. in his April 16, 1963, *Letter from Birmingham City Jail*—have appealed to this doctrine. The human rights of individuals can be derived from the natural inclinations of men as interpreted by reason when that is not clouded by sin or passion. Pius XI repeats these ideas in his encyclical against the communists, telling them and us,

"Only man, the human person, and not society in any form is endowed with reason and a morally free will" (Pius XI 1937a, para. 29). "Society is for man and not vice versa," to which he adds "that this must not be understood in the sense of liberalistic individualism, which subordinates society to the selfish use of the individual; but only in the sense that by means of an organic union with society and by mutual collaboration the attainment of earthly happiness is placed within the reach of all" (para. 29). There is an echo here of personalist corporatism with its "proper hierarchic structure of society" (para. 32), but that hierarchy does not come at the expense of or even in sharp contrast with the liberalism of the later UDHR.

For Pius also tells us that everyone has "the right to life, to bodily integrity, to the necessary means to existence; the right to tend toward his ultimate goal in the path marked out by him for God; the right of association, and the right to possess and use property" (Pius XI 1937a, para. 27); all these rights are also itemized in the Universal Declaration. Since "it was Christianity that had raised manual labor to its true dignity," Pius had no trouble following Leo XIII's vindication "for the workingman of the right to organize" (para. 37), which we find reiterated in UDHR Article 23(4). Pius believed that "a 'charity' which deprives the workingman of the salary to which he has a strict title in justice, is not charity at all, but only its empty name and hollow semblance. The wage-earner is not to receive as alms what is his due in justice. And let no one attempt with trifling charitable donations to exempt himself from the great duties imposed by [social] justice . . . from which neither employers nor working men can escape" (para. 49). If this is the kind of personalism Moyn has in mind, it in no way detracts from standard liberal Catholicism, which calls for respect of individual economic rights for both workers and owners. There is no fight here with a supposed "atomistic individualism," for it fits right in with Article 17 of the declaration, which tells us that "everyone has a right to own property alone as well as in association with others," and with Article 23's claim that "everyone who works has the right to just and favourable remuneration ensuring for himself and his family an existence worthy of human dignity, and supplemented, if necessary, by other means of social protection."

Moyn proposes the philosopher Jacques Maritain as the link between personalist papal thinking on human rights and the wider human rights community, including in the United Nations. Maritain saw Catholic natural law as "the proper framework for human rights" but brought his earlier personalist agenda to that new framework. Writes Moyn, "Crucially for its postwar European fate, Maritain rallied to rights in communitarian terms, exalting the moralistic human person against the atomistic individual as their bearer" (Moyn 2010, 54). There is, however, no sign of that kind of atomistic individualism having eclipsed Roosevelt's Four Freedoms, which spread the idea of human rights across New Deal America. Nor is it evident in Maritain's work with the UNESCO survey of world intellectuals. Moyn notes three facts as if they are linearly connected: that Maritain was the main publicist for Christian personalism, that he worked with UNESCO on the philosophical foundations of human rights, and that that kind of Christianity defined the worldview of three main UDHR drafters (John Humphrey, Charles Malik, and Eleanor Roosevelt). We are led to believe that this is how Christian personalism became victorious at the 1940s moment of human rights. But the connections do not stand up to scrutiny. Though all the statements are true, they are not connected in the way Moyn implies. Maritain's 1943 book *The Rights of Man and Natural Law* is indeed a clear statement of the classical natural law doctrine overlain with a strong dose of personalism. The second statement is also true but has little connection to the first or the third. The results of UNESCO's survey were published in 1949, long after the Human Rights Commission had done its work. In chapter 1 I explained that Eleanor's Commission on Human Rights found out about this survey of intellectuals, rejected it, and refused to have anything further to do with it. Not surprisingly, the survey shows that the world intellectuals surveyed could not come to an agreement on what the philosophical foundations of human rights are, which is what UNESCO set out to discover. So the survey was a failure. However, in its summation of the process, the UNESCO committee concluded that despite the conflict of ideas and the "highly divergent doctrinal grounds" articulated by these intellectuals, agreement was possible.

In his introduction to the survey results, Maritain—who was not a member of the committee—put his finger on the source of the committee's confidence. He believed that there was "a kind of plant-like formation and growth of moral knowledge and moral feeling, in itself independent of philosophic systems and the rational justifications they propound, even though there is a secondary interaction between them and itself" (Maritain 1973, 12). This cuts out ideology, including personalism, as the main source for our belief in human rights, which is what I have also argued. Our moral sentiments and intuitions more than our intellect or reason guide us to a knowledge of moral basics. I link these sentiments to our inborn altruism and argue that this kind "pre-scientific" and "pre-theoretical" moral knowledge is what allowed delegates from fifty-six nations to agree on the list of rights they wanted to declare (Morsink 2017, part 3). It is therefore highly unlikely that what brought these fifty-six UN delegates together was the conservative Catholic personalism that I admit was, like a great many other intellectual positions, "in the air" in the 1930s and 1940s. What brought them together and made the UDHR drafters search their pre-theoretical consciences were Hitler's evil practices. As Malik, a devout Catholic, put it, the declaration "was inspired by opposition to the barbarous doctrines of Nazis and fascism" (UNOR GA, Third Session, 857).

Moyn's third point is that the worldview of several of the main drafters (John Humphrey as the first human rights director in the Secretariat, Charles Malik as chair of the Third Committee, and Eleanor Roosevelt as chair of the commission) was a Christian personalist one. Leaving out the personalist element, which is highly unlikely for at least two of these three, having Christian convictions is true of far more than just the three persons Moyn mentions. Many Catholics could be found in the delegations from Latin American nations. Some twenty-two nations from South and Central America met for the Ninth International Conference of American States in Bogota, Colombia, in April 1948, just eight months before the adoption of the Universal Declaration. This conference agreed to adopt the American Declaration of the Rights and Duties of Man (E/CN.4/122), also known as the Bogota Declaration, which Moyn does not mention. Not seeking to represent all four continents, this Bogota Declaration is more metaphysical and mainline (but not personalist) Catholic than the soon to follow Universal Declaration. While the UDHR preamble speaks of "equal and inalienable rights of all members of the human family," the preamble of the Bogota one calls for the "protection of the essential rights of man and the creation of circumstances that will permit him to achieve spiritual and material progress and attain happiness." While the UDHR preamble does not elaborate on the term "inalienable," the Bogota document tells us, "The American states have on repeated occasions recognized that the essential rights of man are not derived from the fact of one's being a national of a certain state, but are fundamental attributes of the individual." Bogota's Article 1 was drawn up before UDHR Article 1, and it reads just like the latter, except that in the UDHR the reference to natural law has been suppressed for reasons I explain later. Bogota reads like this: "All men are born free and equal, in dignity and rights, and, being endowed *by nature* with reason and conscience, they should conduct themselves as brothers to one another" (italics added). These same twenty-two mostly Catholic nations voted a few months later for the benign secularism of the Universal Declaration.

These natural law Catholics were supported by an active Protestant lobby that Moyn claims helped bring about a victory for conservative "Christian Human Rights" in their postwar moment. There was indeed a liberal Christian influence, but it was not a conservative personalist one. Two Protestant organizations attending the UDHR drafting sessions were the International Federation of Christian Trade Unions and the Commission of the Churches on International Affairs (CCIA). This last group was established in 1946 as a joint agency of the World Council of Churches and the International Missionary Council, and Traer tells us that "churches in the ecumenical movement increasingly channeled their communications on U.N. matters through the CCIA" (Traer 1991, 175). The director of this organization, Dr. Frederick Nolde, became an important conduit for the flow of Protestant influence on the writing of the declaration. The full, detailed story of this large ecumenical Christian push for human rights in the 1940s has been told by John S. Nurser in his book *For All Peoples and All Nations: The Ecumenical Church and Human Rights* (2005). In his conclusion, Nurser notes, "The successful outcome of the struggle for global human rights institutions in the period 1944–48 was influenced to a surprising degree by the part one person, Dr. O. Frederick Nolde of Philadelphia, was able to play" (Nurser 2005, 173–74). Since Nolde wrote numerous memoranda, had a good relationship with Eleanor Roosevelt and her advisers, and attended all the meetings of the Human Rights Commission, Moyn's personalism (if there was such) had to contend with another Christian advocacy group. Other liberal Protestants were active in other organizations that had the same status as the CCIA: the American Federation of Labor, the International Abolitionist Federation, the International Committee of the Red Cross, the International Council of Women, the Women's International Democratic Federation, the International Federation of Business and Professional Women, and the World Federation of United Nations Associations. These were not religious organizations in any formal way, but liberal Protestants were active in them then, as they are today.

Though Nolde's organization was at one point concerned about the lack of a reference to God in the declaration, it all along realized that Christians "cannot expect the United Nations to accomplish by legal fiat that which must be the expression of a prevailing conviction" (Traer 1991, 176). Even that was not quite the right way to put it. Voting on particular human rights was acceptable, but voting on philosophical issues in a UN context was not appropriate, with one exception. Commenting on his work at the second session of the commission, Nolde wrote, "It was neither to be expected nor desired that the Christian faith should be made to prevail by a majority decision in the United Nations. As the drafting of the Universal Declaration progressed, the CCIA unflaggingly emphasized the principle that governments could not grant human rights, but could only recognize human rights which man, by virtue of his being and destiny, already possessed" (Nolde 1948a, 38). This fits with the idea of "inherent" and "inalienable" rights that the UDHR drafters mention in their preamble and with Article 1's idea that people are "born with" these rights instead of getting them from their governments. Nolde's organization also believed that making religious liberty "meaningful" involved and required the practice of many other human rights. Among these were "the right to freedom of opinion and expression across all frontiers; freedom of assembly and association which has direct bearing upon the corporate life of the churches and their organization for public activities; education, family and the prior right of parents in the education of their children; and in freedom from the retroactive application of the law" (Nolde 1948a, 39). The ecumenism of the Protestant influence on the declaration text was in no way partisan or parochial; it fit right in with the drafters' goal of inclusiveness and universality. It in effect helped support what I call the benign secularism of the declaration (Morsink 2017, chaps. 1, 5).

Even in the 1940s, the liberal Christian worldview of the World Council of Churches outflanked the Christian conservatism that Moyn suggests won the battle for the meaning of "human rights" in those years. The centerpiece of his narrative is the 1948 meeting in Amsterdam that reconvened the World Council of Churches after the war, representing 147 church organizations from all over the world (Bell 1949, 412). In Moyn's story, John Foster Dulles (from the US), George Bell (from the UK), and Gerhard Ritter (from Germany) spearheaded this transatlantic campaign. Moyn sees Ritter, because of his lecture titled "The Origin and Nature of Human Rights," given in November 1948, as "The First Historian of Human Rights" and traces his life and thought in a chapter by this title in his 2015 *Christian Human Rights* book.

Unlike the UDHR drafters, Ritter did not see human rights as "a response to the Holocaust" (Moyn 2015a, 103) but grounded the concept in Occidental Christianity. Ritter apparently thought that Christian social ethics "must assume the task of informing human rights to avoid their secular or revolutionary perversion" (116). Two things stand in the way of Ritter's playing this kind of role in the alleged victory of Christian personalism in the 1940s battle of meanings. First, he did not give his groundbreaking lecture "The Origin and Nature of Human Rights" till November 1948—and published it a year later—which is just one month before the adoption of the benignly secular Universal Declaration. Second, Moyn admits that Ritter was not aware and did not know about the crucial role that Nolde played as a conduit for the ecumenical movement that Ritter had also joined. I quote Moyn on this point: "Surprisingly, the otherwise well-informed Ritter seems to have been unaware of FCC [Federal Council of Churches] activist Frederick Nolde's participation in 1944–45 at San Francisco in adding human rights to the United Nations Charter or his work after" with the Commission of Human Rights, which wrote the declaration and acquiesced in that text's secular tone (Moyn 2015a, 215n41; Morsink 2017, part 1).

Dulles served on the 1946 CCIA, which was set up by "men prominent in church affairs" from seventeen nations in August 1946 and for which Nolde from Philadelphia served as vice chairman. Representing the CCIA in May 1948, Nolde contributed to the Amsterdam assembly his report "Freedom of Religion and Related Human Rights." Speaking for ecumenical Christians, he blended Aristotle and Thomas Aquinas by asserting that "whether viewed from the standpoint of science, or of an eternal dispensation, to every man is given an appointed potentiality. The realization of his potentiality rests with man and with society" (Nolde 1948a, 174). Asserting man's natural potential for human rights does not fit well with the distinctly Barthian tone one gets from perusing the rest of these Amsterdam proceedings, but it fits well with the benignly secular approach taken by the UDHR drafters.

Like Dulles, George Bell, Bishop of Chichester, was also a member of Nolde's commission and on the Subcommittee on Resolutions and Pronouncements. Moyn quotes the bishop's 1940 comments on the world situation: "Of course you can dress up the ideas of 1789 and adapt them to the conditions of 1940. But the present situation is the result of secularism. To add a further dose of secularism to what the patient has already absorbed is to add poison to poison. . . . No amount of secular Declarations, no number of claims for human rights, without spiritual sanctions, will save us from destruction" (Moyn 2010, 75). On the same page, Moyn cites a much later address the bishop gave on the Amsterdam proceedings at Chatham House in June 1949, a year and a half after the adoption of the Universal Declaration. He cites the bishop's view that the church should "affirm that all men are equal in the sight of God, and that the rights of men derive directly from their condition as children of God and not of the state," but he does not cite the first part of this sentence, nor what the bishop says in the next two sentences: "It must of course often be the case that a stand has to be made by the Church to meet a sudden challenge. And the method of making it must vary with the circumstances" (Bell 1949, 409). Nor does he let on that the bishop said these things right after he lifted up the voice of conscience of even the "disinterested" unbeliever, who "gradually discovers by his personal experience the existence of the spiritual, and the proposed demands of the moral law for the good of the Nation, for international concord, and for the pacification of the world" (Bell 1949, 408). The bishop ended his talk with a ringing endorsement of Catholic natural law theory: "Recourse to Natural Law is the one and only way open to the world if we are not to see the globe transformed into the worst of jungles. The Natural Law has for its basis faith in God. That basis is unique and unshakable" (Bell 1949, 414). But the bishop also knew that this law is accessible to nonbelievers and non-Christians as well.

During the debates on the preamble and Article 1 of the Universal Declaration, the world's churches and all other religious traditions were forced to take a stand on the source of human rights as religious or not. They ended up supporting the birth of our modern concept of human rights as a benign secular concept, meaning nonreligious and not malignant. How that happened leads to the heart of our counternarrative to Moyn's victory of conservative Christianity over secularism. The rejection and withdrawals of several theistically inspired amendments (Morsink 2017, introduction) was welcomed by the Protestant ecumenical movement that channeled its views through Frederick Nolde, the World Council of Churches secretary for international affairs. "Discussing the rejection of the UN of reference to man's divine origin and destiny, Dr. Nolde said he felt that no specific reference to God could be made in a document which applies to so many nations of so many different faiths and to numbers who are atheists." The latter is a reference to communist delegations who objected vigorously to any suggestion of there being a divine origin for human rights. Nolde added that adoption of these kinds of religiously inspired amendments "would have made the document hypocritical" (Nolde 1948b, 17).

Because they speak of a tension between materialism and the life of the spirit, I do not reject Moyn's citations from these Christian leaders in the 1940s. That tension most certainly existed. But as I said at the start of this particular alternative reading, my opposition is aimed at the purposes to which Moyn puts them. Nothing in these citations precludes fifty-six delegations from all over the world, including those representing the world's major religions, from supporting a nonreligious code for the moral reconstruction after the war (Morsink 2017, part 1). The UDHR drafters chose the middle road between atheistic materialism and overt propositional religiosity. Delegates from nations that were not averse to a theological foundation were willing to give up their plank in the platform because, as they saw it, the text left plenty of room to find a kind of immanent transcendence. The declaration still included in the recital language of "inalienable rights" and Article 1's crucial claim that human beings "are born free and equal in dignity and rights." Piggybacking the rights in the declaration on the birth of people into the human family made these rights genuinely universal and therefore transcendent to local, national, and even international circumstances. In this way the language of human rights ended up serving as a middle ground between extremes at either end.

Beyond Westphalia

Throughout this chapter I have mentioned that in Moyn's story, rights have been kept captive within nation-state frameworks since the end of the seventeenth century, with no transcendent element to lift them beyond those limits until the birth of the human rights movement in the 1970s. In chapter 1's discussion of the views of other historians on rights before the 1940s I indicated that this generalized Westphalian imprisonment is far too severe a position to take. Moyn puts a similar Westphalian reading on the founding of the United Nations. In his view, neither the charter references nor the declaration they yielded put any kind of dent in the armor of the sovereign states that created that organization; only symbolic gestures were made. "The space opened by the Charter for a mass movement to coalesce around the new concept remained hypothetical only," meaning that those charter references to human rights are not seeds of transcendence brought to fruition by the commission that Eleanor chaired. "Though surely proclaimed by an international organization, the Universal Declaration retains, rather than supersedes, the sanctity of nationhood, as its text makes clear" (Moyn 2010, 81). We are not told how the text does this.

In an earlier work, I have defended the thesis that "the cosmopolitanism of the Universal Declaration steps across the boundaries of nation-states and emphasizes the inherent moral rights individuals have as members of the human family" (Morsink 2009, 148). The evidence for a supranational and cosmopolitan birth is overwhelming if only the researcher is willing to consider meetings attended and votes taken in consultation with dozens of NGOs by huge numbers of international civil servants speaking for their peoples and governments from nations on four continents. These numbers cannot be dismissed with the observation that "the existence of a global diplomatic elite, often schooled in Western locales . . . helped tinker with the declaration at a moment of symbolic unity" (Moyn 2010, 66). No serious and sustained reaction to the Holocaust can be demoted this easily. While the UDHR preamble acknowledges that human rights are essential for "the development of friendly relations among states," the body of the document makes only two references to the role of the state: one in Article 16(3), in which the state is called on to protect the family, and one in Article 30, in which we are told that no "state, group or person [has] any rights to engage in any activity or to perform any act aimed at the destruction of any of the rights and freedoms set forth herein." If that is not an announcement of the transcendence of the UDHR rights beyond the state, I do not know what would be. Of course, what is lacking in the declaration is a regime of enforcement should any state, group, or person violate this prohibition. After the declaration had been adopted, the international community worked some twenty years at setting up these regimes of enforcement. I discuss them in chapter 4.

There were, of course, delegations involved in the UDHR process that did not like this overt transcendence, the communist ones being a case in point. For the great occasion of the General Assembly debate, the Soviet Union chose as its main spokesman Andrei Vishinsky, who is better known as the infamous prosecutor in Stalin's purge trials. Vishinsky took the positivistic stand that Moyn claims held rights imprisoned until the 1970s. He noted, "Human rights could not be conceived outside the State; the very concept of right and law was connected with that of the State" (UNOR GA, Third Session, 924). Some of the delegates, he said, had maintained that in the Soviet Union, "the individual was some sort of cog in the all-powerful State along the lines of Hobbes' *Leviathan*" (928), but they had forgotten that in the Soviet Union, the tension between classes had disappeared and there was no "contradiction between the government and the individual, since the government was in fact the collective individual" (929). In his country "the State and the individual were in harmony with each other, [and] their interest coincided" (929). There was therefore no need for the declaration to transcend the interests of individual states. In keeping with this Marxist thinking, the Soviet Union had more than once proposed amendments to UDHR articles that, if adopted, would have allowed the content of the right in question to be wholly determined by individual states. For example, with respect to Article 13's "right to leave any country, and to return to his country," the Soviet Union proposed that this be granted "in accordance with the established laws of that country" (Morsink 1999b, 74). This was rejected and left the international right to move between countries as open and undefined as the right to move within a country. Similar attempts were defeated in connection with the wordings of Articles 12, 15, 17, and 18 (2.1, 2.2, and 7.1). My reader can well imagine that with respect to almost all the rights in the declaration, this question of how the practice of a human right squared with the domestic laws of the member states was a bone of contention. This issue came to a head when the time came to adopt Article 29.

UDHR Article 29(2) says, "In the exercise of his rights and freedoms, everyone shall be subject only to such limitations as are determined by law solely for the purpose of securing due recognition and respect for the rights and freedoms of others and of meeting the just requirements of morality, public order and the general welfare in a democratic society." The presumption here is that individuals have the moral rights enunciated in the declaration but that in the practice of them, there are certain limitations to be observed. More than once Alexei Pavlov, the Soviet representative, observed that "it was the laws of States that fixed the limits for the exercise of human rights and freedoms," and he therefore wanted to add at the end of 29(2) "and in accordance with the just requirements of the democratic State" (Morsink 1999b, 250). An addition like this raised the issue of what is meant by "democratic state," on which point there was no consensus among the drafters (Morsink 1999b, section 2.4). Did the Marxist-inspired "peoples democracies" just then being set up in Eastern Europe represent the ideal type, or do Western-type liberal democracies have that honor? Even though earlier drafts of Article 29 had included the phrase "democratic state," this time around it was rejected both in the third session of the commission in the summer of 1948 and again that fall in the Third Committee. The Cold War and the Berlin Airlift were making their presence felt in the drafting chamber, but as I noted above, this presence did not amount to an "extended . . . mortification of their [human rights'] birth" (Moyn 2010, 81). From the start it had been clear that human rights needed protection against the absolutism of the Nazi state. That in fact was the point of drawing up the declaration. Now, toward the end of the proceedings, it became very clear that they also needed protection against the absolutism of communist states.

I noted in my *Origins* book that "the drafters were so set against having references to the state in their document that they even refused to put one at the very place where it would have been most natural to do so, namely in the article where limitations were being discussed" (Morsink 1999b, 250). Article 29(3) states that "these rights and freedoms may in no case be exercised contrary to the purposes and principles of the United Nations." At the time of adoption, a choice had to be made between an Egyptian proposal that these rights "not be exercised contrary to the purposes and principles of the United Nations" (UNOR [1948] A/C.3/267) and a French proposal that they "serve the purposes and principles of the United Nations" (UNOR [1948] A/C.3/345). Eleanor said she thought the Egyptian way of putting the case might lead to confusion, so she preferred the French text, meaning the United States admitted that its own domestic legal system might be made subservient to the purposes and principles of the United Nations, a view that does not now prevail in legal circles if it ever did. Article 29 is about the duties that "everyone" also has toward "the community in which alone the free and full development of his personality is possible" (29[1]). Given that fact, it is remarkable how few objections there were to this assertion that the exercise of these rights should serve the purposes of the United Nations. One of the very few objections came from the British delegation. Its delegate, Percy Corbett, thought that "the purposes and principles of the United Nations as stated in the Charter applied largely to the conduct of States and not to individuals" (Morsink 1999b, 252).

The fact that by thirty-four votes to two, with six abstentions, the Third Committee adopted this third paragraph of Article 29 shows that in the late 1940s, Westphalianism no longer had a firm grip on the international community of nations. Slippage like this is everywhere apparent in the early years of the United Nations, referred to as the norm-setting period. With the adoption of the declaration, a supra-state element was injected into the very concept of what a human right is. Moyn overstates his case with his thesis that modern human rights did not escape Westphalianism till the birth of the movement in the 1970s. The individual not only has rights that stretch across borders, he or she also has correlative duties that stretch in the same way.

The purposes and principles of the United Nations included putting an end to absolutist regimes of either a fascist or a communist kind, the former openly and the latter just below the surface. To avoid possible recurrences of the fascist menace, UDHR Article 30 was amended to include not just states or persons but also groups as being barred from aiming their activities at "the destruction of any of the rights and freedoms set forth" in the declaration. This insertion of groups into Article 30 resulted from a French proposal based on the rationale that "it was rarely States or individuals that engaged in activities that aimed at the destruction of human rights; such activities in recent times had been pursued by groups sometimes acting on the instructions or with the connivance of states" (UNOR [1948], Third Committee, 666). Alexei Pavlov, the delegate from the Soviet Union, immediately backed this French proposal "because experience had shown how dangerous were the Nazi groups which . . . by constant infiltration and propaganda had paved the way for the fascist regimes of Hitler and Mussolini" (670). Pavlov thought that these dangers had by no means disappeared after the war and pointed to the Ku Klux Klan in the United States as one such dangerous organization. Referring to repeated US attempts to have Article 30 deleted, he added that "naturally attempts were made to belittle the importance for those organizations on the ground that their membership was very small and their activity of little consequence. He recalled the same attitude had formerly prevailed concerning the fascist organizations of Hitler and Mussolini, the disastrous consequences of such indifference was unfortunately all too well known" (667). The word "group" was inserted by forty-two votes with a sole US abstention, and the whole article was adopted unanimously (672–74).

Like the other delegations, the Soviet one also badly wanted to condemn fascism and the horrors perpetrated by the Nazis. To do that they, like the others, also needed a platform from which to launch their condemnations. "Give me a place to stand, and I will move the world," Archimedes is supposed to have said. The communists or any other delegation could not condemn the Nazis if they held to a strictly positivist view of law and morality. In that case there is no universal morality woven into domestic law, not even that of H. L. A. Hart's minimum content of natural law expressed in a system of "mutual forbearances which underlies both law and morals" (Hart 1961, 195); I discuss the implications of this further in chapters 4 and 5. In theory the purists among the communists should have voted against most proposals and certainly at the end against the text as a whole. But their suffering at the hand of the Nazis made them participate in this international act of condemnation. So they too took a stand outside the confines of domestic legal systems and (after a great deal of participation) abstained instead of casting a negative vote. They followed their consciences instead of their theories. Moyn is surely right in claiming that "the concept [of human rights] never did percolate in public and around the world with anything like the currency it required later" (Moyn 2010, 44). Even so, for a plane to reach great heights and speed, it first needs to take off, which is what happened for human rights in the UDHR drafting years of 1946–48. After President Truman had promised the San Francisco delegates that the world as a whole would soon have an "international bill of rights" the way the US had its own bill of rights, ECOSOC made the writing of this international bill the first task of the Commission of Human Rights. That commission presented the UDHR to the Third General Assembly in December 1948. It took more than the "yearlong debate" mentioned by Moyn, and from the start the result had far more "supranational" elements than he would have us think. In fact, its entire conception was not just *inter*national, but *supra*national, meaning universal.

Takeoff and Later Breakthrough

I do not reject the suggestion that the international human rights movement primarily took off in the 1970s, as Moyn and others have argued it did. But I do not think that the spiking of the movement—largely because of the new recruitment methods used by Amnesty International (AI)—was as "sudden" or "surprising" as Moyn makes it look. The big event was the linkage between the Holocaust and the declaration in the second bin in our flowchart: idea → Holocaust + UDHR text → system ↔ movement. The background presence of both the UDHR text and the system it spawned makes the birth of the movement in the 1970s far less sudden than the contingencies and discontinuities of history on which Moyn's reading of events relies. With these two parts of the chart in place, I dispute Moyn's thesis that the movement was primarily born out of a contest of ideologies. In fact, I do not consider the ideology of human rights a utopian one at all. Born out of the Holocaust, the human rights movement both at the start and in its later stages does not generally coalesce into any kind of political party or platform. In that sense it has more in common with the earlier historical universalisms of value than with contemporary socialist or neo-capitalist party platforms. So I agree with Moyn that there is some kind of "purity" to the movement of human rights in the 1970s, but instead of seeing that as a new development, I trace this purity back to the mother text as master frame of the movement. The drafting of the UDHR also—as Moyn suggests the movement did in the 1970s—went beyond the "politics of the state to the morality of the globe" (Moyn 2010, 43). Both periods lifted the cause of human rights above and beyond regular domestic and international politics. The purity Moyn lauds in the third chapter of this *Utopia* book was there all along, even in the 1940s, when the declaration rose above the Westphalianism that according to him kept human rights imprisoned until the "breakthrough" in the 1970s. This is not to say that no politics are or were involved, but in my view these are mediated by the *system* link of the flowchart that I discuss in chapter 4. I do not think that the birth of human rights is primarily the result of a tough contest of ideologies, utopian or otherwise. All along, both the *text* and the *system* were germinating in the background and ready to have an effect on world affairs by way of the NGOs or HROs that made up the movement before and at its alleged "implosion" in the 1970s. My cutting back on the "surprise" element of what Moyn says happened in the 1970s (though not on what actually did happen) should help my readers see more clearly the importance of the late 1940s as *the* moment of human rights.

Moyn has presented the rapid, sudden, and tremendous growth of the human rights movement in the 1970s as a "breakthrough" for the *concept* of human rights. That breakthrough, as he sees it, was a totally new way of defining, using, and fighting for the modern idea of human rights. To him "the percolation of the phrase got nowhere before the stakes of defining it clearly turned out to be low and not high" (Moyn 2010, 55). I have shown how high the stakes in the 1940s were. They were higher than in the 1970s, for in 1948 the modern concept with its many examples was presented to the world and its master frame was born. Moyn feels that "the [1940s] trip toward definition" turned out to be "a negligible line buried in the proposal for a Social and Economic Council and without any serious meaning" (56). On the contrary, that simple line created a very effective Human Rights Commission that in a relatively short time of two years defined human rights through a long list of examples. Moyn thinks that even at the time of its birth "the Universal Declaration emerged as an afterthought to the fundamentals of world government it did nothing to affect" (82). That was before the system of human rights law was created in the 1960s and 1970s and before use of the phrase "human rights" spiked in the news media and broke the popularity barrier in 1977 (appendix). So it went until "commitment to human rights crystallized as a result of [increased] Holocaust memory, but only decades later, as human rights were called upon to serve brand new purposes" (83). I argued in this chapter, and present more evidence in the next, that that Holocaust memory—defined both narrowly and broadly—was not absent in the 1940s, which means that the human rights purposes of the 1970s were in no way "brand" new. The movement in the 1970s relied on previous links in the chain: idea → [1940s] UDHR text → system → [1970s] movement. Moyn's breakthrough interpretation ignores these arrows and lets the movement fend for itself.

My view of the same trajectory goes like this: as described in this and the next chapter, the human rights plane took off in the 1940s. It was a solid text of a plane, well built by engineers from all over the world. Then, for some twenty years (discussed in the next chapter), it flew quite low and under the radar of world popular opinion, all the while gaining *systemic* strength and speed—until, in the decade of the 1970s, for many different reasons, it broke the popular barrier. Many people started to notice the plane, appreciated it, and supported its trajectory. As if by collective remote control, they directed it to various hot spots where human rights violations were occurring or had occurred, especially the disappearances in the cone of Latin America and the continuing repression in communist bloc nations.

In his contribution to the volume *The Breakthrough: Human Rights in the 1970s*, Jan Eckel notes, "Human rights do not notably figure in these [economic breakdown] descriptions of the [1970s] decade. Yet the 1970s saw a vigorous surge in the popularity of the idea and an impressive proliferation of political practices associated with it" (Eckel 2014, 227). The majority of the essays in this *Breakthrough* volume deal with associated political practices of the dissident movements under the repressive regimes in Eastern Europe and the Soviet Union and the opposition movements to brutal dictatorships in the cone of Latin America. The volume ends with a structural analysis by Eckel of what happened in that decade. Its title is "The Rebirth of Politics from the Spirit of Morality: Explaining the Human Rights Revolution of the 1970s." Eckel's explanation has two parts to it. The first part consists of six "extraneous causes and contexts": decolonization, détente, mass media, mass mobilization and the presence of suffering, the transformation of the political Left, and the transformation of the churches (241–52). Readers can easily imagine how factors like these might influence and create different political practices associated with human rights. Before he lists them, Eckel tells us that "while the overarching trend in the decade's human rights history was a forceful global upsurge, a closer survey thus reveals a much more fractured picture. The human rights revolution of the 1970s can clearly not be viewed as a uniform shift," as one might have thought reading Moyn's (2010) chapter "The Purity of the Struggle" on that same decade.

This course correction is important. I do not dismiss the variety of causes and contexts or the "multiple chronologies" that shaped the political use of human rights in the 1970s, but given my interest in the UDHR, I am intrigued by the second section of Eckel's explanation. It is titled "The Intrinsic Appeal of Human Rights." He tells us that "without the intrinsic appeal of the idea [of human rights], the resonance would hardly have been as widespread and as intense as it actually was" (Eckel 2014, 252). I interpret an unexplained assertion like this in terms of our flowchart, in which the 1948 *UDHR text* led to a worldwide *system*, both of which then were able to feed the *movement* when the time was ripe, as it apparently was in the 1970s. Without this intrinsic appeal, the extraneous causes and contexts would not have had the uniformity and hence effectiveness they did have. At the end of chapter 1, I argued that a successful movement needs a master frame and that the UDHR contains such a frame. Since its birth in the 1940s, the phrase "human rights" has traveled with a deep affective content that it received through its connection with the Holocaust. To all those familiar with the occasion of its birth, the declaration and by extension any use of the phrase collectively or for a single violation carries with it a seriousness that cannot be set aside.

Eckel discusses "the intrinsic appeal" part of his explanation for the rise of human rights in the 1970s under the headings of "Disillusionment and Rehabilitation," "Beyond the Cold War," and "Morality as a Political Resource" (Eckel 2014, 252–59). The heading that best fits our flowchart is the last one, for that one treats human rights as they were treated when the Universal Declaration was drafted and adopted. The first heading does not fit as well because Soviet dissidents were not giving up on or disenchanted with good socialism. They wanted the real thing without corruption and cruelty. It is also not clear that Latin American leftists gave up on socialism. For tactical and humane reasons, they wanted the disappearances and torturing to stop.

I said earlier that it does not seem as if the birth of human rights, even in the 1970s, came out of a battle between giving up old utopias to adopt the latest new one. Utopias are visionary political schemes that often are not realistic. As the always advancing but admittedly slow human rights historical trajectory shows, human rights—because they were not sold as a political solution—were always realistic. When early samizdat writers mention human rights, they are not searching for a new utopia; they want the rights that are listed in the Soviet constitution to be respected without corruption and no delays. Later dissidents wanted the Helsinki Accords lived up to. The same holds for Eastern European dissidents. Eckel believes that "the fact that dissidents seized upon human rights was certainly as much a matter of tactical choice as of ideological alignment, or even more so" (Eckel 2014, 253). As for the heading "Beyond the Cold War," there is an important time difference between *before* the Cold War, when the 1946–48 debates about the declaration took place, and *after* the Cold War, when politicians like Jimmy Carter and Joop Den Uyl, the prime minister of the Netherlands, wanted to move beyond Cold War politics. Both activists and politicians seemed to want to shift to "a universal morality," which leads them straight to the mother text of the human rights movement.

At a point like this, both Moyn and Eckel are hard put to explain what that "universal morality" (Eckel) or "purity of the struggle" (Moyn) consists of without invoking the text of the Universal Declaration as an important or even crucial element. A universal morality of human rights took off in 1948 and systematically gained strength till this moment of the 1970s. What else might be meant by "morality as a political resource" other than the morality of the Universal Declaration? For a morality to function as a resource, it must be available to those who wish to use it, from prime ministers up high to activists down low. Clearly the elite were familiar with the then-evolving system of international human rights law that had been spawned by the declaration. For the increase in activists, both Eckel and Moyn point to the tremendous growth of Amnesty International membership in those years.

Moyn reports that when human rights activists saw in the late 1960s that it would not do to work through governments, they instead turned to AI's "new style of mobilization" with its local chapters' seeking the release of prisoners of conscience. He quotes Peter Benenson, AI's founder, as offering a "common base upon which the idealists of the world can co-operate. It is designed in particular to absorb the latent enthusiasm of great numbers of such idealists who have, since the eclipse of Socialism, become increasingly frustrated; similarly it is designed to appeal to the young searching for an ideal" (Moyn 2010, 130). That there was mass participation in this new AI campaign to free prisoners of conscience is certain, but no one knows how many of the thousands of new members in those years were disappointed socialists and how many were just searching for a good cause. Moyn reports that in the 1970s AI provided a "substitute utopia" (146–47) that shot up its membership to 300,000 in the US alone. Add to that the fact that "almost 90 percent of local groups resided in Great Britain, Sweden, Denmark and the Federal Republic" (Eckel 2014, 229n6). We cannot be sure that any kind of substitute ideology was involved in these huge membership numbers. Why people vote and why they join certain organizations or campaigns is notoriously hard to find out.

Regarding "the long postwar period," Moyn holds that "human rights were not a promise waiting to be realized but a utopia first too vague then too conservative to matter. To capture the world's imagination they would need profound redefinition in a new ideological climate" (Moyn 2010, 47–48). Human rights were never presented as a utopia, the examples in the UDHR are not vague, and the presence of social and economic rights makes the text far from conservative. No "redefinition" of human rights was necessary after the text that lists them had taken off in 1948 and gained systemic strength for two decades, until AI and other organizations helped make them popular in the 1970s. Eckel rightly thinks that "not all the reasons for the rise of human rights resided in the meaning of the idea itself and its ideological or political substance" (Eckel 2014, 242). He cites AI activist Roger Baldwin as saying, "Sending a card . . . will not change the world very much. But it is surely worth investing a little time and postage to try and help two other individuals to secure justice, or at least to find courage" (254). That is not the motivation that animates someone with a new political ideology. It is the voice of someone who stopped by a table in his university center, read bits of the UDHR, and wrote a letter that AI said it would mail, which was done a great deal in the 1970s at the university where I was teaching and where I manned such tables.

While the AI numbers are impressive, we should be careful not to overdo the idea of a "breakthrough." Several of the essays in the volume by that name suggest that "multiple chronologies" are involved in the 1970s activism associated with human rights. The activism lines between the 1960s and 1970s in the Soviet Union and Eastern Europe are clearly blurred. While the 1973 military coup in Chile marked "the decisive caesura" in the Latin American cone, these lines are also blurred (Eckel 2014, 233). The anti-apartheid campaign that started in the 1950s and served as lead-up to the "breakthrough" surely had something to do with the background presence of the *text* and the *system* in our flowchart. It should also not go unsaid that at Amnesty International's founding in 1961, the only international text that stipulated that everyone in whatever country or living under whatever type of regime has the rights to freedom of expression and to a fair trial was the Universal Declaration of Human Rights.

There are other signs as well that the second and third bins of our chart played a role in the growth of the movement in the 1970s. For instance, after he has described the enormous diversity in the upsurge of human rights groups in the decade of the 1970s, Eckel notes that contemporary observers "sardonically spoke of a 'human rights industry' building up before their eyes" (Eckel 2014, 228). He took this phrase from a handbook for human rights organizations published in 1979. That handbook listed numerous human rights organizations in Britain and the United States, but it had only one appendix: the Universal Declaration of Human Rights. Another important example of the behind-the-scenes influence of the UDHR text is the fact that the two international covenants it spawned (the ICCPR and the ICESCR) are mentioned in the 1975 Helsinki Final Act and in that way came to shape the dissident movements in the communist countries, such as Charter 77 in Czechoslovakia and Solidarity in Poland. Through its moral and legal offspring in these Helsinki Accords, the UDHR brought the communist empire to its knees. It may be that the effect of the Helsinki Accords within the very communist nations that signed them with great pride was totally unforeseen. While the role of the declaration in these and similar events remains to be explored, it is already clear that it cannot be said or implied that there is no deep connection between the birth of human rights in the 1940s and their upsurge and "popularity" later in the 1970s.

3

THE 1940s MOMENT OF HUMAN RIGHTS

The focus of this chapter is on the second complex link of the moral (not the criminal) flowchart that I used as an outline in chapter 1. I ended the *movement* link of that chapter with citations from Samuel Moyn's work to the effect that the 1940s were not all that important in the telling of the human rights story. These citations sought to bypass the second link of our diagram and locate the birth of "human rights" in the 1970s instead. I here respond to that challenge. The second link of our chart is quite complex in that it connects the text of the declaration to the events of the Holocaust. I hold that the connection between this text and this event is central to our contemporary understanding of human rights. With this evidence in hand, in part 2 of this book, I unpack the moral and philosophical import of this historic moment for modern human rights. The by now familiar diagram is shown in figure 3.1. After I discuss the connection between the Holocaust and the UDHR text, I place side by side two proposed articles—one for the Genocide Convention on cultural genocide and one for the Universal Declaration on minority rights—and show that these much-needed articles were rejected in 1948 mostly because of assimilationist headwinds in the Americas. I conclude that even though the declaration has some obvious blind spots, ethics has not failed us.

Holocaust

↓↓

idea → [1948] UDHR text → system [1948–68] ↔ [1970s] movement

FIGURE 3.1: Amplified flowchart

The Holocaust and the UDHR Text

I should begin with the observation that sixty-odd pages (36–91) of my book *The Universal Declaration of Human Rights: Origins, Drafting, and Intent* (1999) are specifically devoted to giving evidence for the connection that I here claim is endangered. I collected that evidence under the title "World War II as Catalyst." When I first studied the *travaux préparatoires* of the UDHR in the 1980s, I noticed that when seeking to make a case for a certain article or clause, a delegate often would reference the horrors of the war that had ended just three years earlier. I collected these references and here repeat some of them to show that there is a real connection between the Holocaust—broadly understood as the evil Nazi practices that included but were not limited to murdering millions of Jews in concentration camps—and the adoption of the Universal Declaration. At the time I broke up the articles of the declaration into six groups: Personal Security and the Camps (Articles 1–5); Nazification and Legal Human Rights (Articles 6–10); The Problem with the Nuremberg Trials (Article 11), which I used in chapter 1 to keep the moral human rights system separated from the criminal system; Democracy, Free Speech, and Hate Speech (Articles 18–21 [with a relapse to Article 7] and 27–29); Special International Rights and the Role of the UN (Articles 13–15, 22, 28, 29, and 30, because they all call for a "new world order"); Social, Economic, and Cultural Examples (Articles 22–27). I am not sure that doing the work today I would use these exact same categories or rubrics. But I think they work well enough, and I encourage my reader to consult these and other UDHR articles (see Morsink 1999b, app.) against the background narratives I gave them in this earlier study. Here I first want to lift up a piece of evidence that I should have made more of when I first did this work. I will also give a few examples from the *travaux* to shore up the endangered connection.

In June 1946 ECOSOC instructed the UN Secretariat "to make arrangements for the collection and publication of information concerning human rights arising from trials of war criminals, quislings and traitors, and particularly from the Nuremberg and Tokyo trials" (E/CN.4/29/1) that had either just finished or were still ongoing. The Secretariat asked the United Nations War Crimes Commission, which had researched information needed for criminal charges in the war crimes tribunals, to prepare this special report for the Human Rights Commission. The UNWCC accepted that responsibility and in August 1947 furnished the UN Secretariat with a progress report of its findings and a tentative outline of the final report. This report (E/CN.4/W20), titled "Information concerning Human Rights Arising from Trials of War Criminals," runs more than 300 hundred pages and was "designed to serve the specific purpose of contributing to the task of the Commission of Human Rights, in preparing an international bill of rights, or international declarations or conventions on civil liberties" (vi), though, as I note later, it includes plenty of social, economic, and cultural matters as well.

I noted in chapter 1 that Dan Plesch's book *Human Rights after Hitler* perfectly describes the Holocaust cauldron that gave rise to two international tracks: one of international criminal law and tribunals and one of international human rights law and its treaty bodies. Plesch is puzzled "that this recorded history [of the UNWCC] is overlooked in most scholarships concerning the Holocaust, Nazi crimes in general and the history and law of war crimes" (Plesch 2017, 2–3). In correspondence Dan Plesch pointed out,

> The interconnection of the UNWCC and the drafters of the Universal Declaration consisted of the personnel who moved from the UNWCC in London to work on the Universal Declaration. To give three examples: Egon Schwelb, a legal officer of the UNWCC, joined Humphrey's staff. René Cassin was at the founding meeting of the UNWCC in 1943 and was closely engaged in its work for several years, and the then–Norwegian foreign minister Trygve Lie

> was at the founding meeting of the UNWCC and, of course, later became the first UN secretary-general.

Plesch's book on these "more than thirty-six thousand individuals and units indicted as war criminals by the commission" is therefore quite a revelation to most scholars, me included. While I had been aware of the work that the War Crimes Commission did to help the Human Rights Commission, I was unfamiliar with the wide scope of the UNWCC, which included China, India, Ethiopia, and the Philippines in its discussions. In that context, Plesch notes, the UNWCC had "a clear operational need to provide a universal discourse that required a shift in language from protection of 'Christians' to the broader notion of 'humanity'" (193). From that insight it is only a small step to universal human rights.

In its report (E/CN.4/W20) to the Human Rights Commission, the UNWCC notes that it considered three draft documents of preliminary bills of rights that had already been submitted to the Human Rights Commission's Drafting Committee: Panama's, the United Kingdom's, and the Secretariat's (meaning John Humphrey's). I discussed these sources in chapter 1 of the *Origins* book but here draw attention to the draft by John Humphrey, who was the first director of the UN Secretariat's Division of Human Rights (1946–66). Humphrey's draft (E/CN.4/AC.1) drew heavily on the Panamanian one. It had forty-eight articles and had been informed by a survey his Division of Human Rights had made of the extant constitutions of UN member states to see what rights they contained. That survey allowed members of the Drafting Committee to see whether a UDHR-proposed international right was domestically "popular" or not. These two sources of information available to the Human Rights Commission—the War Crimes Commission report and the Humphrey draft—clearly make the connection between the Holocaust and the Universal Declaration that this book defends.

The War Crimes Commission report (E/CN.4/W.19/20) of May 1948 (but previewed in August 1947), which was specifically drawn up for the Human Rights Commission, makes for fascinating reading because it points out to the commission that the Germans had violated every one of the rights that were being considered for inclusion in the Universal Declaration of Human Rights. To help my reader match the rights in the UDHR with the main headings of the 350-page War Crimes Commission report, I share the abbreviated headings of the report's table of contents, putting relevant UDHR articles in parentheses: to life, liberty, and security (Art. 3); from slavery (Art. 4); from torture and degrading punishment (Art. 5); to recognition as a person before the law (Art. 6); to equality before the law (Art. 7); to remedy by a competent tribunal (Art. 8); from arbitrary arrest and exile (Art. 9); to fair public hearing (Art. 10); to be considered innocent until proven guilty (Art. 11); from interference with privacy, family, home, and correspondence (Art. 12); to free movement in and out of the country (Art. 13); to asylum in other countries from persecution (Art. 14); to a nationality and the freedom to change nationality (Art. 15); to marriage and family (Art. 16); to own property (Art. 17); to freedom of belief and religion (Art. 18); to freedom of opinion and information (Art. 19); to peaceful assembly and association (Art. 20); to participation in government and in free elections (Art. 21); to social security (Art. 22); to desirable work and to join trade unions (Art. 23); to rest and leisure (Art. 24); to an adequate living standard (Art. 25); to education (Art. 26); to participation in the cultural life of the community (Art. 27); to a world social order that articulates this document (Art. 28); to community duties essential to free and full development (Art. 29); from state and personal interference in the above rights (Art. 30). Just glancing at these headings of the table of contents of the UNWCC report, the UDHR drafters could see that Germany had massively interfered with the rights they were about to adopt into their declaration.

Not surprisingly, both layers of the bifurcated flowchart I introduced in the preceding chapter play a role in this War Crimes Commission report that was prepared for the nonmilitary Human Rights Commission called for in the UN Charter. I repeat some of the more telling full headings, with the parentheses showing detailed violated rights: Human Rights Protected by the Laws and Customs of War (including the murder and ill treatment of civilians; the taking and killing of hostages; slave labor; plunder of private and public property; wanton destruction of cities, towns, and villages); Violations of the Rights of the Victims of War Crimes (among whom were the Allied inhabitants of occupied territories who had rights to life, to freedom of movement, and to a fair trial, plus family rights, property rights, civic rights); Violations of the Rights of Prisoners of War (to life and health, to integrity of the person, to freedom of movement, and to a fair trial, plus religious rights, property rights, and civic rights); Rights of the Accused at the Time of Trial (to know the charges, to be present at the trial, to have aid of counsel, to have the proceedings be made intelligible). Part 2 of the report contains information arising from the relationship between the state and persons under its jurisdiction. Chapter 1 (pages 310–59) details the "Jurisdiction over Violations of Human Rights of German Citizens and Stateless Persons within the Territory of the German Reich." It repeats most of the human rights already mentioned but places them in a strictly domestic context.

There is no way of escaping the conclusion that this UNWCC report asked those charged with drafting "an international bill of rights" to inform themselves of the kinds of human rights violations that had been perpetrated by the Third Reich. We cannot tell, of course, how many of the UDHR drafters carefully read or perused this report. It is clear, though, that these UNWCC findings percolated below the surface of the adoption debates for the UDHR. At times they broke through to the surface, as I indicate in the following paragraphs by highlighting certain phrases.

In the first session of the Drafting Committee in February 1947, Geoffrey Wilson, the UK representative, reminded his colleagues of "the historical situation" they found themselves in. "Germany and other enemy countries during the war had completely ignored what mankind had regarded as fundamental human rights and freedoms. The committee met as a first step to providing the maximum safeguard against that sort of thing in the future" (Morsink 1999b, 36). Close to two years later, in December 1948, after the War Crimes Commission report had had a chance to sink in, Wilson's colleague from Lebanon, Charles Malik, told the Third General Assembly that the document "was inspired by opposition to the barbarous doctrines of Nazism and Fascism" (Morsink 1999b, 36). Jorge Carrera, the delegate from Ecuador, also observed that "Nazism and fascism having been destroyed, so had the brutal totalitarian States," which created room for a new "democratic internationalism" based on human rights (UN Doc. GA [1948] 918/9).

In *Origins* chapter 2, I matched Hitler's racism in *Mein Kampf* with observations that the French delegate, René Cassin, made about UDHR Article 1. Cassin told his colleagues that he had sought to craft the article around "the fundamental principle of the unity of the human race" because Hitler had "started by asserting the inequality of man before attacking their liberties" (Morsink 1999b, 38). To any reader acquainted with the historic antagonism between fascists and communists, it will be no surprise to hear that Alexei Pavlov, the USSR delegate, believed "the principle of nondiscrimination," which is spelled out in UDHR Articles 2 and 7, was "the most important one to be included in the Bill of Rights" (39). Dr. F. R. Bienenfeld frequently addressed the drafters on behalf of the World Jewish Congress. He objected, for instance, to a clause ("except in cases prescribed by law") in an early version of UDHR Article 3, which speaks of the "right to life, liberty and security of person." After Bienenfeld had pointed out that "under the Nazi regime thousands of people had been deprived of their liberty under laws which were perfectly valid" (39), the clause was deleted. Count Carton de Wiart, the Belgian delegate, thought that "it was more than ever necessary to affirm the right to life, as the right has been so gravely violated by the Nazis" (40).

Stephan Demchenko, the delegate from the Ukraine Socialist Republic, supported Article 4's ban on slavery in all its forms in part because "it could not be denied that . . . slavery had been reintroduced by the Nazi regime" (Morsink 1999b, 41). The previously mentioned War Crimes Commission report told the UDHR drafters "that the murders and ill-treatments of civilian populations [in Ravensbrück, Buchenwald, Natzweiler, and Auschwitz] were carried out, among other means, by the performance of experiments, by operations and otherwise on living human beings" (44). This supported Cassin's raising in connection with Article 5 (banning torture and cruel treatment) the question, "Do some human beings have the right to expose others to medical experiments and do any have the right to inflict suffering upon other human beings without their consent, even for ends that appear good?" (42). While the UDHR was being written, the same drafters worked on a parallel legal covenant. Article 7 of that covenant read: "No one shall be subjected to any form of physical mutilation or medical or scientific experimentation against his will" (42).

In my larger narrative, I match the legal human rights in the declaration (Articles 6–11) with the story Ingo Müller tells in his 1991 book, *Hitler's Justice: The Courts of the Third Reich.* The concept of being "a person before the law" and having a legal personality puzzled some of the drafters. Cassin explained to them that indeed UDHR Article 6 would not be necessary "had not certain heads of state such as Hitler sought in the last ten years to revive the ancient idea that an individual considered as a slave had no right to marry, to be a creditor or to own property" (Morsink 1999b, 44). Pavlov, Cassin's colleague from the USSR, also explained "apart from attempts against whole groups, such as those against the Jews in Germany, account must be taken of the fact that some civil legislation contained restrictive provisions regarding juridical personality of individuals" (44). The Canadian delegate, H. H. Carter, noted that "Nazi Germany offered an example" of persons being deprived of their juridical personality by an act of their government (44). The drafters had a long discussion about whether they should have just one article on nondiscrimination or the two that they gave us (Articles 2 and 7). The basic difference was thought to be that whereas Article 2 spells out the general principle, Article 7 adds specifics, such as protection "against any incitement to such discrimination." This addition was the result of a USSR push in the Subcommission on the Prevention of Discrimination and the Protection of Minorities. In the larger Human Rights Commission, Bogomolov, the USSR delegate, defended it with the observation, "Between Hitlerian racial propaganda and any other propaganda designed to stir up racial, national or religious hatred and incitement to war, there was but a small step" (70).

Alberto F. Cañas, the representative from Costa Rica, captured the rationale behind Article 8 (on an independent judiciary) by arguing that "Hitlerite Germany had shown that a state which placed its interests above those of its individual citizens entered upon a path which led to war" (Morsink 1999b, 49). As was the case with other articles, Article 9 (on arbitrary arrest) at first included the clause "except in cases prescribed by law and after due process." Once again Dr. Bienenfeld objected and warned of the danger "of using the word 'law' . . . because strictly speaking the actions of the Nazis were legal" (50). The second session of the commission received a report from the Institute of International Law pointing out to the UDHR drafters that

"National-Socialist law was marked by the removal . . . of these fundamental rights (*Grundrecht*) of man which are beyond the reach of political decisions by governments" (E/CN.4/40/5//Org.347/nt44). We do not know how carefully the drafters read reports like this, but the high level of the debates suggest that they aimed UDHR Article 10 (on the need for an independent judiciary) in part to prevent a repeat of anything like the Third Reich's Nazification of the German legal system. In chapter 1 I pointed out that the *system* link of our flowchart really is a bifurcated one, and I used the UDHR debates behind the term "international" in Article 11(2) to support my objection to the conflation of the international moral norms found in the declaration with the new international criminal norms enacted in the Nuremberg trials and further worked out in the international criminal law system. I do not see merit in the popular and professional "criminalization" of our concept of human rights. The half of the system here under discussion, though fed by the same research, is not a list of criminal norms.

The International Law Institute made a connection between "fundamental rights," like Article 18's freedom of opinion and expression and Article 19's freedoms of association, and the nature of government, which according to Article 21(3) is to be grounded in "the will of the people" expressed "in periodic and genuine elections which shall be by universal and equal suffrage and shall be held by secret vote or by equivalent free voting procedures." The reader may have noticed that the words "democracy" and "Nazism" or "fascism" do not appear in the Universal Declaration. In the Article 18 debate, Jamil M. Baroody, the Saudi delegate, observed "that the term fascism, like that of democracy, was too liable to different interpretations to be used in a legal document" (Third Committee [1948], 425). In the debate on Article 19, the Greek delegate, Alexander Contoumas, also noted that "he had not been able to support the USSR amendment because of the use of certain terms which were too vague, such as 'democracy' and 'fascism'" (446). Yet it is obvious from the tenor of the debates that these three political articles are meant as a "democratic" response to the Nazi practice of grossly violating the political rights mentioned in these articles. The Third Committee had received from the commission versions of these articles that were much like what we have. However, in each case the Soviet delegation proposed amendments openly aimed at preventing any resurgence of fascism. For Article 18 it submitted a long text that included this sentence: "Freedom of speech and the Press shall not be used for the purposes of propagating fascism, aggression, and for provoking hatred as between nations" (E/800). The *travaux* tell us that "this sentence was not adopted, 19 votes being cast in favour and 19 against, with 8 abstentions" (Third Committee [1948], 423). For Article 19 the Soviet delegation again submitted a long text that had this sentence in it: "All societies, unions and other organizations of a fascist or anti-democratic nature, as well as their activity in any form, are forbidden by law under pain of punishment" (E/800). The *travaux* tell us that "the text was *rejected* by 28 votes to 7, with 12 abstentions" (Third Committee [1948], 443).

If they had been successful in suppressing the rights to freedom of expression and association for Nazis and fascists, the communists would not have needed to amend Article 21 on the machinery of democratic (though without the term) government, and they did not. But that does not solve the problem of how intolerant an otherwise tolerant government should be of opposition groups that themselves are intolerant. A joint amendment submitted by Colombia and Costa Rica (AC.3/248) made that point when it approved of opposition only "by legal means with equality of electoral opportunities and of access to the means of propaganda." Cañas from Costa Rica told his colleagues

> that the right of everyone to take part in the government should be completed by a statement of the right to oppose the government and to promote its replacement by legal means. If the latter right were lost all human rights would be lost. The Nazi and fascist governments—like all tyrannical regimes—had been able to deprive the people of all fundamental human rights precisely because they had first deprived them of the basic right to oppose the government. States that had shown such an interest in preventing a renewal of fascism should realize that the amendment would serve that purpose, for the right it laid down was in itself a negation of fascism. (Third Committee [1948], 449)

Pavlov, the USSR delegate, answered with the recollection that "it was because Hitler and Mussolini had been allowed to oppose their respective governments that they had eventually been able to come to power. The USSR delegation therefore hesitated to accept the amendment, for it might provide the possibility for fascist elements to overthrow the government" (449).

At a later point, the Belgian representative added the important issue of the need for "several lists of candidates" and asked that the clause "with several lists" be added after the phrase "and by secret ballot" (Third Committee [1948], 453). And later yet, in an exchange with Pavlov from the USSR, he said he "would like the words 'according to the party system' to be inserted after the word 'periodic'; that would permit the introduction into article 19 [21] of the idea of duality or plurality of parties, which was to essential functioning of the democratic system" (470). Moments later and even closer to the end of the debate, he repeated this request and sought to turn it into an amendment of his own. The chairman responded that "it would be impossible in practice to introduce that amendment into the English text" (471). Pavlov quickly pointed out that the Belgian amendment "was absolutely irreconcilable with the social structure of certain Member States." Then the *travaux* record the surprising resolution of an important and dramatic showdown on how "the will of the people is to be authority of government." "Mr. Dehousse (Belgium) withdrew his amendment as a conciliatory gesture" (471). Article 21(3) with the rest of the details still in it (but not those of a multiparty system) was adopted "by 39 votes to 3, with 3 abstentions" (472). After all the different votes on Article 21 had been taken, Pavlov said that "the USSR delegation was particularly pleased to see that its wishes on a number of points had been taken into account; gaps had been filled, and a statement of the principle of freedom of elections had been inserted into the text"; then the meeting rose (473). Pavlov probably was not thinking of the fact that when Article 21 is combined with the list of nondiscrimination factors in Article 2, which includes "political opinion," the political rights of Articles 19–21 do allow for a dual- or multiparty system.

We have given Holocaust references for four of the six original categories under which I explored World War II (and, as we saw, with it the Holocaust) as a catalyst for the birth of the Universal Declaration: Personal Security and the Camps, Nazification and Legal Human Rights, The Problem with the Nuremberg Trials (dealt with in chapter 1), and

Democracy, Free Speech, and Hate Speech. That leaves me with a debt of two more from which to draw Holocaust examples: Special International Rights and the Role of the UN, and Social, Economic, and Cultural Examples. I already covered these categories in chapter 2's discussion of Daniel Moyn's alternative readings of the declaration's origin under the headings "Beyond Westphalia" and "Domestic or Universal Labor Rights."

Before I leave the discussion of Holocaust references in the UDHR debates themselves, I want to make one further point about the background against which these references must be understood. In chapter 1 I noted that the drafting of the Universal Declaration and the Genocide Convention significantly overlapped; the UN adopted the documents only one day apart in December 1948. That overlap led to an unfortunate omission from each of these texts: Article III was omitted from the Genocide Convention and an article on minority rights was omitted from the declaration. Article III condemned cultural genocide and not just physical or biological genocide. Naturally the debate about it led delegations to make references to their own experiences with Hitler's practice of cultural genocide during the war. Before I discuss this overlap in detail in the next section, I here paint it with a few broad strokes to emphasize the larger context within which the declaration was written. Understanding that the UDHR was written at the same time as another document with an even stronger connection to the Holocaust strengthens the UDHR text's connection to the Holocaust. Both documents were drafted at the same time in the same United Nations, albeit in different committees.

Several delegations were strong proponents of Article III of the Genocide Convention. Platon Morozov, the USSR delegate, argued in the Sixth Committee, which deals with jurisprudential matters, that if genocide was "the intent to destroy a group in whole or in part, the physical destruction of members of the group was one way of carrying out that intention, and the destruction of the culture of a group was another" such method (GAOR, 6th Comm., 3rd Sess., 205). He pointed out that the "Nuremberg verdicts had shown that the destruction of the culture of certain groups might constitute a method of destroying those groups; there had been examples of that in Czechoslovakia, Poland and Luxembourgh" (205). To those delegations that argued cultural genocide should be dealt with in the Universal Declaration, he responded that "biological genocide—the destruction of physical persons—was also already covered in the Declaration's rights to life, liberty and security of person, yet no one disputed the need for a convention on physical genocide" (205). Why should cultural genocide be any different?

N. M. Khomussko, the Byelorussian Soviet Socialist Republic (BSSR) representative, also argued that "acts aimed at the destruction of the language, religion or culture of a group . . . were always a feature of persecutions having as their object the destruction of groups—as the crimes perpetrated under Hitler showed" (GAOR, 6th Comm., 3rd Sess., 202). On another occasion he told his colleagues how Hitler had used ghettos, concentration camps, and finally gas chambers in Minsk to "hasten extermination of the population" (GAOR, 3rd Sess., Plenary Mtgs., 829). The Belorussian people knew, he said, "that the destruction of cultural and national centers accompanied the mass destruction of people, cities and villages. The Germans had burned the Academy of Sciences, the State University, the State Library, the schools of medicine and law, the Ballet Theater, the National Library, whose books had been plundered and destroyed, and over one thousand school buildings in the region of Minsk alone" (842). He said that the same thing had been done in the Soviet Union, Poland, and Czechoslovakia.

Perez Perozo, the Venezuelan delegate to the Ad Hoc Genocide Committee, argued that

> adequate justification for the protection of human groups from cultural genocide could be found in present-day history; everyone was aware of the violent outrages committed by the Nazis upon the cultural or religious life of the groups they intended to destroy; everyone knew of the burning of synagogues and Jewish libraries; nor could anyone forget certain events which occurred during the first World War, such as the burning of the university of Louvain and the destruction of the cathedral of Rheims. (GAOR, 3rd Sess., 6th Comm., 195)

In the next section, I flesh out this wider Holocaust context and show how the omission of this Article III on cultural genocide was intertwined with the omission of a minority rights article from the Universal Declaration. Any reader who would like even more details than I give here should go to an earlier account of the same events (Morsink 1999a).

Cultural Genocide and Minority Rights

I trace the common fate of Article III—which dealt with cultural genocide—of the 1948 Genocide Convention and of a minority rights article proposed for the Universal Declaration. There was a clear consensus that one of these two proposals deserved passage. However, the overlap between the drafting processes for the two documents created confusion and misunderstandings, with the unfortunate outcome that assimilationist headwinds caused both proposals to be rejected. Because of these headwinds, the Universal Declaration contains a blind spot that (as I relate in chapter 5) was not corrected for some twenty years. Citations from the debates on these two proposed articles support the contention that for the majority of both groups of drafters, group-differentiated rights (whether the right to culture or to minority rights generally) did not have a high priority. Communist delegations saw minority rights as a prelude to both cultural and physical genocide, which is why they wanted both proposals to go forward. But the majority in both groups of drafters had assimilationism as their working hypothesis. They were also scared off by Hitler's abuse of the Minority Rights Treaties of the League of Nations. For them the principle of nondiscrimination was the best way for states to respond to claims of any group-differentiated rights, which is why they expanded the UN Charter's four items of nondiscrimination (race, sex, language, and religion) to the much longer list we now have in Article 2: "without distinction of any kind, such as race, color, sex, language, religion, political or other opinion, national or social origin, property, birth or other status . . . or international status of the country or territory to which a person belongs." Owing to the hesitation of the French delegate (René Cassin) and a bad ruling of the chair (Eleanor Roosevelt), the much-needed minority rights article of the UDHR was "put aside" in the third session of the commission and not given a chance at rehabilitation in the later Third Committee proceedings.

On December 11, 1946, the very first General Assembly of the United Nations passed a resolution declaring genocide to be "the denial of the right of existence of entire human groups" (A/Res/.96[I]). Following up on that resolution, two years later the Economic and Social Council of the UN created an ad hoc committee to prepare a draft Convention on the Prevention and Punishment of the Crime of Genocide for adoption by the 1948 General Assembly. The convention itself was "to prevent the destruction of racial, national, linguistic, religious, or political groups of human beings" (UN Doc. E/447 [1947]). Toward that end the Ad Hoc Genocide Committee submitted what was called Article III to the Sixth Committee, where unfortunately it was deleted for reasons I explain later. In figure 3.2 I have placed Article III (UN ECOSOC, 3rd Year, 7th Sess., Supp. No. 6, 6) in the first column. Next to it I have put what I shall refer to as the Humphrey-Lauterpacht minority rights article, which almost made it into the UDHR. The slightly altered text of the Humphrey-Lauterpacht article shown in Figure 3.2 (E/CN.4/Sub.2/SR.11/11) was passed on to the second session of the Human Rights Commission, which met in December 1947 in Geneva, by its Subcommission on the Prevention of Discrimination and the Protection of Minorities. The subcommission had relied heavily on John Humphrey's Article 46 (E/CN.4/21/23), which Humphrey in turn had taken from Hersch Lauterpacht's influential 1946 proposal for an international bill of rights (E/CN.4/89/Art. 12, 38). There is a clear overlap in time and substance between these two proposed articles. The reader can see that Article III is written in legalese, while the slightly amended Humphrey-Lauterpacht proposal reads more like a statement of principles.

On its second reading in the Ad Hoc Genocide Committee, Article III was adopted with four votes for (USSR, Venezuela, Lebanon, and Poland) and three abstentions (France, the US, and China) (ECOSOC, 3rd Year, 7th Sess., Supp. No. 6, 7). The ad hoc committee met from May 5 to 10 at Lake Success, New York, which places the initial adoption of this cultural genocide article between the second session of the Human Rights Commission of December 1947 and the commission's third session in May and June 1948. Hence considerations of the UDHR minority rights article in this third session overlapped with similarly intense discussions about whether to include a cultural

Article III, Genocide Convention	Minority Rights Article, UDHR
In this Convention genocide also means any deliberate act committed with the intent to destroy the language, religion or culture of a national, racial or religious group on grounds of national or racial origin or religious belief such as: 1. Prohibiting the use of the language of the group in daily intercourse or in schools, or the printing and circulation of publications in the language of the group; 2. Destroying, or preventing the use of, libraries, museums, schools, historical monuments, places of worship or other cultural institutions and objects of the groups.	In States inhabited by a substantial number of persons of a race, language or religion other than those of the majority of the population, persons belonging to such ethnic, linguistic or religious minorities shall have the right, as far as compatible with public order and security to establish and maintain schools and cultural or religious institutions and to use their own language in the Press, in public assembly and before the courts and other authorities of the State.

FIGURE 3.2: Two rejected proposals from 1948

genocide article in the Genocide Convention. Adding these two venues (the convention process and the UDHR process) together, the matter of minority rights was discussed in the United Nations at least seven times in the spring and fall of 1948, most of the effort being for naught.

The reader will not be surprised to hear that there was a great deal of back-and-forth about these two articles in their respective adoption debates. How could there not be an underlying connection between the protection of minorities and the condemnation of cultural genocide? Protecting minorities is an important way of avoiding cultural genocide, and as Hitler's use of cultural genocide shows, it can be a prelude to physical genocide, which is the crime of all crimes. Protecting minorities can, therefore, be seen as a way of implementing the Genocide Convention, which is what some delegates in these overlapping debates did indeed think. But even without an explicit Article III to remind us, it is hard to imagine physical genocide without any kind of cultural genocidal prelude. The links between violating minority rights, committing cultural genocide, and then committing physical genocide lie, I believe, just below the surface of these debates, and they still reverberate in present-day international legal debates. The way minorities and endangered majorities preserve their collective identities is through the cultural expressions listed in the two proposed articles: building libraries and houses of worship, printing material in their own language, using their native language in courts of law and "other authorities of state," and creating works of arts and monuments. In theory and practice, we project a natural progression from the denial of minority rights to cultural genocide and from there to physical or biological genocide. While some delegates affirmed all or several of these connections, others denied them. In any case, there was a clear consensus that one of these two articles had to be included in either of these two texts. The shame is that neither article was adopted because both faced the same assimilationist headwinds. I tell the story mostly in terms of the votes taken on the proposed Article III of the Genocide Convention, ending with the simultaneous deletion of a minority rights article from the UDHR.

The Connection between Cultural and Physical Genocide

Though adopted by the ad hoc committee, Article III was deleted in the fall of 1948 by the Sixth Committee in a vote of twenty-four to sixteen, with four abstentions. Because of the previously mentioned connections between cultural genocide and minority rights, I think we can count those who voted for deletion of Article III as also being against or lukewarm toward minority rights. Later votes on the declaration's minority rights article bear this out. The negative votes on Article III came from South Africa, the UK, the US, Australia, Belgium, Bolivia, Brazil, Canada, Chile, Denmark, the Dominican Republic, France, Greece, India, Liberia, Luxembourg, the Netherlands, New Zealand, Norway, Panama, Peru, Siam, Sweden, and Turkey. We can count the nations that voted for retention of Article III in the convention as being likely proponents of minority rights. They were the

USSR, Yugoslavia, the BSSR, China, Czechoslovakia, Ecuador, Egypt, Ethiopia, Lebanon, Mexico, Pakistan, Philippines, Poland, Saudi Arabia, Syria, and the Ukrainian Soviet Socialist Republic (UKSSR). Venezuela, Afghanistan, Argentina, and Cuba abstained (GAOR, 3rd Sess., 6th Comm., 206).

Venezuela was the sole Latin American nation on the Ad Hoc Genocide Committee. As a member of that group, it had voted for the inclusion of Article III in the convention, and it became one of the most articulate defenders of that position. Though he abstained in the Sixth Committee vote because delegations had not been allowed enough time to state their views, Venezuelan delegate Perozo started out with a lengthy statement. He pointed out that "Sub-paragraph 5 of article II [of the Genocide Convention] had been adopted because the forced transfer of children to a group where they would be given an education different from that of their own group, and would have new customs, a new religion and probably a new language, was in practice tantamount to the destruction of their group, whose future depended upon that generation of children" (GAOR, 3rd Sess., 6th Comm., 195). He went on to argue,

> Adequate justification for the protection of human groups from cultural genocide could be found in present-day history; everyone was aware of the violent outrages committed by the Nazis upon the cultural or religious life of the groups they intended to destroy; everyone knew of the burning of synagogues and Jewish libraries; nor could anyone forget certain events which occurred during the first World War, such as the burning of the university of Louvain and the destruction of the cathedral of Rheims. (196)

These examples, he said, showed that "crimes against the culture or the religion of certain groups could shock human conscience in the same way as did crimes of physical genocide" (196). At this point the chairman reminded him that "each speaker was limited to a maximum of ten minutes" (197).

The communist delegations came from countries where Hitler's forces had practiced cultural genocide; thus, they believed in an "organic connection" between theories about superior and inferior races and acts of cultural genocide aimed at wiping out supposedly inferior cultures, races, or groups. I previously cited Morozov's observation that besides physical genocide, "the destruction of the culture of a group was another" method by which to destroy that group and Khomussko's observation that "acts aimed at the destruction of the language, religion or culture of a group . . . were always a feature of persecutions having as their object the destruction of groups—as the crimes perpetrated under Hitler showed" (GAOR, 3rd Sess., 6th Comm., 205).

Sardar Bahadur Khan, the Pakistani delegate to the Sixth Committee, said that "for his country cultural genocide was a matter of vital concern, for thirty five million people, bound to Pakistan by ties of religion, culture and feeling, but living outside its boundaries, faced cultural extinction at the hands of ruthless and hostile forces" (GAOR, 3rd Sess., 6th Comm., 193). He argued that biological and cultural genocide were "complementary crimes insofar as they had the same motive and the same object, namely, the destruction of a national, racial, or religious group as such either by exterminating its members or by destroying its special characteristics" (193). He reversed the usual order of things with the argument that "cultural genocide represented the end, whereas physical genocide was merely the means." The chief motive of genocide was, he said, "a blind rage to destroy ideas, the values and the very soul of a national, racial or religious group, rather than its physical existence" (193). The two kinds of genocide were therefore "indivisible," which meant that "the goal of Article III could not be attained by provisions of the Universal Declaration of Human Rights or of a Convention on Minority Rights." Addressing those delegates who "appeared to consider cultural genocide as a less hideous crime than physical or biological genocide," he said that "for millions of men in most Eastern countries the protection of sacred books and shrines was more important than life itself; the destruction of those sacred books or shrines might mean extinction of spiritual life." He concluded by observing, "Certain materialistic philosophies [of the West] prevented some people from understanding the importance which millions of men in the world attached to the spiritual life" (194).

Many of these pro and con arguments on the desirability of banning cultural genocide were repeated later when the Third General Assembly took up adoption of the Genocide Convention. Both Venezuela and the USSR submitted amendments to the text that repeated positions they had taken in the Sixth Committee. Perez Perozo noted, "The Venezuelan amendment [A/770] was very simple: it retained three factors in the original article III and deleted all those which might lead to confusion. Those three factors were: religious edifices, schools and libraries of the group" (GAOR, 3rd Sess., 178 Pln. Mtg., 816). The USSR resubmitted its own version (A/766) of Article III. Neither attempt at rehabilitating the ideas of Article III succeeded.

In our own day, the importance that millions of people attach to their cultural or spiritual life was reaffirmed when on March 24, 2016, the International Criminal Court found Ahmad Al Faqi Al Mahdi "criminally responsible for the war crime of directing an attack" in Timbuktu on "buildings dedicated to religion and [on] historic monuments which were not military objectives" (ICC-01/12-01/15/Charges/para. 23). Al Mahdi "participated personally in the destruction of at least five sites . . . that were regarded as and protected as a significant part of the cultural heritage of Timbuktu and of Mali" (para. 20). According to the indictment, "the community in Timbuktu was involved in their maintenance and used them for their religious practices" (ICC-01/12-01/15/Findings/para. 36). At the time of the attacks, Timbuktu was under the control of the armed group Al-Qaeda in the Islamic Maghreb, which together with an affiliate had set up "an administrative structure for the city" (ICC-01/12-01/15/Charges/para. 31). As part of that "occupation," Al Mahdi had been appointed head of the Hisbah, which was given the mission "to prevent vice and to promote virtue." That task included destroying sacred sites to "discourage the population from following their established practices concerning the mausoleums" that had been built on ancient ancestral tombs. Three years before Al Mahdi's indictment was handed down, Lydia Polgreen (2013) had reported that Ali Imam Ben Essayouti had bundled 8,000 volumes of fourteenth-century manuscripts and spirited them to safety before the carnage took place because "they belong to all of humanity." I return to these crimes of cultural genocide as best harbored under the category of international cultural heritage law and not under the rubric of international human rights law.

The Minority Rights Approach to Cultural Genocide

Some delegations argued that protection of minority rights and protection from cultural genocide are fundamentally the same and that therefore it was not necessary to adopt both proposed articles. This argument led to the suggestion that the UDHR was the better place to protect the cultural rights of members of minority groups. India and China were strong supporters of this position.

Responding to the Pakistani position, M. C. Setalvad, the Indian delegate, "fully sympathized with the idea underlying Article III." However, he pointed out that there were "comprehensive provisions in [India's] constitution for the protection of minorities" and that therefore "the anxiety expressed by the representative of Pakistan concerning the fate of the thirty five million Muslims [was] quite unfounded" (GAOR, 6th Comm., 3rd Sess., 201). But Setalvad's delegation also did not think that there was a connection between what the convention on physical or biological genocide was trying to do and the protection of the cultural rights of minorities. "The protection of cultural rights of a group should be guaranteed," he said, "not by the convention on genocide, but by the declaration of human rights" (201). Setalvad's colleague, K. V. K. Sundaram, repeated this suggestion in the General Assembly, arguing against all attempts to reinstate Article III on the grounds that "the cultural rights of groups should be assured by the declaration of human rights, which would shortly come before the General Assembly" (GAOR, 3rd Sess., Plenary Mtg., 824). This Indian defense of a minority rights article for the Universal Declaration implied a rejection of overt assimilationism.

C. H. Wu, the Chinese expert, explained to his colleagues on the Subcommission on the Prevention of Discrimination and the Protection of Minorities that "in the whole of China's history there had been no religious or racial persecution. There were five main races in China, but none had been added by military conquest. The minorities in China were," he said, "given more than equal representation" (E/CN.4/Sub.2/SR.3/4). In a similar vein, but stressing the cultural genocide part of the equation, Tsien Tai, the Chinese delegate to the Sixth Committee, supported the inclusion of Article III because while cultural genocide seemed less brutal, "it might be even more harmful than physical genocide or biological genocide, since it worked below the surface and attacked a whole population, attempting to deprive it of its ancestral culture and to destroy its very language" (GAOR, 3rd Sess., 6th Comm., 98). These same considerations led China to support a minority rights article for the Universal Declaration. To those who were looking for a convention on just minority rights, Tsien pointed out "that at the present no such convention existed even in the form of a draft" (98).

Assimilationist Headwinds from the Americas

With the strong exception of Venezuela, most Latin American delegations and the United States consistently showed a lack of interest in the protection of the rights of members of minority groups. All these countries had a policy of denying that there was any kind of minority problem on the American continents. In the 1930s and early 1940s, the nations of Latin America had been worried about the war spreading to their own continent, and that fear was connected to their experience of waves of immigration from Germany. On at least three separate occasions, they as a group publicly worried about the influx of undesirable aliens into their nation-states: at the Eighth International Conference of 1938, at the February 1942 Latin American Ministers of Foreign Affairs Conference, and at the March 1945 Inter-American Conference on the Problem of War and Peace (just before the San Francisco Conference). At the March 1945 conference, under the heading of "Post War Immigration," the group stipulated that "it is highly undesirable that there should reside in the territory of any of the American States aliens disposed to conspire against the historic democratic ideal common to those States or . . . intended to foment wars, conflicts, or disturbances of any nature . . . or who pursue aims in the name of doctrines contrary to the ideals and principles of liberty sustained by the peoples of the Hemisphere" (E/CN.4/Sub.2/3 [1947]). These worries and the formal declarations to which they led lasted far beyond the war, and they reinforced an already existing policy of assimilation.

The reader can well imagine that Article III of the Genocide Convention was a difficult bone to swallow for these Latin American nations, and most of them did not vote for it. Bolivia, Brazil, Chile, the Dominican Republic, Panama, and Peru all voted against Article III in the Sixth Committee; Ecuador and Mexico voted to retain it; and Venezuela, Argentina, and Cuba abstained (GAOR, 3rd Sess., 6th Comm., 206). As a member of the Ad Hoc Genocide Committee, the United States had voted against Article III, and it had asked that a formal declaration of US opposition be added to the ad hoc committee's report. In the later ECOSOC discussions, the US delegate, Willard Thorp, repeated his country's opposition to Article III. He said that its presence would be "a dilution of the purpose of the Convention which might render it much less effective." He admitted that it "was obvious that such fundamental rights as those envisaged in the article on 'cultural genocide' must be safeguarded, but he did not think that that end would best be achieved by including them in a convention on genocide" (GAOR, 7th Sess., Supp. No. 6, 725).

It was to be expected that the United States would vote in the Sixth Committee to delete Article III from the convention. However, the rationale given by Ernest Gross, the US delegate, is surprising. He thought that Article III might not even help the very minorities it sought to protect. "There were," he said, "in fact grounds for asking whether it was more important to protect the right of a group to express its opinions in the language of its choice [which is what Article III did] or to protect its right to free expression of thought, whatever the language. If the object were to protect the culture of a group, then it was primarily freedom of thought and expression for the members of the group which needed protection" (GAOR, 3rd Sess., 6th Comm., 203). This line of thinking misses the close connection that exists between language and culture and, in some important respects, misses the very point of the article.

Unredeemed Promissory Notes

So far the score of the vote on Article III in the Sixth Committee is two blocks for protection of cultural minority rights (the communists and most Middle Eastern delegations) and one large block of mostly South American nations against such protection in the convention. If Article III of the Genocide Convention was going to have a chance—and by implication the minority rights article in the Universal Declaration as well—the balance had to come from the North Atlantic bloc of votes. The votes of this bloc went almost totally against Article III's inclusion in the Genocide Convention. The countries opposing Article III included South Africa, the UK, Australia, Belgium, Canada, France, Luxembourg, the Netherlands, New Zealand, Norway, and Sweden. They shared the view that there was a huge difference between physical or biological genocide and cultural genocide and that the latter was too vague a concept to be included in the Genocide Convention. They further thought that including cultural genocide would probably prevent many nations from becoming signatories to the convention and that such abstentions would turn the whole project into a self-defeating one. They therefore held out for only a possible insertion of minority rights in the UDHR, but even that support they failed to organize, the result being that assimilationism won out by default.

France had been one of the two objectors in the first reading of Article III in the Ad Hoc Genocide Committee, and it had not changed its stance. In the ECOSOC discussion that preceded the Sixth Committee discussions, Pierre Ordonneau, the French representative, said that his delegation "did not accept the idea of cultural genocide presented in Article III. It considered such an idea too vague, and thought that the council should not confuse two extremely different concepts and risk going beyond the purpose of the Convention by transforming a minor infringement of human rights into an international principle" (ESCOR, 3rd Year, 7th Sess., Supp. No. 6, 723). Ordonneau's delegation proposed "that the attention of the Third Committee should be drawn to the need for the protection of language, religion and culture within the framework of the international declaration of human rights" (GAOR, 3rd Sess., 6th Comm., 199–200). This set the tone for others to also hold out for inclusion of minority rights in the declaration instead of the convention.

Speaking in the Sixth Committee, the Belgian representative thought that the matter raised in Article III "came within the province of the domestic affairs of States," while later in the Third Committee the Belgian delegation became a strong supporter of the Humphrey-Lauterpacht proposal (GAOR, 3rd Sess., 6th Comm., 204). The Danish representative thought that the concept of cultural genocide "was not clearly defined" and that in any case there was a huge difference between "mass murderers" and "the closing of libraries" (198). Hugues Lapointe, the Canadian representative to the Sixth Committee, announced that "no drafting change of Article III would make its substance acceptable to his delegation." This was his reason: "The people of his country were deeply attached to their heritage, which was made up mainly of a combination of Anglo-Saxon and French elements and they would strongly oppose any attempt to undermine the influence of those two cultures in Canada. . . . [His delegation] felt that the idea of genocide should be limited to the mass physical destruction of human groups" (199–200).

It is interesting to note just how many of the North Atlantic delegations went out of their way to make the point that the kinds of rights discussed in Article III of the Genocide Convention might be better dealt with in the Universal Declaration or in a special convention on the rights of members of minority groups. Per Federspiel, the Danish delegate, said that if "he had voted for the exclusion of provisions concerning acts of cultural genocide, it was not because he disputed the criminal nature of these acts but because he considered the question came within the sphere of human rights" (GAOR, 3rd Sess., 6th Comm., 198). The Dutch delegate said that "cultural genocide fell rather within the sphere of the protection of human rights or the rights of minorities" (202). The Swedish delegate thought it "desirable to establish the cultural protection of minorities on a more general international plane than had been the case with the League Treaties," which led him to suggest that there be a special convention on "the cultural protection of minorities" (197).

Having heard firsthand reports of how Hitler practiced cultural genocide before he built gas chambers, it was difficult for those who were opposed to Article III to simply vote against it. They could not deny that Hitler had practiced cultural genocide and that it had been a prelude to physical genocide. As objectors to Article III, they rightly felt the need to propose another way of dealing with the phenomenon of cultural genocide. They did that by making the just mentioned promissory notes. A minority rights article in the Universal Declaration was the perfect compromise between rejecting Article III in the convention and doing nothing at all. But when the time came to redeem these promises, Cold War issues and colonialism stood in the way of their redemption.

The upshot was that the Universal Declaration was adopted with a blind spot on the protection of members of minority religious, linguistic, or ethno-cultural groups. Although the Humphrey-Lauterpacht minority rights article had been thoroughly researched and prepared by the Subcommission on the Elimination of Discrimination and the Protection of Minorities, it ran into trouble in the second session of the Human Rights Commission that met in December 1947. Neither proposed article listed side by side in figure 3.2 made it into the final text of these historic documents. I begin with the trouble for the minority rights proposal in the working group on the declaration in the second session of the commission and end with its nonacceptance in the Third Committee.

Although there were different ethnic and linguistic groups in her country, Roosevelt told her colleagues that "in the United States there was no minority problem" (E/CN.4/SR.9/17). Other delegates suggested changes, but all of them approved of the minority rights article in concept. Cassin said that his country "had always been an immigration country . . . but would vote for the whole of Article 36, provided the word 'persons' was changed to 'citizens of the country', which suggestion was accepted" (19). To communist attempts to raise the issues of federalism and colonialism, Cassin responded, "There were certain countries where different peoples, Christians, Mohammedans and Jews, had lived side by side for centuries; as in North Africa, for instance, and where such a [territorial] text would be inapplicable. There were some non-self-governing or trust territories where, no doubt, a problem of self-government existed, but there was no minorities problem" (20). We see here how Cassin seeks to separate what in chapter 5 I call the territorial or "land factor" from issues of nonterritorial minority rights as proposed in the Humphrey-Lauterpacht article. Listening to these complications and being worried about having a declaration that was "not applicable to all states," Roosevelt proposed to delete "the whole of the [Humphrey-Lauterpacht] text" (EC.4/SR.9/19). We then read in the *travaux* of the Working Group of this second session that Roosevelt's proposal was voted down and that "the text of Article 36 was therefore retained" (19).

I interpret this rejection of Roosevelt's proposal as an implicit adoption of the Humphrey-Lauterpacht text before the commission. When

Roosevelt as chairperson called for a vote on the original Article 36 with the added change from "persons" to "citizens of the country" (as called for by Cassin), "one can feel," I wrote in my *Origins* account, "history slip through the fingers of one hesitant man" (Morsink 1999b, 272). The *travaux* tell us: "Professor Cassin (France) withdrew his amendment, since he considered that the text of this Article was not yet final and should therefore be held over" (E/CN.4/SR.9/21). But as I see it, his wanting to hold it over did not overrule the earlier rejection of the US proposal to delete the whole, which rejection meant, as the record shows, that it was "retained." In my reading of the record, Cassin's withdrawal means that the Humphrey-Lauterpacht article, as it had come down from the subcommission (without the change from "persons" to "citizens of the country"), was "retained" and therefore adopted by the Working Group of the commission's second session. A chairman from a delegation of a country more friendly to minority rights might have gone with this reading of the situation. Unfortunately, Eleanor Roosevelt was in the chair and ruled that Cassin's withdrawal meant the article was being "held over," as if he by himself could undo an official vote of the Working Group. The result was that the second session itself also "left it aside" (E/CN.4/SR.40/16). It was in this sorry state that the article was passed on to the third session of the Commission of Human Rights. Toward the end of its meetings, the third session received the first draft of the Genocide Convention, which at that point still included Article III.

The delegates to the third session of the Human Rights Commission therefore had grounds to think that minority rights were taken care of by the Genocide Convention. Some of them may not have felt any urgency about also including these rights in the UDHR. As a result, the Humphrey-Lauterpacht article was dismissed in this third session, after the US, the Belgian, and the Indian delegations all spoke up against the need to include this kind of article in the declaration. Hansa Mehta, the Indian delegate, said that "members of minority groups were protected as human beings by other articles of the Declaration," and the Belgian delegate added the warning that Hitler had used the presence of German minorities in other countries as a pretense to meddle (SR.73/6). The French, British, and Uruguayan delegations, all of which had initially supported the Humphrey-Lauterpacht article, now opposed its inclusion in the declaration (SR.73/10). As I said, these reversals of position might have been caused by the fact that at this point the Genocide Convention still contained an Article III banning cultural genocide. Article III was rejected a few months later by the Sixth Committee, while at the same time the rehabilitation of the UDHR minority rights article failed in the Third Committee.

The Third Committee failure must be ascribed to a combination of factors. Because Stalin and Tito had just had a falling-out, the communist delegations did not come up with a unified campaign for the adoption of any of the three rehabilitation proposals before the Third Committee, one from the USSR, one from Yugoslavia, and one from Lebanon. In my earlier account (Morsink 1999a), I showed that the votes for a minority rights article would have been there but had not been pulled out into the open; therefore, the article was defeated by a combination of mostly (North and South) American assimilationist and European colonialist forces. While no delegation sought to retrieve the set-aside Humphrey-Lauterpacht article, three delegations—the USSR (E/800), Denmark (A/C.3/307/Rev.1/Add.2), and Yugoslavia (A/C.3/307/Rev.2/Add.2)—sought to rehabilitate the idea of group-differentiated rights in various ways. But all of them were eclipsed by a Haitian motion to refer the entire question of minority rights back to the subcommission from whence it had come (A/C.3/373).

Proponents of the Haitian motion did not want any of these rehabilitation attempts to be voted on because they thought that "a thorough study of the problem of minorities" should be conducted before the General Assembly could commit itself on such a "complex and delicate" question. The motion made a crucial point that to this day is still a focus of United Nations discussions: it is "difficult to adopt a uniform solution in this complex and delicate question, which has special aspects in each State in which it arises, without endangering the national unity of the Member States and without creating a new source or cause of aggravation of the discriminations outlawed both by the United Nations Charter and by the present Declaration." The motion went on to point to "the universal character of the declaration of human rights" and asked the General Assembly "not to deal in a specific provision with the question of minorities in the text of the present declaration." The "specific" provision here refers to the

Humphrey-Lauterpacht article that was set aside. The motion ended with a request that a "thorough study" be made of the problem that minority rights presented to UN member states. The Haitian motion was voted on in parts, with the most relevant part ("Decides not to deal in a specific provision with the question of minorities in the text of the present declaration") being accepted by a vote of twenty-two for, nine against, and ten abstentions (Morsink 1999b, 279). This was a last-minute proposal passed over strong communist objections. Evidently, a uniform solution to minority rights issues was not to be found in 1948, as it also was not in later UN decisions, except with great difficulties. Those decisions are the subject of chapter 5 of this book.

Parting of the Ways

I remind my reader that in chapter 1 I complicated our initial diagram by giving it two layers: a top criminal one and a bottom civil one. The two proposals discussed in this section that were rejected for inclusion in their respective texts have since had a very uneven legal development. The idea of minority rights found new life when it was incorporated as Article 27 of the ICCPR on the lower track. Legally (though not sociologically), the idea of cultural genocide has over time been subsumed into the idea of physical and biological genocide, as spelled out in the Genocide Convention, which is one of the leading texts on the upper track of our by now familiar bi-furcated chart.

E*lisa Novic has investigated the merger of cultural genocide into* physical genocide in her 2017 book The Concept of Cultural Genocide: An International Law Perspective. She shows how, "from the perspective of international law, the terms of the debate—culture, genocide, and group—have radically evolved since its emergence in the 1940s such that both the questions and answers must now be rethought in a contemporary context" (Novic 2017, 10). She traces the newer concept of cultural genocide in both its narrow sense of being a means to physical genocide and in its broader sense as a crime in its own right. She wants to "rethink the terms of the debate. Rather than just acknowledging that 'cultural genocide' is not currently addressed as such by international law, it [her book] proposes to reverse the [dominant] approach in order to determine whether contemporary international law possesses the tools to address the so-called concept of 'cultural genocide'" (12). She discusses this dominant merger approach in her third chapter and the hoped-for new tools in the other chapters of her book.

The new tools in Novic's book consist primarily of the human rights approach to cultural genocide (Novic 2017, sec. 4.1), the cultural heritage approach (sec. 4.2), the development of the concept of "cultural persecution" (chap. 5), "State Responsibility for Cultural Crimes" (chap. 6), and "Reparation for Intended Cultural Harm" (chap. 7). Overall it seems that the idea of cultural genocide, so obvious in the Hitler campaigns, has mostly fallen below the radar of international criminal law, making an appearance only as an ac*cesso*ry or means to the crime of biological genocide and then only in a rare case like the 2007 IC*TY Kr*stić case related to crimes perpetrated at Srebrenica. Novic cites Ana Vrdoljak's view that the Krstić progressive interpretation of cultural genocide as a technique of genocide has a built-in "inconsistency" in that "a group must have a distinct identity to attract the protection afforded by the [Genocide] Convention but acts which target their cultural heritage (and wh*ich rend*er the group distinctive) are not prohibited per se. Confining such acts to establishing the mens rea of genocide alone, serves only to highlight the inconsistency rather than remedy it" (94). The difficulty of proving the mens rea, or intentionality, of any crime creates a gap between a state's supposed intention to destroy the whole or part of a group and its policy of actually doing so, and this gap dominates the international criminal law of biological genocide. Once the mens rea is pushed aside, it becomes quite easy for the crime of genocide to be categorized as a crime against humanity, for which the emphasis is not on intentionality but on numbers and systemic procedures. Most scholars seem to think this is what has happened to the crimes of biological and cultural genocide. Novic's exploration of the cultural genocide trajectory is therefore much needed.

At first it would seem that of the new tools she explores, the minority rights approach to cultural genocide is the most promising. While Novic's discussion picks up where the overlapping debates discussed in this chapter leave off, it does not bring these two ideas back together again. Because the Humphrey-Lauterpacht article was incorporated into international human rights law with the adoption of Article 27 of the International Covenant on Civil and Political Rights, the idea of minority rights has fared better than the idea of cultural genocide. I show in chapter 5 that this adoption of ICCPR Article 27 did not reach back and embrace the 1948 idea of cultural genocide, letting that idea fall below the radar of international human rights law. While some cases decided by the ICTY provide glimmers of hope, the parting of the two ideas more or less continued throughout the postwar criminal tribunals. My own objection to the human rights approach is focused on the individualist ontology of human rights that is not hospitable to the collectivist dimension of cultural rights.

The best tool, therefore, would seem to be the cultural heritage approach to the protection of cultures. I argue in chapter 5 that for Holocaust-related reasons only flesh and blood human beings can have human rights. Since a group or a culture is a different form of collectivist entity and is not an individual human person, it does not fit the paradigm of the Universal Declaration, which gives human rights to members of the human race only and not to the race itself or to any segment thereof. International cultural heritage law, at least in its tangible versions, accommodates this philosophical difference. Novic cites courts that have ruled on the collective possession of rights for items of material culture, such as mosques, temples, churches, tombs, statues, and the like, that can, depending on the case, be seen as the heritage of mankind or more frequently of a (religious) segment thereof. The destruction of the tombs and mosques in Timbuktu, Mali, which I mentioned earlier, is a case in point. I conclude that since cultural genocide of the material or tangible kind requires a collectivist philosophical underpinning rather than the UDHR individualist one, it is best pursued on the different track of cultural heritage law. As to the intangible dimension of cultural heritage, that too has a collectivist dimension, but unlike the tangible one, it can be more readily broken up into the interest and behavior of the members who produce and keep alive that dimension (like a language). If that is so, it can be seen to fit the UDHR individualist paradigm of what a human right is. I explain this way of looking at the intangible dimension of cultural heritage more fully in chapter 5. David Nersessian has also argued that the human rights approach to cultural genocide is not a good one. He therefore calls for a "new treaty dealing specifically with cultural genocide" because it is "a unique wrong" that human rights jurisprudence is *not flexible enough to handle (Nersessian 2005).*

Conclusion: Has Ethics Failed Us?

In his 2015 book, The Failures of Ethics: Confronting the Holocaust, Genocide and Other Mass Atrocities, John K. Roth defines ethics as the "careful deliberation about the difference between right and wrong, encouragement not to be indifferent toward that difference, cultivation of virtuous character, and action that defends what is right and resists what is wrong" (Roth 2015, 16). The idea of "careful deliberation" fits a good many theories of ethics, but I agree with Roth when he cites historian Raul Hilberg's observation that we have a knowledge of good and evil "in our bones" as it were (21) and that moral deliberations start after those basic intuitive judgments are felt or publicly made. The failure of ethics Roth has in mind occurs because millions of people "stand by," "watch in silence," or "try not to see at all" (12–16) when Holocaust-type horrors are repeated in other genocides and mass atrocities, as we know has happened on a regular basis. Working with a three-term taxonomy of perpetrator, victim, and bystander, Roth derives the failure of ethics after World War II from the fact that almost all the time almost all the people fulfill the role of being bystanders to these repeated horrors. We play this role even though "in our bones" we have a knowledge of good and evil. This can mean only that, as Roth himself puts it, "ethical insight, conviction, and resistance are rather easily overridden" (23). It seems true that the moral insights we have are often easily overridden, but the very adoption of the UDHR three years after the war and the tremendous growth of both the human rights system and movement belie his claim that after the war we have seen nothing but failures of ethics (18).

I also do not agree with Roth that the suppression of those deeper moral intuitions by a sick racist ideology on the part of Heinrich Himmler and his cronies—which led them to believe that there was nothing wrong with "the wanton killing of European Jews"—makes even a weak case for moral relativism (Roth 2015, 22). What the Nazi and all later massacres—as well as our own continued standing by—show is not that ethics has failed us but that our deeper moral intuitions can be and often are blocked from operating properly. This has been true for the entire recorded history of the world. Since the dawn of civilization, people have more often than not suppressed their moral instincts. I also do not see how the supposition that "the heritage of many years, which implies a social or evolutionary formation of ethics," raises doubts about those Hilberg-type intuitions (21). The evolutionary backdrop of ethics does not weaken my view that Himmler and his cronies were morally sick people. Hilberg's view "that social history or evolution produces a deep-seated consciousness and, in that sense, timeless qualities" (21–22) that over time begin to appear universal and absolute seems to me correct, even in the shadow of the Holocaust.

Roth speculates that the Holocaust "may have deepened conviction that a fundamental, nonrelativistic difference exists between right and wrong. Its destruction may have renewed awareness of the importance of ethical standards and conduct" (Roth 2015, 22). I have held that view ever since I started investigating the origins of the Universal Declaration in the 1980s. But then Roth adds a puzzling qualifying sentence, only the last clause of which I think has some merit: "Nevertheless, the Holocaust continues to cast disturbing shadows over basic beliefs concerning right and wrong, human rights, and the hope that human beings will learn from the past" (22). The shadow I see with some regularity is the last one: doubt that human beings will learn from the past. In my own reading and more than twenty years of teaching human rights courses, I did not encounter the Holocaust casting "disturbing shadows" over either the discipline of ethics itself or over belief in human rights. That belief in fact was strengthened by our study of the Holocaust. All the shadows I saw fell over human beings and their failures to do what they know is morally right. We are one and all plagued by what the Greeks called moral weakness. The Holocaust itself and the continued occurrence of other genocides and mass atrocities have raised doubts about our ability as human beings "to learn from the past" (22). We agree that this makes ethics "an expression [and] a reflection" of human existence. These continued atrocities give us what has come to be called "the human rights project." But that does not mean that that project is a "human projection" (24). A discovery of facts is not by that token a projection of anything in the mind of the discoverer. When it comes to the very basics, this is probably even more true in the moral sciences than in the physical ones. The values laid bare in the Holocaust are not projections of the human imagination either of individual UDHR drafters or of them as a collectivity. As I argued elsewhere, the drafters read most of the rights in the declaration off from the moral facts on their drafting room floor (Morsink 2009, chap. 3, sec. 3).

The relationship between the Holocaust and the discipline of ethics is not that the former weakened the latter but that it strengthened it and gave it a new direction. I think of ethics as the search for a coherent set of moral principles for people of a certain community to live by. Throughout history, ethicists—who search for those rules and seek to organize them into a coherent set—have aimed their work at communities of different sizes, which then later led to disagreements between these entities. Greek theories of morality were mostly designed to fit Greek city-states. In the Hellenistic world and in the Middle Ages, the ethicist's community became the Roman or Byzantine Empires. In the modern world, it was the nation-states that made up the Westphalian system. And today, in the twenty-first century, it is the global village or the one world community, which includes all humanity with the global problems it faces. The question behind this book—that informs my defense of the connection between the Holocaust and the Universal Declaration—is whether the rules proposed for this global village can or will have influence over the Westphalian system or not. My view is that the 1948 Universal Declaration gave us a good set of rules for the global village to live by and that its birth out of the Holocaust gives these rights or rules a depth, *seriousness, and integrity they would not otherwise have had. To me, ethics after World War II has not* been a failure; it is a human rights success story.

Roth thinks ethics after World War II has failed because it did not adequately confront the Holocaust, genocide, and other mass atrocities—like Rwanda, Darfur, the Democratic Republic of Congo, the Central African Republic, Kosovo, Bosnia-Herzegovina, Cambodia, and others (Roth 2015, 14, 20). This to me conflates the two parts of the bifurcated system that came out of the Holocaust cauldron. It unnecessarily criminalizes both layers of that system, including the lower level of human rights law. It is understandable why anyone would fall silent and turn their gaze the other way when asked to see or listen to what happened in the Nazi camps or in Rwanda courtyards. In his moving last two chapters ("The Politics of Testimony" and "Death and Meaning"), Roth tells us how Charlotte Delbo, an Auschwitz survivor and memoirist, "and her worn-out prisoner companions returned to camp after a long and punishing day of slave labor. This time, her work detail carried the bodies of Berthe and Anne-Marie, two comrades beaten to death—helplessly, hopelessly—when they collapsed from exhaustion that afternoon" (193). These bodies had to be carried along because the Germans wanted all the prisoners (alive or dead) to be accounted for at that night's "roll call." Roth then quotes Delbo's memoir: "A corpse. The left eye devoured by a rat. The other open with its fringe lashes. Try to look. Just see" (194).

Roth also tells us how Elie Wiesel, another survivor and memoirist whom he cites, "was forever changed as he saw children, alive or dead, thrown into flaming pits" upon his arrival at Birkenau, the main killing center in the vast Auschwitz complex. "Never shall I forget," Wiesel repeats seven times. "Never shall I forget those things, even were I condemned to live as long as God Himself" (Roth 2015, 165). Wiesel also can never forget the face of a boy whom the Germans suspected of sabotage. "Along with two adults, the tortured boy was executed while the assembled prisoners had to watch and then march past the victims. The two adults died quickly, but the boy lingered, 'struggling between life and death, dying in slow agony under our eyes. And we had to look him full in the face'" (202). For some twenty years, I taught an international human rights course that I always began by watching the BBC documentary *Liberating the Camps*. It shows hundreds of corpses being dumped into death pits by German guards. We tried to look but often were forced to avert our gaze. The class was totally silent except for sniffles and some tears. We always filed out silently. After that, we studied the human rights system as it developed since the end of World War II, using primarily human rights texts as filters between our agony and the urge to act.

It is difficult to come to grips with the Holocaust and other mass atrocities directly and full-fronted, which is why it helps to use human rights texts as filters. Roth is good at showing how difficult it is to extract meaning from absolute evil, which is why crying or silence is our natural reaction. Even the testimony of survivors is one step removed from the horrors. It needs to be interpreted and placed in context, as does all oral and written testimony. Survivors' testimonies can never reach the depth of the horrors they and the dead experienced. Silence, Roth points out, "involves a range and complexity that disaggregate the untellable into the unsaid and the incommunicable, the unbearable and the irretrievable" (Roth 2015, 177). "It is that way because testimony both reveals and hides the worst" (177). Just as individual memoirs are by definition incomplete, so individual philosophies and theologies are by definition idiosyncratic and fail to confront the full depth and scope of the Holocaust. So, I argued in the first two chapters, have the new historians failed us. And so have, I argue in chapters 4 and 5, important international legal scholars.

In a section titled "Good Days and Bad Days," Roth writes, "After World War II and the Holocaust, good days of ethics occurred on December 9 and 10, 1948, when the General Assembly of the United Nations adopted the Convention on the Prevention and Punishment of Genocide and the Universal Declaration of Human Rights" (Roth 2015, 18–19). At this point our reading of postwar history diverges. Writes Roth, "Two good days for ethics in December 1948 called for more of the same, but as far as the Holocaust is concerned, such days—during and after that disaster—have been too few and far between. . . . Notwithstanding the UN Declaration the Holocaust had ruptured the notion of universal human rights as the Third Reich's genocidal policies trapped Jews and other victim groups in one 'choiceless choice' and lethal dilemma after another" (19). I have argued in this chapter that whatever notion of human rights was "ruptured" (Roth's term) by the Holocaust was a very weak one because neither of the locomotive texts of the two layers of our chart had been constructed. Focusing, as Roth does, on the top layer of our chart is not sufficient for the telling of the human rights story. We need to study the whole cauldron (see figure 1.1 on page 25) and what came out of it.

Ethics before and after the Holocaust is *not* the same. It is not a question of the modern human rights story being ruptured. It is one of its being born for the first time and inaugurated. It is the collective writing of the two texts, the Genocide Convention and the Universal Declaration, and their joint indebtedness to the events of the Holocaust, which infused both texts with an objectivity that is hard to circumvent and that prevents the story of ethics after World War II from being a failure.

Roth focuses most of his attention on the criminal top layer of this chart. He considers ethics a failure when seen in light of this top layer. That is not my area of expertise, but as I noted in chapter 1's plea that we not criminalize "the system," even there I believe that ethics has not failed us, though Hopgood and others join Roth in thinking it has. The guilty verdicts and jail sentences handed down by the Criminal Tribunals of the former Yugoslavia, Rwanda, and other regions are to me a testimony to the victory of good over evil in our world. The plethora of truth and reconciliation commissions operating on different continents also testifies to good prevailing over evil. Those victories on the upper level of the bifurcated chart are not the story I relate in this book. Instead I tell the story of the lower-level moral/legal chart (Holocaust → 1948 UDHR text → ICCPR → ICESCR → CEDAW → CRC → Etc.) by reinvigorating the international human rights system and its concomitant movement with moral vigor drawn from the same cauldron that produced the other track.

In this chapter I reconnected the Universal Declaration—which is the moral heartbeat of both the system and the movement—to the events of the Holocaust. That connection is needed to inject a new moral seriousness into both the international human rights system and its movement. The two chapters of part 2 of this book defend the Universal Declaration as a supranational code of ethics that informs international morality and legality as a consistent set of moral rules that lies outside but nevertheless is shaped by the legal framework created and maintained by the Westphalian system of nation-states that dots our planet. Part 1 of this book has laid the groundwork for elucidating that later philosophical impact by spelling out chapter and verse the connection between the Holocaust and the declaration. We have been mixing the cement used to build the later system.

Part II

THE PHILOSOPHIC MOMENT

4

THE MORAL ENGINE OF THE SYSTEM

In this chapter I explore the third item in the flowchart that I have been using in this book. I argue that the Universal Declaration is the moral engine of the legal system of international human rights. The declaration both inspired the creators of that legal system and also functioned for them somewhat as a moral mirror to look at in their international legal endeavors. Figure 4.1 below shows an emphasis on the system discussed in this chapter.

The argument of part 2 of this book is that the 1940s historic moment of human rights discussed in part 1 is at the same time a philosophic moment for human rights. I trace the philosophic effects of the historic moment to the background presence of the Holocaust, both positive (giving the system a moral foundation, discussed in chapter 4) and negative (keeping the list of genuine human rights shorter than is usually thought, discussed in chapter 5). These two moments—historic and philosophic—implicate each other and are inextricable. Precipitated by the Holocaust, the historic moment for human rights was the creation of a moral text that stipulated what human rights are and how diverse they are. Much in the way court decisions often stipulate what a disputed right is or involves, so with the adoption of the Universal Declaration, the international community by way of the Third UN General Assembly in 1948 stipulated what it is to be a human right in the modern world. And since the Holocaust was a key

Holocaust

⇊

idea → [1948] UDHR text → system [1948–68] ↔ [1970s] movement

FIGURE 4.1: Amplified flowchart

factor in the drafting of this historic text, it also is a key factor in the attendant philosophical meaning of that moment and document.

Unfortunately—like the historians mentioned in the preceding chapters—legal philosophers have mostly ignored the Holocaust as a key factor in their definitions of what a human right is. And like the historians, legal philosophers also have not taken the Universal Declaration as seriously as they should. That in turn has skewed their definitions of what a modern human right is. The Holocaust has found even less of a place in philosophical reflections on the meaning of the phrase "human rights" in the modern world than it has in historical reflections. In my 2009 book, *Inherent Human Rights: Philosophical Roots of the Universal Declaration*, I connected the philosophy of the declaration, insofar as it can be said to have one, to the events of the Holocaust. I argued that the evil Nazi practices made the UDHR drafters tap into "the conscience of mankind" and realize that human beings, as such, have certain moral rights that no state, whether or not a member of the newly founded United Nations, may violate. This conscience of mankind played a role in the Nuremberg trials and in other famous international law cases before, during, and after the war. It shaped the test of "manifest illegality," according to which some deeds are so manifestly immoral that anyone would know that an order mandating they be done would have to be illegal. For example, Article 7 of the Nuremberg Statute disallows defendants the defense of "superior orders." That denial supposes that in some situations superior orders must be disobeyed, which can be done only if the defendant obeys his own conscience instead of "superior orders." Courts generally argue that any "normal" defendant in similar circumstances would need to disobey orders like those in the case at hand. The UDHR drafters were "outraged" by what they heard and read the Nazis had done to ordinary citizens and prisoners of war. The sovereignty of no state gives it license to violate the list of pre-state moral rights the UDHR drafters thought "all human beings are born with" (Art. 1).

Human beings have the moral rights listed in the declaration by birth and not because of any domestic or even international procedures. If that were not so, soldiers who had shoddy training would not know that it is wrong to kill children, prisoners of war, or hostages, and they might not know that medical experimentation on captured enemies or the bombing of hospitals or the working of prisoners to death in factories next to camps are all obviously immoral deeds. Nor would they know that brainwashing children with a racist ideology is obviously wrong. These immoral acts should never have been done, whether or not they were ordered. Knowing that these kinds of deeds (and the Nazis did many) are wrong, the UDHR drafters drew up their list of moral birthrights. No international processes "created" these human rights. The drafters "recognized" and then "proclaimed" them as "inherent" in "all members of the human family." Their language harks back to Enlightenment ways of thinking about rights and was at this historic moment crucially reinforced by common knowledge of various evil Nazi practices. Their knowledge of how the Nazis had conducted their aggressive wars gave the UN founders and the UDHR drafters a common platform of revulsion from which to condemn these practices in World War II and for all time to come. They called these rights "universal" both because all people have them and because they are valid for all times, cultures, and political, economic, religious, ethnic, and language systems.

The thesis of this chapter is that the inherence in human beings of these moral rights as they are spelled out in the UDHR is the engine of the international legal human rights system. The moral heart of that system is not the legal procedures and practices that have evolved since the end of World War II, crucial and important as these procedures are. Those practices and procedures are the veins of the system, but what pushes the blood through those veins is the Universal Declaration adopted in 1948. In his 2013 book, *The Heart of Human Rights*, Allen Buchanan has taken a view opposite of the one I just spelled out. He argues that the heart of international legal human rights is not their morality but their international legality. At the center of our disagreement lies the question of what reading we are to give to the 1948 Universal Declaration of Human Rights. I look at the declaration as at first separate from the rest of the system—of which, I agree, it has over time become a unique and special part that inspires expansions of the system—Buchanan does not quite see it that way. He does not give nearly enough credence to the separate influence the UDHR had and still has over the rest of the system. For him the declaration is not a unique part of the system as the heart is when it pumps the blood through our veins. As I see it, just as the UN Charter is unique, so is the declaration because it is the authoritative explication of the seven human rights references in the UN Charter. In that way it shares with the charter a foundational influence on the system unlike any other legal human rights text.

From 1946 to 1966, John Humphrey was the first director of the UN Secretariat's Division of Human Rights. In that capacity he more than anyone had his finger on the pulse of human rights development in the first twenty years of the UN, all the way from the seven charter references through the 1966 adoption of the two international covenants, the ICCPR and the ICESCR. In a 1967 essay, "The Charter of the United Nations and the Declaration," Humphrey traced that entire UN human rights story. He placed the UDHR at the very center of it, noting, "No other act of the United Nations has had anything like the same impact on the thinking of our time, the best aspirations of which it incorporates and proclaims" (Humphrey 1967, 51). By the time Humphrey wrote this, the main pillars of the international legal human rights system—the ICCPR and the ICESCR—had just been erected, each mirroring one half of the declaration.

Buchanan's merger of the UDHR text into or with the rest of the system conflicts with how the UDHR drafters themselves saw their task. It is fitting that upon the suggestion of the French delegation, the title of the document was changed from "International Declaration" to "Universal Declaration of Human Rights," thereby elevating it above international legal arrangements (GAOR, 3rd Sess., 3rd Comm., 775). The day before the declaration was adopted, the French delegate, René Cassin, presciently noted that "the chief novelty of the declaration was its universality. Because it was universal, the universal declaration could have a broader scope than national declarations and draw up the regulations that were essential to good international order. It was for states to conclude conventions between themselves for the preservation of that order; otherwise it would establish itself over their heads, for men could not be indefinitely deprived of the necessary protection of their rights" (A/PV 180/866). The size of the elephant I introduce in the next section shows that states did just that; they have concluded numerous conventions that implement the declaration legally. And in that way the universality of the declaration lords itself over the fragmentary system of international human rights law because each convention implements only a part of the declaration. On the tenth anniversary of the declaration, Cassin wrote that the UDHR formed "the basis for a list of minimal common right[s] and offered a common moral code to each member of the human community" (Morsink 2009, 57). No other legal international human rights text is authoritative in this special universalistic way. Whether legal theorists and philosophers like it or not, the historic moment of human rights in the 1940s has had philosophical implications they cannot ignore and still be true to the modern notion of what a human right is. I begin with Buchanan's disparagement of what he calls the "preambular rhetoric" that one finds in a great number of international legal human rights texts. To me these preambular references to the declaration are more than mere "rhetoric," they are indicative of an authoritative moral pulse that beats throughout the system that is the third bin of our chart: idea → Holocaust + UDHR text → system ↔ movement.

The Moral Mouse and the Legal Elephant

The Universal Declaration of Human Rights is a small booklet obtainable from the United Nations and other outlets for two dollars or less. It can be printed out on just one page from the websites of numerous human rights organizations. To make the point that it is nevertheless a moral giant, I have dubbed it the mouse and called the system of human rights law, to which it helped give birth, the elephant. My argument is that this little mouse of a text gave birth to or inspired this huge international elephant. The difference between Buchanan and me is that he has the elephant swallow up the mouse, while I let the mouse keep its own separate life. That requires that I explain the unusual birth of the elephant out of this mouse of a text, which is the objective of this chapter and involves the philosophical import of the Holocaust. As a moral text, the Universal Declaration was adopted in 1948, while the international legal system to which it gave birth got its real start with the adoption of the two famous international covenants (the ICCPR and the ICESCR) in 1966. Apparently, there was a long gestation period. This gap itself suggests some kind of separation of the mouse from the elephant to which it, in my view, gave birth.

The international legal human rights system has three main parts and a great many secondary parts. The three main parts are first the 1948 Universal Declaration and then the two international covenants adopted in 1966 that came into force in 1976: the International Covenant on Civil and Political Rights and the International Covenant on Economic, Social, and Cultural Rights. These three documents are thought to head the rest of the system. Initially, the visionaries of the 1940s who created the United Nations and soon thereafter adopted the declaration also planned to adopt a legally binding convention that would spell out in more detail what the obligations of states would be. Unfortunately, they ran out of time, and toward the very end of the proceedings, the Cold War started to intervene. The United States and the Soviet Union no longer saw eye to eye legally, which led to the Third General Assembly's adoption of just the Universal Declaration as a moral text. However, instead of abandoning hopes for a legally binding convention, Eleanor Roosevelt stayed on and the Commission of Human Rights continued to work on that legal convention text. Because the Cold War was intensifying, the one planned convention was later split into two: one on civil and political rights and one on social, economic, and cultural rights. While this split is important, it should not obscure the fact that the two covenants did get adopted at the same time in 1966 and that they did both come into force in 1977. Today each of these legally binding conventions has been ratified by more than 160 of the world's nations.

What sets these two covenants or conventions apart from the rest of the system is that between them they translate all the moral rights in the declaration (except Article 17 on property) into international legalese. While the declaration has only one article, the twenty-ninth, devoted to duties, these two conventions are mostly about the duties the ratifying states have to legally implement the UDHR moral rights in the territories under their jurisdiction. The ICCPR repeats all the UDHR's civil and political rights in legal terms, while the ICESCR does the same thing (except for the right to own property) for all the UDHR's social, economic, and cultural rights. Before they commit themselves to change and adapt their domestic legal system to these international standards, states want to know in some detail what they are obligated to do or not do. These conventions therefore repeat in far more detail what the Universal Declaration declares only in principle and more abstractly. Adding this detail was not an easy process and took almost twenty years.

Many of the books in the third bin of our flowchart (idea → Holocaust + UDHR text → *system* ↔ movement) are about the drafting, meanings, inner workings, and effectiveness of these and other international texts. Over time the committees that oversee these conventions have come to focus on how the international community can know that states are living up to the promises they make when they ratify these conventions. In addition to these two main conventions, the size of the elephant discussed later shows that there are a great number of smaller ones that take just one or several UDHR articles and turn those into more specialized legal treaties, going into great detail to satisfy the legitimate curiosity of states as to what is involved in, for instance, an international legal obligation to treat handicapped citizens and aliens without discrimination. These covenants and treaties contain the legal embodiments of the moral rights of the Universal Declaration, much the way the world of flux for Plato contained the physical embodiments of his Forms or Exemplars. These legal embodiments are not perfect and can be altered and, as we know from the committees that oversee states' records of adherence, often still need to be interpreted as to what they mean in local circumstances.

My reader will find the texts of most of these international legal documents in Ian Brownlie and Guy S. Goodwin-Gill's *Basic Documents on Human Rights* (2006). The chronological list starts with the Charter of the United Nations and thirty-four procedural resolutions and declarations (of which the Universal Declaration of Human Rights is the third) before it comes to the first legal convention, the Convention on the Prevention and Punishment of the Crime of Genocide of 1948. Brownlie and Goodwin-Gill end their list at 125, the Additional Protocol for the European Convention on Human Rights and Biomedicine, Concerning Biomedical Research of January 25, 2005. In between these two endpoints of the 1945 UN Charter (which is a legal convention) and the Biomedical Research Protocol of 2005, we find listed in chronological order an enormous variety of eighty-nine legal international treaties with their dates of adoption, their dates of entry into force, and the number of nations that had ratified them by 2006, as well as thirty-five declarations (like the UDHR) and other procedural resolutions that were adopted by a vote and do not need signatures of legal ratification. We have tabulated the references made to the UN Charter and to the Universal Declaration for both types of texts in Brownlie and Goodwin-Gill's list, nonlegal and legal. Of the nonlegal texts, six make a preambular reference to just the declaration, while sixteen make a preambular reference to both it and the UN Charter. For the legally binding texts in this list that start at 36 and end at 125, we found that some twenty make a preambular reference to just the UN Charter, some thirty make a preambular reference to the declaration but not to the charter, and sixteen make a preambular reference to both texts. In terms of its influence on the human rights system, the Universal Declaration outranks even the United Nations Charter. That makes sense because the declaration was conceived as an expression of the seven charter references to "human rights and fundamental freedoms for all."

These numbers clearly show that the Universal Declaration is used as a moral authority and inspiration (often together with the UN Charter) for the international system of legal human rights. The very fact that the UDHR is mentioned more frequently than the UN Charter tells us a great deal about the moral suasion the declaration has had on international civil servants, lawyers, and diplomats. They have used the declaration as a moral mirror for the international legal work they do, which is why they credit that text so frequently. The argument of this chapter is that without its connection to the Holocaust, the declaration would have lost much of its suasion and might not have been the inspirational force for the international legal system that it has been. If we seek a moral justification for the international legal human rights system, we should stop and look at these preambular acknowledgments. Those who created this international legal human rights system clearly were inspired by the Universal Declaration and used it to guide their international legal enactments. The charter itself contains only seven general references to "human rights and fundamental freedoms for all," sometimes adding "without distinction as to race, sex, language, or religion," as in Article 1. The declaration contains thirty articles that in detail spell out what these charter generalities mean. Because it contains only this kind of general human rights language, the UN Charter could not have done what it has without the help of the details spelled out in the Universal Declaration. The preambular statements scattered throughout the international legal human rights system are therefore highly significant. They are not just "rhetoric" on the part of those who wrote up and then brought these hundred (and still counting) treaties into force; they point to the moral source of their legal activities and hence of the ensuing system. In figure 4.2 I dramatize the difference between the moral rights in the mouse and the international legal system to which the mouse gave birth in the years 1948 through 2006.

A typical preambular reference to the declaration is found in the Convention Against Torture and Other Cruel, Inhuman, or Degrading Treatment or Punishment, which came into legal force on June 26, 1987, some forty years after the declaration was adopted (Brownlie and Goodwin-Gill 2006, doc. 51). The preamble of this torture convention makes three references to the UN Charter's obligations regarding human rights and then states, "Having regard to Article 5 of the Universal Declaration of Human Rights and Article 7 of the International Covenant on Civil and Political Rights"—both of which provide that no one shall be subjected to torture or to cruel, inhuman, or degrading treatment or punishment—"the States Parties agree to this Convention." Many such preambular statements refer to more than one moral or legal source of authority and inspiration. Like Lego blocks the human rights system builds on itself with the later treaties being inspired by the UN Charter, the Universal Declaration, and other legal texts that preceded the one being drawn up. The fact that some twenty of these preambular statements of international legal texts do not refer to the UN Charter but *do* refer to the declaration together with other relevant later texts is very telling. The declaration often is the first one mentioned, not just because it precedes all the others in time but also because it clearly is thought

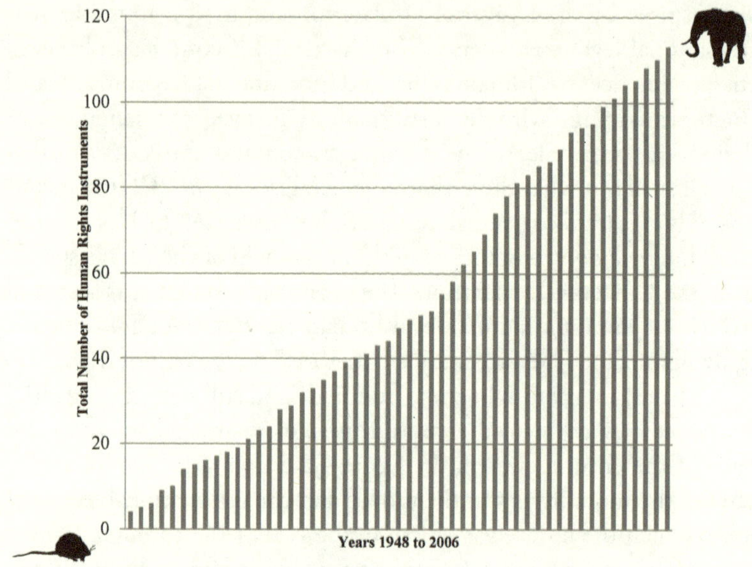

Figure 4.2: Mouse (Universal Declaration) at work creating the elephant (international legal system)

of as morally and often legally authoritative, being mentioned more often than even the UN Charter itself. The Convention against Discrimination in Education came into force in May 1962 and has been ratified by over a hundred states. The very first line of its preamble reads, "Recalling that the Universal Declaration of Human Rights asserts the principle of nondiscrimination and proclaims that every person has the right to education." Understandably, it also refers to UNESCO principles, but the UDHR is the engine that pulls even huge organizations like this one along in its moral wake. Another preambular reference to just the declaration, and no other text, is the 1990 Second Optional Protocol to the International Covenant on Civil and Political Rights, aiming at the abolition of the death penalty. And so on for numerous international conventions open to all UN member states.

Interestingly, regional legal texts, for example, from Europe or the Americas, that are not open to nations from other continents generally do not trace their pedigree to the United Nations Charter. But they do look to the UDHR for moral inspiration to help ground their own regional systems. The 1948 Bogota Declaration was adopted a few months before the UDHR and became the moral foundation of the Latin American legal human rights system, one of the key elements of which is the 1969 American Convention on Human Rights. That convention goes out of its way to twice reference the UDHR: first in conjunction with its own principal texts and then separately in a reference to President Roosevelt's Four Freedoms, as enumerated in the second recital of the UDHR's preamble. The Inter-American Conventions on Forced Disappearance of Persons of 1994 and on the Prevention, Punishment, and Eradication of Violence against Women of 1994 also single out the Universal Declaration as a moral inspiration without linking it to the UN Charter.

The preambular references to the Universal Declaration in the two main international covenants (the ICCPR and the ICESCR) are the most important because they finish the vision of the 1940s drafters who had wanted to but could not adopt a convention at that time. These two treaties list for the international legal domain what the 1940s visionaries put into the moral domain. They are the direct descendants of aborted convention attempts in the late 1940s. In the next chapter's case study, I discuss an example of how the drafters of these covenants held up the UDHR as their standard for what to include and what to leave out. Figure 4.2 shows that there are many more such texts that are also closely connected to one or several UDHR articles and that draw out with legal details the moral content of those UDHR articles. The preambles of these treaties often show that their drafters saw the declaration as their one or main source of inspiration. In my drawing I have included only the most important and most obvious of the 125 that Brownlie and Goodwin-Gill listed in 2006 as part of the system of international human rights law. I have already noted that for the legally binding texts, some twenty make a preambular reference to just the UN Charter, while some thirty make a preambular reference to the declaration but not to the charter and sixteen make a preambular reference to both these texts. It would therefore seem that in terms of its influence on the international legal human rights system, the Universal Declaration is as influential as the United Nations Charter.

The Flow between Moral Rights and Legal Duties

I characterize the difference between the Universal Declaration and the rest of the international legal human rights system as being a matter of the difference in the flow between rights and duties. All these texts speak of both rights and duties, as well they should, because rights and duties are correlated with each other in the way high and low and beautiful and ugly are correlated. You can't have the one without the other. The important question is not whether both exist and need to work in tandem but what emphasis to put on each half of the pair and what the flow between them is. In the case of the Universal Declaration, the emphasis obviously falls on rights and the flow goes from them to only one article on duties, the twenty-ninth, just before the end. The drafters of the declaration had no compunction or discomfort about first enunciating a list of rights and only after that appending an article on the correlated duties. They thought of the human rights they listed as inherent in human beings on account of their humanity, a view I defend in *Inherent Human Rights: Philosophical Roots of the Universal Declaration* (Morsink 2009). Since all human beings share this membership in the human family, "everyone" has the rights mentioned in most of the first twenty-eight articles of the declaration. At the end the UDHR drafters point out that with these rights come certain duties as well, the flow clearly going from rights to duties.

Contrastingly, in the international legal human rights system, the emphasis falls not on rights but on duties, and the flow seems to go in the other direction, from the numerous articles that spell out the duties that ratifying states have to a few correlated rights of individuals that are briefly stated at the start, often hurriedly in the preamble, as if to get on with the real business of the treaty, which is to tell states what their duties regarding these rights are.

When discussing the flow between rights and duties, most legal and even moral theorists take as their point of departure Wesley Hohfeld's (1917) analysis of legal rights as (among other options) claim rights. They consider a human right a moral or a legal claim right. Any kind of claim right has these three elements: (1) a subject that can make the claim; (2) a thing, substance, action/inaction, or service being laid claim to; and (3) the person who must fulfill that claim and deliver what is demanded. Alan Gewirth took the following definition away from his study of Hohfeld: "A claim-right of one person entails a correlative duty of some other person or persons to act or to refrain from acting in ways required for the first person's having that to which he has a right" (Gewirth 1982, 2). This definition has the three elements I mentioned: two persons and the object of the claim, which is here referred to as *that to which* the first person (called *the right holder*) has a right. The other person is called the *duty bearer* and could be one person, a group of persons, an institution, or the state. So, the formula or schema for a claim right is simply this: *A has a right to X against B*, where A is the right holder, B the duty bearer and X the object or substance that A has a right to and that B must make happen. Later I discuss Buchanan's view of philosophical attempts to state the underlying reasons or rationale why it might be said that A has this right to X against B. When they have such a rationale, philosophers may add to this simple schema the clause *by virtue of Y*, where Y spells out the philosophical rationale, which in the case of Gewirth is the generic conditions of human agency. Right now I forgo a discussion of the various rationales philosophers have put forward and point out that this simple formula or schema leaves open the question of how the flow goes between rights and duties. My view is that in *moral* human rights, such as those in the declaration, the flow goes from rights to duties, and that in most *legal* human rights treaties it seems to go the other way—from duties to rights—but with a twist that Buchanan ignores when he refers to the preambular references of these treaties to the declaration as mere "rhetoric."

For some theorists of human rights (whether moral or legal), the flow goes from rights to duties, as the original italics in this citation from Gewirth show: "Respondents have correlative duties *because* Subjects have certain rights, and not conversely; the duties are for the sake of the rights and not conversely" (Gewirth 1982, 14). Gewirth's choice of flow comes from the fact that he is exploring the foundations of human rights as seen in the Universal Declaration and affiliated texts. He says, for instance, that he wrote his book *Community of Rights* "to give a philosophical elucidation and specification of some of the main economic and social rights set forth in the Universal Declaration of Human Rights" (Gewirth 1996, xiii). This direction of the flow between rights and duties represents the declaration's view of that very flow, going from rights to duties and not the other way around. It explains why the UDHR drafters did not abort their plans when they ran out of time and could not also adopt covenant in which the duties, especially those of states, would be spelled out in more detail.

To nail down what duties were taken on by what persons and entities would have taken a great deal more time, which the drafters did not have. It is a good thing that the international community did finally come to those duties when it opened for ratification the two covenants in 1967. In 1948 the UDHR drafters were comfortable first setting down a set of *moral rights* that all human beings have and briefly noting in Article 29 the *moral duties* that go along with those rights. The term "everyone" with which almost every UDHR article starts tells us that everyone has these rights "inalienably" (preamble) because they are "born with" them (Art. 1). Because these rights belong to everyone on account of their humanity and because that feature is not hard to ascertain, we do not require knowledge of complicated legal procedures (domestic or international) to decide who does or does not qualify as a possessor of human rights. I submit that for many drafters it was awareness of the Holocaust that helped them make this "shortcut" to human rights before duties. Everyone qualifies because everyone is a member of the human family.

The duties, however, are conditional. They depend on the circumstances of the case. We know that a child has a human right to food because he or she is a member of the human family. But if parents and relatives cannot feed the child, and if the town and state governments are dysfunctional and the region is in chaos because of a civil war, then my reader and I may need to nudge our own governments or UNESCO or the Red Cross into action so that the child's right can be fulfilled. In the end we ourselves, as extended family members of that child, may have to step into the breach by teaching abroad for a year or sending a check. The breakdown of the system at various points does not lead us to doubt that the victims have human rights; we just need to figure out where the duties in a certain case fall.

The conditionality of the duties involved in each case is the main reason it took so long for the international community to draft the two main covenants that state what legal obligations ratifying states have regarding the rights that are first listed in the UDHR. The difference between the inalienable possession of human rights in everyone because they are born with them and the conditionality of the correlated duties raises difficult questions about the relationship between the Universal Declaration and the rest of the international system of legal human rights, in which the flow is more complicated. It turns out that the relationship between the mouse and the elephant of our drawing is rather difficult to fathom.

The legal treaties in the system begin with a quick reference to human rights and then spend most of their space on the duties that ratifying states have so as to be able to deliver the enjoyment of these human rights to those under their jurisdiction. Because international conventions do spend most of their space outlining states' duties, theorists have been misled into thinking that duties are the beginning point for an analysis of the flow in these international legal texts. We have here a reverse asymmetry of what we saw in the declaration. States' duties mostly ignored in the declaration have pride of place in the international legal system. To complicate matters even more, while the up-front, often preambular, rights in these international legal treaties are those of individuals, the correlated duties are mostly those of the ratifying states. As a theorist, Buchanan—who downplays the preambular references to the declaration as mere "rhetoric"—sets himself the task of explaining and justifying why it is that the international legal human rights system would be structured around *individual* legal rights. The equal basic status (EBS) feature that I discuss later plays a key role in Buchanan's answer. My view is that that is so because they are the *moral* rights that treaties "borrowed" or "copied" from the Universal Declaration; these are the inalienable rights of individuals. The declaration gives more attention to rights of individuals and less to duties, while the international human rights treaties spend more time on the correlative duties of the ratifying states.

These attention-grabbing duties in the system correlate with initial moral individual rights that the treaty preambles often tell us are borrowed or copied from the declaration or—because the UDHR is the formal interpretation of the charter's human rights references—by implication from the UN Charter. So, there is a difference in flow between the founding text or, as I called it at the end of chapter 1, the master frame and the rest of the system. If it is true that these legal treaty rights are borrowed from the list of *moral* rights in the declaration, then it needs to be explained how these same rights come to be *legal* treaty rights of the international system, for in the first instance the UDHR rights are moral and not legal. Somewhere a shift is taking place from morality to legality. For most legal theorists, the presumption is that the creation of legal rights is not effective unless and not before the duty bearers are also identified. In this case we cannot properly speak of international legal "rights" of individuals until states are informed about and accept the duties they incur by ratifying a human rights treaty. In the legal realm, rights and duties are more or less perfectly correlated. They are produced at one and the same time by the same legal processes. At the very time that I receive the deed to my property, you are assigned the duty to stay off it. The processes that define the procedures of the legal system create both legal rights and legal duties. Creators of such a system can start at either end of the spectrum. Since states want to know what their obligations or duties regarding the legal human rights of the system are, that is where the emphasis and space in the drafting of international treaties needs to fall. So, there is a clear difference in the flow between rights and duties as they are seen in the declaration and in the rest of the system. The mouse is one thing and the elephant another. Given this difference, one would think that a text can or should have either the one kind of flow or the other, but not both. Yet we see both flows operating in the international legal human rights system.

In addition to using the three elements involved in Hohfeldian claim rights, Buchanan stresses a feature of moral claim rights that he says sets the *moral rights* in the declaration apart from the *legal human* rights in the rest of the international system. The feature involved is that the moral duties that correlate with moral rights are specifically *directed at the individuals* that have those rights. Not only that, "something" about these individuals is the reason the moral duties are owed to or directed specifically at them. I quote Buchanan:

> In the case of moral-claim rights generally, including moral human rights, the correlative duties are morally owed to the [specific] right-holder, or, as is sometimes said, they are *directed duties*. What must be true if these duties are morally owed to the right-holder? The

> only cogent answer, as far as I can tell, is that there must be *something* about the right-holder that is of sufficient moral importance *to ground the duties* and it is because this is so that the duties are owed to him or her. Or, to put the same point in different terms, in the case of a moral-claim right, the right-holder is morally entitled to the performance of the correlative duties and this can only be the case if there is *something* about the right-holder that makes him or her so entitled. (Buchanan 2013, 58; italics added)

The obvious question is, What is this "something" that causes the direction of the duties to go straight to specific right holders? In the legal realm, that something can be decided by the legislators when they write the laws. It might be the title that I have to the property or the fact that someone is a minor child of mine. In the moral human rights realm, there is no such choice. Those duties are directed at someone because he or she is either a member of the human family or something more specific. As it tells us in its first recital, the Universal Declaration uses the human family membership criterion. Admittedly, this is rather vague, and we wonder in a later discussion how and why the UDHR drafters came to this choice. It is clear, though, that the listed UDHR rights belong to "everyone" as members of the human family or to everyone by virtue of his or her humanity.

Because this is so vague, philosophers have sought to help UDHR drafters by offering various theories for what the "something" is in the earlier citation from Buchanan that grounds human rights in human nature and therefore makes the correlated duties directed. In section 3.B of *Inherent Human Rights*, I myself use Martha Nussbaum's generic capabilities that members of the human family normally share to further explain this elusive something. Most of the first three chapters of Buchanan's book are devoted to his rejection of philosophical help from a group of human rights theorists. We discuss this rejection later in this chapter when we address the idea of equal basic status in the international legal system. For the moment I share with the reader Buchanan's surprising claim that the duties in the international legal system are not and should not be seen or interpreted as specifically directed ones. He rejects the human family membership criterion as too vague and the philosophical help as too constraining on the system.

Before I discuss and defend the declaration's human family membership criterion, I give Buchanan's reason for focusing his analysis on duties before rights. In a section titled "Moral Rights versus Legal Rights: The Distribution of the Costs of Fulfilling Duties," he mentions the flow between moral rights and legal rights, but his focus is on the difference between their respective correlative duties and not on the issue of flow itself. To me the issue of the flow is itself very important, while for him the difference in justification is the key issue. He thinks,

> It is easier to justify a legal right than to justify the corresponding moral rights, at least so far as legal rights are enforceable. *To justify a moral right one must show that the corresponding duties exist, that someone has the duties in question or on some theories of rights, one must at least show that it would be justifiable to impose the duties on someone* [as yet unspecified]. But whether an individual, A, has a moral duty, D, to do X, and whether it is justifiable to require A to do X (to impose the duty on him) can depend on whether A has reasonable assurance that others are going to fulfill that duty. Without this assurance, it may be unfair to require A to do X. If D is merely a moral duty, then A may not have this assurance, in which case he may not have the duty, and it will not be justifiable to impose the duty on him. But if D is a legal duty, and enforceable as such, then A will have the needed assurance and hence it will be justifiable to require him to do X. . . . Because the law can provide reasonable assurance of reciprocity, *legal duties, and hence legal rights, can be more robust than moral rights. That is another reason why the law can be a more effective mechanism for achieving moral ends if it does not restrict itself to giving legal form and enforcement to preexisting moral rights.* (Buchanan 2013, 66; italics added)

This is Buchanan's rationale for saying that "the heart" of human rights lies not in their morality but in their legality. The last clause of the first italicized passage leaves open the possibility of first establishing that someone has a right and then figuring out on whom to impose the duty, just so long as that will be done. I think that this is exactly what the UDHR drafters did when they first drew up a list of human rights, knowing full well that they would have to eventually also spell out the duties. They did that in Article 29 and in the two later covenants, the ICCPR and the ICESCR. Basically, the moral flow for the UDHR drafters went from moral rights to the correlated moral duties, which were later translated into international legal duties.

The second italicized passage in this citation tells us that in the case of legal rights, the flow goes the other way, from the duties to the rights, as is indicated by the use of "hence." The moral flow is reversed. The reason is that the duty bearers need to know that others who have these duties will perform them too so that they will not be left "holding the bag," so to say. There must be reciprocity between all the duty bearers, which happens because the law will enforce the duties they all took on themselves. Because the law enforces this reciprocity, the duties are real, and hence the rights more securely held.

Because his focus throughout the passage is on duties, Buchanan avoids the difference in flow that we think is crucial for a philosophical explanation of the moral human rights in the UDHR, in which the flow goes so clearly from rights to duties. For Buchanan the main issue is that legal duties are more robust than moral ones, and on this point—if enforceability is the test—we agree. That is why it is so important that after the adoption of the 1948 list of moral human rights in the UDHR, the international community went on to establish legal human rights regimes that have more or less enforceable duties. While some scholars have argued that these regimes are in their "twilight" years, we agree with Buchanan that they still are more robust than the moral duties in Article 29 of the UDHR. Among the duties of states and third parties in the international human rights treaties is a call for states to report their progress in implementing in their territories the individual rights listed in the treaties and, upon failures, to be shamed into doing so.

By focusing here on legal duties (from which the flow goes to legal rights), Buchanan leaves untouched the preambular references to the moral rights in the declaration that we find scattered throughout the system. He in effect dismisses them as irrelevant to a proper functioning of the international system of legal human rights. He does not discuss the puzzle of how the flow can go from the *moral human rights* at the start of most international legal human rights treaties to the enforceable *legal duties* we find articulated in those same treaties. He concludes from this enforceability of legal duties that "there is no good reason to assume that a system of international legal human rights must be grounded on a corresponding set of moral human rights and good reason to assume that some important international legal human rights cannot be justified in that fashion but are nonetheless justifiable" (Buchanan 2013, 66–67). This analysis of the international legal human rights system demotes the preambular references in the system to nothing but "rhetoric." There is for Buchanan no place for moral human rights in this system, even though the system repeatedly pulls those rights in when it makes the preambular references. The previously cited comment on the difference between moral and legal duties sucks the morality right out of these preambular references in international human rights treaties. But if the rights referred to are not clearly *moral* human rights—as they don't seem to be for Buchanan—then what makes them *legal* human rights?

Acts of Translation

The difficulty with the international legal human rights system is that many of its texts are hybrids. Unlike the other regimes in the international legal system, the human rights regimes of this system are not self-contained. Human rights treaties often begin with a *moral* right that they copy from the list in the Universal Declaration and then go on to spend most of their time parsing the *legal* duties that correlate with those borrowed individual moral rights. This makes sense because states want to know to what obligations they commit themselves when they ratify a human rights treaty. Most human rights treaties do not create the rights they seek to protect de novo. They pluck them from already existing international texts, like the UN Charter or the declaration, or from other earlier treaties or declarations. One of the main purposes of the preambular references discussed previously is to exhibit these borrowing links.

If we look at the initial act of copying or borrowing a set of moral rights (as in the ICCPR and the ICESCR) or at the act of borrowing just one moral right (as in CAT), then it seems that in these international legal texts, a deeper flow runs from the borrowed moral rights to the incurred international legal duties. In the international legal human rights system, this *recognition* of preexisting moral rights is used as a reason for the *ascription* of the legal human rights in whatever treaty is involved. This transition from recognition to ascription is a matter of puzzlement for someone like Buchanan, who thinks the heart of the system is its legality and enforceability (however weak it is) of the duties involved. In the first chapters of his book, Buchanan seems to want to ignore this preambular copying and just go for the ascription aspect of the human rights treaties. However, the international acts of ascription seem beholden to initial acts of recognition. I see a dilemma at the heart of the international legal human rights system. We could accept the opening act of copying and admit that the purpose of the international legal human rights system is to implement the moral rights found in a document like the Universal Declaration. In that case the preambular references to the declaration in the system's texts are not mere "rhetoric"; they constitute acknowledgments of these borrowing acts. Or we could ignore these borrowing acts and pretend that the legal duties found in these treaties create the legal rights being protected, which is what leads Buchanan to say that the "heart of human rights" is the legal rights so created. For me that heart lies in the moral borrowings that pulse through the system.

If we trace a treaty's opening rights only back to the UN Charter, we might say that the rights in any of these legal treaties are "legal" because the states involved are acting against the background of Article 56 of the charter, which says that UN member states (when they sign the charter) pledge themselves "to take joint and separate action in cooperation with the Organization for the achievement of the purposes set forth in Article 55" of the charter. One of these purposes is to promote "universal respect for and observance of, human rights and fundamental freedoms for all without distinction as to race, sex, language, or religion" (Art. 55c). This is how the Convention Against Torture and Other Cruel, Inhuman, or Degrading Treatment or Punishment anchors the right not to be tortured legally in the UN Charter and morally in Article 5 of the Universal Declaration. Since the declaration is the authoritative interpretation of the charter, references to "human rights and freedoms" and references to the declaration can also be read as turning the rights invoked into legally binding rights and duties for those member states that ratify a treaty. However, since the charter references are so cryptic, more often than not a legal treaty's preamble will invoke the declaration's moral rights to put moral flesh on the charter's legal bones. It can also be said that since the declaration is the authoritative interpretation of the charter's references, any reference to the declaration also has legal and not just moral significance. Historically, this is a difficult point to make since, at the time of its adoption in 1948, the Universal Declaration was by most (but not all) drafters seen as a list of moral and not of legal rights, even though these drafters knew what Articles 55 and 56 of the charter said. That thick moral but not legal hue still hangs over UDHR rights some seven decades later because NGOs often use the declaration not as a legal but as a moral weapon with which to hit states that commit gross violations.

Given a moral reading of these borrowed up-front international rights, one might say that when states ratify a particular treaty, that very act of ratification involves that state in an act of translation the way a member of the clergy or a judge translates a couple from the unmarried state to the married state by speaking the magic words "I hereby pronounce." Looked at this way, every act of ratification is an act of translation. In this case the translation is from being just *moral* rights to becoming international *legal* rights as well. And the more states ratify a treaty the stronger the international legality of the rights involved becomes. The preamble of a certain international legal treaty usually begins by invoking the human rights "principles proclaimed in the Charter of the United Nations." Since those principles are not very specific and only make mention of "human rights and freedoms," a legal treaty will often also immediately mention one or several of the moral rights listed in the Universal Declaration as a reason for the ratification. And later treaties will often mention earlier treaties or General Assembly resolutions, which in themselves have far less legal force. For instance, both the ICESCR and the ICCPR, after they have cited the UN Charter's principles, say in their respective preambles that the rights they are about to protect "derive from the inherent dignity of the human person," which is an extrapolation of the Declaration's first recital, "recognition of the inherent dignity and of the equal and inalienable rights of all members of the human family." This collective act of translation from being moral rights listed in the declaration to becoming through the ratification process legal rights listed in the two main international covenants makes these hybrid texts.

The hybrid character of many of the human rights texts in our elephant, which contain overlapping moral and legal rights, leads me to object to Buchanan's view of them as containing only legal rights that make up "the heart of human rights." When we stand on top of a building and look through a telescope on the roof at the moon, we should not say that we *just* see the moon, for we see it through an image in the telescope. The dropping of the moral UDHR images leads Buchanan to misconstrue the ontological flow between the rights and the duties involved in the international legal human rights system. Anyone who belittles or ignores the declaration's influence on the international system of legal human rights, as I think Buchanan does, or who does not think the declaration has a unique place in that system, as he seems not, will likely have a skewed view of the system. Buchanan is unfaithful to his own occasional references—as on pages 32 and 149—to the Universal Declaration as "the foundational text" of the system, which is the role I give it in the flowchart I use in this book: idea → [1948] Holocaust + UDHR text → system [1948–68] ↔ movement. Here is an example of such a foundational reference: "Articles 22–28 of the founding document, the UDHR, list a number of social and economic rights . . . that we now associate with the welfare state" (Buchanan 2013, 32). Here another: "Apparently, the representatives of weaker states who spearheaded the movement to create the founding document of the modern human rights era, the UDHR, thought that the risks that powerful states would manipulate international legal human rights for their own purposes were less serious than the risks of living in a world without international legal human rights" (149). Like some new historians, Buchanan here fails to take note of the crucial drafting years of the founding document, during which time, I believe, these representatives were more interested in crafting a full list of moral rights and, because of time pressures, less so in translating those moral rights into legal rights.

Although Buchanan often refers to the UDHR—occasionally calling it "foundational"—these references undercut the general tenor of Buchanan's discussions in the opening chapters of his book. He consistently lumps "the major documents" of the system on one undifferentiated pile. For example: "From the outset the major documents, beginning with the UDHR, included rights whose realization requires states to provide positive benefits to those under their jurisdiction" (Buchanan 2013, 31–32). In a passage like this, the elephant of the preceding section is made to swallow the mouse, for from the legal point of view, the Universal Declaration has no domain of "jurisdiction" unless we make it "apply" to the whole world. The passage wipes out the difference between the application or implementation of the moral UDHR text and the jurisdiction that ratifying states have over those who live in their territories. When Buchanan speaks of "the founders of the system," he does not see much difference between those who drafted the Universal Declaration and those who wrote the texts we find in Brownlie and Goodwin-Gill's catalogue, which is our elephant.

Buchanan points out that "the UDHR and the human rights treaties that followed it make it very clear that human beings are social by nature and go out of their way to repudiate any notion that humans are atomistic individuals" (Buchanan 2013, 27n30). That is true. Why then not lift up Article 22 of the founding text, which speaks of "everyone, as a member of society"? Buchanan barely acknowledges the key role this article plays in the structure of the UDHR. He defends the idea that "the primary function" of the international legal human rights system is to regulate "*the behavior of states toward individuals under their jurisdiction, conceived of as social beings*" (27; original italics). Also with his own italics, he repeats that the primary function is to regulate "*the behavior of states toward individuals under their jurisdiction, considered as social individuals, and for their own sakes*" (86). When he writes, "The authors of the UDHR in particular took considerable pains to make clear that the individuals to whom that document ascribes rights are social beings, but they underestimated the resilience of false preconceptions" (87), he does not say what these "false preconceptions" are; these drafting "pains" are not connected to the *travaux* of Article 22. The *travaux* show that the UDHR drafters were keenly aware that the social, economic, and cultural rights in their text required special attention and protection (see Morsink 1999b, sec. 6.4). In chapter 5 I defend the view (which Buchanan also holds) that this group dimension or collective aspect of human rights does not undercut the individualist ontology of human rights derived from the UDHR. We part ways when Buchanan tells us, "There is no use in trying to discern the purposes of 'the founders of the system' as to this matter [of living a minimally good life]" (Buchanan 2013, 35). I think we can discern what the drafters thought on this question (Morsink 2009, chap. 5).

One of the goals of the international system is "to protect people from serious harms inflicted by their own states" (Buchanan 2013, 96). Buchanan takes this to mean that an entirely voluntary system would not be so good. He then adds, "Keeping this in mind it seems likely that the founders of the system looked forward to a time when a set of legal standards that was explicitly embraced by the vast majority of states through treaty ratification would become binding on all states" (97), even those that did not ratify these treaties. That could happen only if human rights norms became an integral feature of customary international law, which so far "include only the rights against slavery, torture, genocide and aggression" (96). Buchanan consistently shies away from singling out the text of the Universal Declaration as truly foundational and from naming its drafters as "the" founders of the system, even if only in a moral and not legal way. This shyness and reluctance leaves the international legal human rights system largely unexplained and therefore also not clearly justified. To that task of explanation and justification I now turn. My focus is on what Buchanan says is by far the most important and central feature and purpose of the international legal human rights system.

Mirroring and Equal Basic Status

The Mirroring View

Throughout his book Buchanan presses some difficult questions on those against whom he is arguing. His opponents are a group of philosophers, among whom I find myself. We have presented different theories of human rights as moral rights based on or derived from the humanity of the subjects who have these human rights. Each of us has picked an aspect, attribute, or property of human beings and gone on to argue that the human rights of people are based on the possession of that particular property or, in most cases (my own included), a particular set of properties. James Griffin (2008) and Carl Wellman (2011) picked normative agency, Alan Gewirth (1978) (whom Buchanan chose to avoid) also (but with very different arguments) picked the generic conditions of human agency, I myself (Morsink 2009) picked human capabilities, and Charles Beitz (2009) picked vital interests. And so on. According to Buchanan, the implication of these philosophical theories, which not all of us spell out, is that the international legal human rights system can be explained and justified only if the rights in the system reflect or mirror the moral human rights that have a place in a particular philosopher's theory. While Buchanan chides his opponents for not expressing enough interest in the international legal human rights system, he nevertheless faults them for implying that "international legal human rights, when they are justified, mirror moral human rights" (Buchanan 2013, 15).

The mirroring view is the idea that to explain or justify any right in the international legal human rights system, it needs to mirror a preexisting moral human right. Depending on how strictly this mirroring view is held, it could be of great help to international lawyers, offering a way to ground the idea of equal basic status, which for Buchanan is the most important feature of the system. But its help is not wanted. As Buchanan sees it, the system with its crucial EBS feature can be explained and justified quite well on semipractical grounds without the use of moral human rights theories. His philosophical opponents are spinning their wheels, for their moral human rights are not needed or sufficient if we want to make sense of the international legal human rights system. This analysis seems to do away with the second arrow in our flowchart (idea → Holocaust + UDHR text → system ↔ movement) because the UDHR, being subsumed under or swallowed up by the elephantine system, has no special role to play.

Buchanan takes on his philosophical opponents seriatim, beginning with Joseph Raz; I follow the critique of Raz with an overview of Buchanan's rejection of the mirroring view. According to Raz, the first feature of the international system is its limiting of states' sovereignty. In the Practice (capitalized by some of these authors) of the international legal human rights system, these limits are established via legal international human rights. To help with establishing these limits, Raz, speaking for his philosophical cohorts, writes, "the ethical doctrine of human rights should articulate standards by which the

Practice of human rights can be judged, standards which will indicate what human rights we have" (cited in Buchanan 2013, 15). Buchanan sneers at this, for he thinks that this limitation of sovereignty cannot be done by just "any 'folk' or philosophical theory of moral human rights. No folk or philosophical theory of moral human rights is determinate enough or widely accepted enough to play the role [of limiting sovereignty] in the Practice that international legal human rights play" (15). Again, "no moral theory of human rights is needed to help us identify which international legal human rights we have; that can be determined by consulting international law. If, instead, the task is to determine which international legal rights we should have, then knowing which moral human rights we have would be essential, *if* international legal human rights are supposed to mirror moral human rights" (17; original italics). Buchanan thinks that the rights in the international legal human rights system are not supposed to do any such thing as mirroring preexisting moral rights. Hence, moral human rights are not needed to tell us which legal human rights we should have, never mind the "preambular rhetoric" that suggests otherwise.

Each philosopher, having picked a particular human characteristic as the foundation stone for the derivation of human rights, approaches the international legal human rights system from a slightly different angle. Each therefore finds a different defect in that legal system as a whole or in the omission or lack of emphasis on one particular right that ranks highly in the philosopher's theory. Writes Buchanan, "On this simplistic conception law is merely an instrument for realizing preexisting moral rights that we can know simply by the power of individual moral reasoning, without relying on the collective, institutionally structured practical reasoning that law supplies" (Buchanan 2013, 50). Words like "simplistic" indicate Buchanan's low view of what his opponents have to offer international lawyers. He thinks these philosophers' views end up being conceptually imperialistic and not nearly pluralistic enough. And even if the mirroring view seems to work for some legal human rights, "legal processes can provide greater determinations with the result that the effort to realize moral human rights in law actually changes our understanding of the content of moral human rights" (51). I doubt this. While the translation from a right existing in the mouse to its concretization in an international legal treaty is one of specification and greater detail as to what having the right entails, I think the right's essential and core content is preserved in the translation. The justification of the international legal human rights system is a "strangely neglected problem" that Buchanan seeks to fix in his book. Certain philosophers' mirroring view is of no help in that task. These philosophers deign to judge and evaluate the system without accounting for the practical considerations Buchanan advances.

The Seven Features of the System

The narrow moral conceptions of his opponents cannot accommodate or explain the seven functions or features of the system as Buchanan sees it. As I lay out these seven functions, I underline the contrast between the broad scope of the system and the narrow gauge of the philosophical theories that Buchanan thinks are constraining and imperialistic. This is where the "new" understanding of a human right presumably enters the discussion. Buchanan thinks that the international legal human rights to, for instance, health care, democratic participation, and due process cannot be justified by an appeal to preexisting moral human rights, which we find in UDHR Articles 25, 21, and 6–12, respectively. The reason is that the moral analogues of these legal rights do not have "the extensive scope of these legal rights" (Buchanan 2013, 52). Buchanan thinks these legal rights are nevertheless justifiable in terms of their overall social benefits of unity and security for the populations involved. Moral analogues are not necessary, because a legal justification for these rights can be made in terms of more practical considerations without falling into the trap of consequentialism that is the standard death of real rights talk. Nor are these moral analogues sufficient. For Buchanan a moral right correlates with *directed duties* that in the case of his examples (health care, democratic participation, and due process) would have to be aimed at individual right holders. But in the international legal system, the duties that correlate with these rights are not aimed at individual right holders. They are instead aimed at bettering the lives of whole populations or large groups of people, an obvious case of which would be a government's policy to inoculate children. Domestic or international bodies put these legal rights on the books, not as a matter of directed moral rights but because they make for good social policy, peace and security, and other moral values not captured with individual moral rights language.

Moral analogues are not sufficient for the justification of the three legal rights given as examples, because those who created these international (or domestic) legal rights were not thinking of their duties as directed at individual human beings. They were thinking about much larger and broader social policies that then led them to stipulate all sorts of legal details of implementation that the defenders' moral analogues never even thought of. My reader should keep these practical arguments against the mirroring view in mind as I lay out the seven functions of the human rights system as Buchanan sees it. The idea is that there is no need or room for moral human rights in that system, for the elephant has swallowed the mouse, without moral remainder. I argue that in Buchanan's description of the seven features of the international legal system, there is an unacknowledged shift from the morality to the legality of the rights involved and that he has not succeeded in banning the moral rights found in the mouse from the system. I speed through the first four features because that shift is most prominent in the fifth feature, EBS, which is the next subject of this section. At the end I explain how my own philosophical approach differs from most others that Buchanan says are constraining. That then leads us back to the role of the Universal Declaration as the founding text of the system.

International law is a huge enterprise that covers the world economy, the oceans, the sky above us, the minerals below us, and a great deal more. All of it limits the sovereignty of the Westphalian states that share our planet. So, the question or uniqueness of international human rights law is not that it limits the sovereignty of states. That is a given for any part of this huge enterprise. As I list Buchanan's seven features, the reader needs to remember that these are features of the legal *human rights* system and not of the entire international law domain. As I see it, the first two features he selects conflict with the hybrid character of human rights treaties discussed previously. The first feature reads: "*The innovation of international human rights law is that it serves to limit state sovereignty, even within the state's own jurisdiction, for the sake of individuals themselves*" (23; original italics). The addition of the last clause is puzzling. I don't see limiting state sovereignty as an "innovation" of human rights law, because this feature can also be found in other parts of international law. The American Society of International Law (ASIL) in 2011 published a second, updated version of a pamphlet called *International Law: 100 Ways It Shapes Our Lives*. The tabulated ways fall into categories such as daily life, leisure, liberty, public health and environment, public safety, and commercial life. For example, millions each year enjoy "seeing the water go over Niagara Falls" because of "the Niagara Diversion Treaty (1950), which restricts the diversion of water from the Niagara River for hydroelectric power." This example is in the "leisure" category, which is very different in this case from the right to leisure referenced in UDHR Article 24. As another example, "flying shorter, more direct routes to international destinations" is a benefit millions each week derive from a well-functioning International Air Services Transit Agreement (1944). ASIL has placed this benefit in the category "away from home," which, again, is not what is meant by the right to movement referenced in Article 13 of the UDHR. Another example, "promoting the equal protection, treatment, and dignity of children," is based on the 1989 Convention on the Rights of the Child. Unlike the first two examples, this example is relevant to human rights. The point is that benefit to individual human beings is not unique to human rights law.

In his second feature, Buchanan lists the three characteristics "of the legal duties that correspond to individual international legal rights created by human rights conventions" (Buchanan 2013, 24). Here Buchanan references what I called "acts of translation," in which suppressed moral rights yield legal duties for states to fulfill. The three characteristics are that these duties are given *primarily* to states, pertain *mostly* to individuals under their jurisdiction, and, when neglected, *may* lead to humanitarian intervention by other states. The terms I itemized will be hard to capture with the philosophical theories that Buchanan regards as too pure for the job of grounding the international legal human rights system. On the supposition that one of the mirroring theories is correct, what might have been a philosophic moment for human rights is in Buchanan's account superseded by the multiple goals for the system that start with international security and world peace and, for a variety of reasons (and not just philosophical ones), include the protection of individual rights. This same mix of human rights and public policies can be found in the preamble of the UDHR, which notes that "recognition of the equal and inalienable rights of all members of the human family is the foundation of freedom, justice and peace in the world." When I chose to make the UDHR, and not any one philosophical theory, the ground of international human rights law, I borrowed Nussbaum's capabilities approach to help ground the list of rights in the UDHR (Morsink 2009, chap. 4). But all along, the text of the declaration remained at the center, and today it is the master frame of the movement. Most of the philosophical theories Buchanan rejects float above the legal details of this system and are too abstract to be useful guides in the drafting of international treaties, or so he argues. But that would not be true of any theory that took the text of the Universal Declaration itself as the moral engine of the international legal human rights system, as I propose we do.

As a third feature, Buchanan lists "the claim to supremacy" that sorts states out into being either monistic or dualistic. Monists give supremacy to any ratified treaty, while dualists say that their own domestic system needs to explicitly accept and incorporate a treaty even after it is signed before it can be considered ratified. In a dualist system, before or without domestic incorporation into its own legal system, a state's ratification process is not complete. The United States completed its ratification of the CAT when the US Congress passed the Torture Act to incorporate the CAT into its domestic legal system. So even though Article 2 (sec. 2) of the Constitution makes the US appear to be a monistic state, practice shows that it always acts dualistically because it adds to any treaty it signs the qualification that no treaty is self-executing, meaning any signature must be followed up by an act of Congress domesticating that treaty.

The fourth feature of the system is titled "The Basic Idea of the System" and repeats much of what the first feature also asserts, namely, that the system is to provide "*universal standards for regulating the behavior of states toward those under their jurisdiction for the sake of those individuals themselves, conceived as social beings*" (Buchanan 2013, 27; original italics). The fourth feature thus adds to the first feature the claim that the system conceives of the individuals it protects "as social beings." In a note here, Buchanan does not refer to UDHR Article 22, which speaks of "everyone as a member of society." He includes this sociality qualification "to forestall an objection, namely, that because of its ascription of rights to individual [*sic*] on the basis of the assumption that individuals count morally in their own right (independently of their contribution to society, usefulness to the nation, etc.), the system . . . is somehow parochially individualistic" (27n30). It clearly is not, but we are not told that individuals count morally because of the independent status that the moral UDHR has in the legal human rights system. It is the Universal Declaration that teaches us that individuals count morally and not just legally. That text also has a cosmopolitan "human family" theme running through it that Buchanan might have emphasized the way Gewirth did in his *Community of Rights* (1996). That would have amplified the wellness feature Buchanan himself stresses.

The Equal Basic Status Feature

This fourth feature leads to a fifth one that, Buchanan writes, "deserves emphasis." It is labeled "The Status Egalitarian Function," and he also often calls it the "equal basic status feature." I often use the abbreviation the EBS feature. This feature "*exhibits a robust commitment to affirming and protecting the equal basic* ***moral*** *status of all individuals*" (Buchanan 2013, 28; original italics). I put the term "moral" in bold to point out that in a description of the international legal human rights system, one would have expected Buchanan to say that all individuals have equal basic legal status and would, for instance, be seen as equal before any law in the system, or something like that. Two pages earlier he wrote that "*the efficacy of international human rights law exceeds its legal reach*" (original italics) and that "the crucial point" of the system is that it "serves as a moral standard that can be employed for political mobilization to change the behavior of states, corporations and other agents, even in cases where it does not impose clear legal duties on them" (26). The system here is given a great deal of moral clout that has found its way into Buchanan's description of the EBS feature with its "*robust commitment . . . to the equal basic moral status of all individuals*" (28; original italics). Clearly, the entry of morality into the heart of the human rights legal system is not inadvertent or an oversight on Buchanan's part. Why then does he play down the special role of the

UDHR for which I am pleading? I submit that the nonlegal, moral clout of the EBS feature is the result of the moral contribution that the Universal Declaration has made and is still making to the international legal human rights system. The hybrid character of the elephantine treaties shows up in the middle of Buchanan's description of the principles that guide the international legal human rights system.

In my discussion of this fifth EBS feature I will often insert this *M* into Buchanan's EBS designation. I do this to alert my reader to what I see as Buchanan's ambivalence about where to draw the line between morality and legality in the international human rights system. He gives us five aspects of the system that are central to "its performing this [EBS] function." All of these five are legal features of the system that in my view feed on the suppressed EB*M*S perspective. I list them and then discuss them:

1. Inclusive (or universal) ascription of rights (international legal human rights are ascribed not just to men, or whites, or so-called civilized peoples, or to believers, or to those who contribute to society, etc., but to all people).
2. Equality of rights for all (the *same* rights are ascribed to all in a very strong sense: They are understood to have [a] the same *content* [including the same correlative duties], [b] the same *weight*, and [c] the same conditions of abrogation, that is the factors that allow abrogation do not discriminate among persons).
3. States are obligated to make *everyone's* rights effective, that is, they are not allowed to make any distinctions among persons that would disadvantage anyone with regard to the effectiveness of their rights.
4. Robust equality before the law (including an extensive set of *equal* due process rights and the requirement that governments are to ensure that domestic legal systems provide effective legal remedies for all when the rights are violated, with no allowance for discrimination among persons as to the legal remedies to be made available).
5. The inclusion of strong rights against discrimination on grounds of race and gender (where this includes both formal legal discrimination and informal practices of discrimination in the public and private sectors). (Buchanan 2013, 28–30)

I see all five of these features as legal ways to implement the moral norms of the Universal Declaration. In the first one, we see a switch from the equal *moral* status in the general EBS statement to "inclusive (or universal) ascription of rights . . . to all people." The use of the noun "ascription" in the first line suggests that we have entered the legal realm. Moral rights are not the kinds of things that are typically ascribed to people; they depend on philosophical arguments or are intuited to exist, as I have argued the UDHR drafters did in light of the horrors of the Holocaust. Legal rights typically are ascribed to all those of a certain group or to all the citizens of a country by its legislature or highest court. But no worldwide legislature has the power to universally ascribe any rights "to all people" in the human family, as this quote might suggest. The only way universal ascription could happen in international human rights law is if the *ergo omnes* conception covered not just a few human rights but the whole range of them. Or if there were an international human rights treaty that all nations signed and ratified. The difference between "universal" and "inclusive" in the first aspect is the difference between the realm of moral rights described in the *Universal* Declaration and the realm of legal rights ascribed to all people included in a certain group, presumably those that a certain human rights treaty seeks to protect. The term "universal" harks back the inalienable moral rights that all members of the human family are born with, while the term "inclusive" fits any and all of the treaties that make up our elephant.

The "to all people" at the end of the first point harks back either to the Universal Declaration or to inclusive treaties like the ICCPR or the ICESCR, in which case we still must add the phrase "to all people under their jurisdiction." If we take as example a treaty that deals with the rights of immigrants or alien workers only, then we must add "to all those fitting the category of people protected by this treaty." Every international human rights treaty has this built-in limitation of applicability to just those that fit the category of persons that the treaty seeks to protect. No human rights treaties protect all the members of the human family. Right after he gives us these five legal aspects of EBS, Buchanan points out that "the modifier 'status' here is intended to signal that what is at stake is not distributive equality (equality in the distribution of resources or opportunities or outcomes), but something more basic, a notion of equal standing" (Buchanan 2013, 30). More basic than legal equality must mean moral equality as stipulated in the UDHR with its emphasis on the inherence of human rights in all "members of the human family."

The same underlying morality can be felt in Buchanan's discussion of the duties states have regarding "equality of rights," which make up the second legal aspect of EBS. This equal possession must also be spread out over the various treaties that make up the system. In the notes that support this nondiscrimination aspect, the UDHR and the ICCPR are given equal billing. However, the former is not separated from the latter as it should have been; it is not singled out as the cause of the equal moral status of all individuals in the system. Sometimes these two kinds of equality (moral and legal) are mentioned in one sentence without explanation, as when we are told that "a proper public recognition of the equal basic *moral* status of all individuals requires that competent individuals are to have *legal* entitlement to participation, as equals" (Buchanan 2013, 164). We see a hint here of the mirroring view Buchanan rejects. My explanation of this switch in terminology would be that UDHR Article 21 requires equal moral status for participation in government and that, for instance, Article 25 of the ICCPR spells out the requirements of equal legal status. Buchanan uses equal basic moral status here without acknowledging that the UDHR is the moral locomotive of the international legal system. He seems to be pulling a moral rabbit out of an international legal hat. The preambular "rhetoric" turns out to penetrate deeply into the substance of the system.

With his philosophical opponents in mind, Buchanan admits that it "is tempting to focus simply on the fact that a *set of rights is ascribed to all* and then note that the realization of these rights serves certain important interests that all humans typically have" (30), which then gives them all equal moral standing. His philosophical opponents have sought to articulate "the important interests that all humans typically have" and, with those interests in place, to explain and justify the idea of *rights ascribed to all* that we find in the five-aspect quotation. Buchanan rejects this transfer from morality to legality because the moral arguments of his opponents cannot factor in the elements of the same content, same weight, same conditions of abrogation, same effectiveness, same equal due process rights, or same robust protection against discrimination based on race and gender that he says fit the EBS feature. Legal details like these can be provided only by rulings that take place within legal systems. They themselves are not part of the moral arguments that purport to show "the important interest that all human beings typically have." Buchanan's opponents cannot bridge this gap between equal basic moral status and equal basic legal status. But, it seems to me, neither does he himself bridge it when he slides over from a general EB*M*S feature to just an EBS feature with five legal aspects.

To our question of how or when the international legal human rights system came to embody this EBS feature, Buchanan responds with a long note (Buchanan 2013, 28–29n31) that cites all of UDHR Article 2 ("Everyone is entitled to all the rights and freedoms set forth in this Declaration, without any distinction of any kind, such as race, colour, sex, language, religion, political or other opinion, national or social origin, property, birth or other status. Furthermore, no distinction on the basis of the political, jurisdictional, or international status of the country or territory to which a person belongs, whether it be independent, trust, non-self-governing or under any other limitation of sovereignty.") and refers to several articles in the ICCPR and ICESCR that speak of nondiscrimination and equality before the law. Notes 32, 33, and 34 make the same point about the key to the EBS feature being a matter of nondiscrimination and equality before the law.

My view is that this emphasis on nondiscrimination does not adequately unpack the idea of EB*M*S, which I agree with Buchanan the system exhibits. The prohibition of discrimination invites the question of discrimination with respect to what issue or which right, for not all discrimination is bad. It is good to reserve seats on a bus or train for handicapped persons, and many political theorists think it is quite acceptable to set aside a certain number of seats in a legislature for women. UDHR Article 2 bans discrimination in terms of "the rights and freedoms set forth in this Declaration," which the document lists in specific articles that follow. This means that nondiscrimination clauses are not self-explanatory the way Buchanan's notes make it look. They need to be backed up by a statement of the characteristic(s) in terms of which discrimination is barred. UDHR Article 2 comes after Article 1, in which the drafters indicate that all human beings are born "free and equal in dignity and rights"; these rights are then spelled out in most other articles of the declaration. Before the drafters give that list, they go on record to bar discrimination in terms of any of the rights that follow. This naming up front of birthrights, in terms of which discrimination is banned, is a function that in the international human rights system is performed by the preambles of those legal documents or by some of their opening articles, and all these texts bar discrimination in terms of selected moral rights. None of them simply say "don't discriminate," for that is of no help if we are not told regarding what issue or right we are not to discriminate. Nondiscrimination cannot be stipulated in a legal void. It makes sense only against the background of an already stipulated set of rights in terms of which discrimination is forbidden. In a preambular or other fashion, international human rights treaties first indicate what rights are at stake. The Universal Declaration performs that function for the international legal human rights system. Without such further stipulation, the equal basic status feature is left without support. That is why I regard the declaration as the moral engine of the system.

In his book *The Moral Dimensions of Human Rights*, Carl Wellman notes that "one primary function, although not the only one, of the two international [human rights] covenants as well as most global human rights treaties is to incorporate moral human rights into international law" (Wellman 2011, 58–59). Wellman did not call this a "mirroring" of moral human rights by legal rights in the system, but he did say that moral and legal rights were "analogous" (56) and that this relationship of analogy "often" (59) is a justification for creating a legal human rights system. Factors such as threats, availability of legal resources, effective means, and absence of harmful side effects also play a role. To justify this analogy, Wellman observes that "General Assembly declarations proclaim many [moral] human rights that presumably ought to be incorporated into international law, and [as a result] conventions sponsored by the United Nations or other international organizations confer real human rights under international treaty law. Although these [legal] international human rights are distinct from moral human rights, this does not imply they are completely unrelated" (53).

Presumably, frequently a "real" legal human right reflects a preexisting moral human right. As his first example, Wellman cites and discusses the preamble of the UDHR, which "presupposes that it is proclaiming preexisting moral human rights" (Wellman 2011, 54). Following Beitz, Wellman admits that "human rights politics also seek to "propagate ideals and motivate social change . . . and [that] international human rights could well be morally justified as requirements of global justice" (55). Both these theorists are right in not holding the mirroring view with any kind of purity, for Buchanan has rightly drawn attention to the numerous "nonrights norms" that are included in all major human rights texts, including the Universal Declaration of Human Rights (Buchanan 2013, app. 1). But that fact does not mean we should not draw a clear line between preexisting moral rights articulated in the UDHR and their translation into legal rights by the nations that have ratified the 1966 covenants. Of those later treaties, Wellman writes, "Like the Universal Declaration of Human Rights, both treaties presuppose the existence of moral human rights analogous to the legal human rights they define. The preambles of both treaties begin by citing from the UDHR its own first preambular statement that 'recognition of the inherent dignity of the equal and inalienable rights of all members of the human family is the foundation of freedom, justice and peace in the world'" (Wellman 2011, 56). What underlies Buchanan's equal basic *moral* status idea is the supposition that people everywhere, because of their membership in the human family, possess inherent and inalienable moral human rights. That possession does not depend on those rights being granted by any domestic or international organ or legislature. The question is how we might come to know that people share this EB*M*S feature. Is it by way of one of the arguments Buchanan's philosophical opponents have offered, or is some less idiosyncratic path available? Before I consider that question I need to briefly finish the last two of the seven features Buchanan identifies in the system.

The sixth feature or function of the system is "The Well-Being Function." According to Buchanan, his philosophical opponents stress this feature the most—at the expense of the fifth feature of the system, EBS. Writing about the modern postwar era of human rights, he notes, "From the outset, the major documents, beginning with the UDHR, included rights whose realization requires states to provide positive benefits to those under their jurisdiction—to contribute to their well-being in ways that go beyond refraining from harm and abuse" (Buchanan 2013, 32). The system has from the outset assumed

> that the responsibility of states include *basic welfare state functions*—provisions for public health and medical insurance, protections against unemployment, public education, and so on. Articles 22–28 of the founding document, the UDHR, list a number of social and economic rights, including rights to "social security"; to rest and leisure; to an adequate standard of living, understood as including food, shelter, clothing, education, healthcare, and social services—in brief all the rights we now associate with the modern welfare state. (32; original italics)

This is a summary of the second half of the UDHR, and the world consensus about these rights was picked by Moyn as more important than the Holocaust as a reason for the birth of human rights in the 1940s, a view I disputed in chapter 2. No one doubts that the international legal human rights system translated these particular moral rights in the second half in the UDHR into legal ones when the International Covenant on Economic, Social, and Cultural Rights came into force on March 1, 1976. The welfare functions that states have duties to perform are, according to Buchanan, part of the system's "two-pronged well-being function," which "protects people from harms and abuses inflicted by their own states and it requires all states to provide the goods and services characteristic of the modern welfare state" (32).

Buchanan's seventh observation on the international human rights system is that the listed features are concerned with description and not prescription. What he means is that most of the rights in the system "can be seen as either affirming and protecting equal basic status for all individuals or as helping to ensure that all individuals have the opportunity to lead a minimally good and decent life" (Buchanan 2013, 37). This makes the EBS feature and the two-pronged well-being feature the two most important features of the system. Buchanan himself values the EBS over the well-being function, and his philosophical opponents focus more on the well-being function; thus, according to Buchanan, his opponents are unable to explain and justify the system as it now exists because they minimize the EBS feature. When I argued in chapter 2 that the Universal Declaration sits on a three-legged motivational stool, I said that the Holocaust was the most weight bearing of the three legs. In that motivational way, I take sides in these debates, for the three-legged stool will not allow the EBS feature of the system to be second to the welfare function. However, I also rely on the Universal Declaration as foundational but do so neither as a purist nor as a conceptual imperialist, which is how Buchanan sees his opponents. For me the moral heart of the legal human rights system is the UDHR, which is why I stress the second arrow in this chart: [intellectual] idea → [moral] UDHR text → [legal] system ↔ [social] movement. That second arrow raises the question Rowan Cruft poses in his review of Buchanan's book: Must the EBS be seen as an independent feature of the system? Cruft points out that "someone who wanted to take the protection of minimal wellbeing as the sole function of human rights law seems able to accommodate equal status rights without regarding 'securing equal status' as an independent function for human rights law" (Cruft 2015, 238).

Cruft reverses the priority between the two main functions of the system, which is something Moyn also sought to do. While Buchanan sees the EBS feature as the most basic, Cruft suggests the minimum welfare function is the most basic, and he locates the justification of the EBS feature within the minimum welfare function. I do not see the EBS function as subordinate to the welfare function, though, because the drafters of the declaration saw both halves of the UDHR text as having equal human rights status. The Holocaust provided the initial and main drafting impulse, but the resulting text was well balanced between the EBS (as seen by Buchanan) and the welfare functions. The debate about inserting UDHR Article 22 as a bridge article between the two halves of the document testifies to the equal status of these halves (Morsink 2009, sec. 6.4). With respect to the "minimum" character of the welfare rights here under discussion, I have elsewhere argued that the concept of a human right has a threshold built into it (Morsink 2009, sec. 5.B). I take this position of the equal status for both halves of the UDHR regardless of the good arguments each side offers for its choice of priority. The desire to respond to the Holocaust ran throughout the entire debate on all parts of the text, so the EBS feature (which is linked to the nondiscrimination theme in the text) also underlies the whole text. When it comes to human rights, I am an originalist who takes his cue from the UDHR text, what its authors had in mind, and what motivated them. Thus, I take Buchanan's side regarding the alleged independence of the EB*M*S feature in the system. Because of its Holocaust connection, I do not see the EB*M*S feature as in any way derivative, which is what it would be under Cruft's suggestion of the basicality of minimum welfare. Buchanan needs this "M," and by keeping it he can have morality underlie both his own EBS feature and Cruft's minimum welfare feature.

The EBS Feature and Consequentialism

The title of Buchanan's fourth chapter is "The Case for a System of International Legal Human Rights." In it "The Importance of Affirming and Protecting Equal Basic Status" takes a central place. The discussion of EBS is part of Buchanan's third argument for having a system of international legal human rights. The first argument for the system consists of a list of "seven valuable benefits" that the system provides the states involved. Briefly, they are (1) encouraging and improving domestic bills of rights, (2) providing backups when domestic bills fail, (3) providing independent adjudication of claims citizens make against their own states, (4) providing supranational processes that help improve domestic constitutional rights, (5) supplying resources for the development of international humanitarian law, (6) constituting a unified legal framework for coping with genuine global problems, and (7) helping correct the tilt of democratic states, which often favor their own citizens' rights over the rights of foreigners (Buchanan 2013, 108). Buchanan does "not claim that the founders of the international legal human rights system had all of these benefits in mind" (109). Having read only the *travaux préparatoires* of the UDHR and not the hundreds of other relevant texts, I can say only that the drafters of the Universal Declaration, while they did, with their preamble, link their effort to "justice and peace in the world" (first recital) and to "friendly relations between nations" (fourth recital), they did not stress these kinds of benefits as they crafted the text. As time goes on, more and more of these benefits will no doubt come to play a role in the creation of new parts of the system.

After he has explained these practical, state-oriented benefits in some detail, Buchanan offers his second argument for having this system: "International Legal Human Rights [are] a Necessary Condition for the Justifiability of the International Order" (Buchanan 2013, 121). The necessity for justification becomes clear once we realize the big flaws of the international legal order before the modern human rights movement gave it a new shape. These flaws were (1) the "veil of sovereignty" that kept other states from interfering with what states did on their own territory; (2) the rights of states to control their own resources; (3) the rights of states to borrow without restrictions; (4) the rights of states to control immigration into their territory; (5) the practice of counting as a government any group that has "effective control" over a territory; and (6) the crafting of the international order "to further the interests of the powerful states" (124–25). My reader understands this sixth flaw from the veto power in the UN Security Council proceedings. The second argument for having our present international legal human rights system (or some other like it) is that "taken together, these six flaws are so severe as to make the system *morally unjustifiable*, unless they can be significantly mitigated. The system . . . has the potential to ameliorate the damage caused by all these flaws . . . with the exception of the last one, or so I shall argue," writes Buchanan (125; emphasis added). I forgo discussing the details because for the most part I agree.

Buchanan's third argument for the system is that states and their governments have a "special obligation" to "cooperate to remedy the flaws that make the international order morally unjustifiable. The obligation falls on states and their governments for two reasons: They are the chief beneficiaries of the international order . . . and they are in the best position to correct its flaws because the international order is created and sustained by them" (Buchanan 2013, 130–31). Again, for the most part I agree, though I argue in the next chapter that the authority states have to fix the defects of their systems is not as wide as Buchanan and other international theorists claim it is. Why is it, I now ask, that this remedy of these flaws needs to be done in terms of individual rights?

Buchanan admits that he needs "to show that the prominent role accorded to individual legal rights in the existing system is justified"

(Buchanan 2013, 132). Note a shift here from the international order being "morally unjustifiable" in the last citation of the preceding paragraph to "individual legal rights" needing justification in the preceding sentence. We are given three arguments for the presence of these individual legal rights in the system. First, rights are often connected to human agency and so give flexibility to the system. Rights provide protection to the individual without paternalistic overtones. It "is up to the individual to actuate the protections or not" (132). I do not think this captures the idea of inherent human rights, the actuation of which more often than not is done by others who seek to protect marginalized persons or groups. Second, individual legal rights make the system efficient since "all that is required to prompt enforcement of the duties is a complaint by one individual" (133). Would that were so. The third argument for having individual legal rights is a justification of the EBS feature in the system: "There is a third and more important reason for assigning a prominent role to individual rights in the system: Doing so best serves the status egalitarian function" (133).

Buchanan has charged his philosophical opponents with using the phrase "human rights" ambiguously for both moral and legal rights. In the citation that follows, he also mixes up these two senses: "A robustly egalitarian system of international *legal* rights of all individuals helps to affirm the equal basic *moral* status of all by creating a universal *legal* status that applies to all people everywhere" (Buchanan 2013, 133; italics added). He owes his readers an explanation of how he gets from equal basic *moral* status to "international *legal rights* of all individuals." The next sentence repeats the ambivalence but does not answer the question: "But by according a prominent role to individual *legal* rights, the existing international *legal* human rights system not only encourages states to act in ways that affirm and protect equal basic *moral* status, it also does so using norms that are themselves partly constitutive of that status in its most visible, public aspect" (134; italics added). I see the EB*M*S feature lurking behind the EBS feature. Buchanan devotes the rest of this fourth chapter to clarifying and justifying this EBS feature of the system without linking it to the *M* I think it needs. The two features are linked to the previously discussed acts of translation that states engage in when they ratify a human rights convention and thereby add to the list of international individual legal human rights.

Buchanan comes close to bridging the gap between moral and legal human rights but never quite makes it happen.

Because he uses the previously listed benefits states receive from the system and the flaws they themselves leave in it, Buchanan is open to the charge of being a consequentialist and hence an opponent of rights talk. We saw that the system gives plenty of benefits to the states that created it, still maintain it, and also have the duty to correct the system's many flaws. This talk of benefits and flaws sounds very much like the philosophical theory of consequentialism or utilitarianism, which is often considered the traditional opponent of rights theories. A theorist must be either a consequentialist who judges states' behaviors by the consequences (read "benefits and flaws") of their actions or a deontologist who judges states' behaviors by standard sets of rights that are not the result of such calculations but are grounded in other kinds of moral and rational arguments. To get out of this bind, Buchanan has made the EBS feature the key feature of the system as he sees it. I quote a "word of caution" (with added italics on "moral") that he gives his readers at the end of all his talk of the system's benefits and flaws. He writes:

> I am not endorsing consequentialism. On my view the justification for any particular international legal human right is subject to an important anticonsequentialist constraint: the commitment to equal basic *moral* status for all. The kind of justifications I have sketched above are not consequentialist. To say that it is legitimate to appeal to interests in addition to those of the right-holder in order to justify having a legal right does not commit one to the thesis that maximizing aggregate interests is what matters. The justifications I have sketched are faithful to the core idea that each individual matters, *morally* speaking, on her own account—in that sense they are *moral*-individualistic justifications. They merely also acknowledge that appeals to the interests of large numbers of such individually important individuals can justify a wider range of duties than any appeal to the interest of the right-holder herself can. (Buchanan 2013, 171–72; italics added)

In his justification of individual rights in the international legal human rights system, Buchanan downplays the role of the moral rights in the UDHR text as shown in treaty preambles. Instead of the morality of the Universal Declaration, he uses the morality of EBS to justify the system, into which this quotation injects "an equal basic moral status."

This EB*M*S feature, and not any particular philosophical theory, saves him from the charge of consequentialism, or so he thinks. I believe Buchanan faces a dilemma. Having banned the mirroring view, the duties of which are directed ones to individuals who have the correlative moral rights, he cannot allow that the rights that "all" individuals have are moral rights, for that presumably would cut off the flow of wider duties that Buchanan rightly says the system has. Instead, he writes that "large numbers of such individually important individuals can justify a wider range of duties than any appeal to the interest of the right-holder herself can." Presumably, this works because the rights involved are legal, and in that case there is no conflict between states' having taken on a much wider range of duties than just the satisfaction of the interests of many individuals. To create good public policy, states often need to take on duties that are not totally and specifically directed at legal right holders. That being so, why then does Buchanan speak of "equal basic moral status for all"? My explanation is that the swallowed-up mouse lives on in the belly of the elephant. We see here the same shift that we saw earlier when Buchanan moved from the EB*M*S in the general statement of the system's fifth feature to the five legal ways the system has developed in the performance of "The Status Egalitarian Function."

This "much wider range of [states'] duties than just the satisfaction of the interests of a large number of individuals" indicates that the international legal human rights system has in it far more duties than those that would normally correlate with moral rights, which in Buchanan's view of his philosophical opponents would only be directed at and owed to the subjects of these rights and not to thousands of persons who benefit from the nonrights duties of states in the system. Since the scope of states' (and third parties') duties in the system is so much wider than the directed duties of moral rights, those built-in limitations of moral rights are too constraining to play an important role in explaining or justifying the international system. As I see it, this objection works for some of the theories of Buchanan's philosophical opponents but not for Wellman's theory. It also fails to account for my own theory of inherent moral rights based on the text of the UDHR, which I agree with Buchanan includes nondirected duties that go way beyond being aimed at a specific individual to also include large numbers of other people, all to the benefit of the larger society.

When Buchanan's philosophical opponents argue for moral human rights as prerequisites for legal ones, they usually pick a particular human property or aspect that they argue all human beings (potentially) share or have in common. I noted that Griffin picked the property of moral agency, Beitz the one of vital needs, Gewirth the one of rational agency, and Nussbaum and I generic capabilities. Buchanan himself at one point also picked *the capacity for responsiveness to reasons* as the threshold property that gives those who possess it special moral standing (137), but now he has come to believe that none of these properties can do the job of underpinning the EB*M*S found in the international system. The reader can readily imagine how any of these properties *could* play a role in explaining and justifying the core EB*M*S feature of the international system, if only Buchanan would let them. If, to use Beitz's case, moral human rights are responses to the "vital needs" that all humans share, then these rights are universal and belong to all members of the human family, and people will have equal basic moral status. Similarly, if Griffin is right and human rights are derived from moral agency, then all those who have such agency have these moral human rights, which makes them nearly universal. This is assuming, of course, that the arguments of these philosophers work, which is not the issue here. My point is that *if* they work, *then* these arguments could help solidify Buchanan's EB*M*S feature because possessing the relevant property gives equal basic moral status to the possessors of those properties. Buchanan rejects this philosophical help for, among others, philosophical reasons of his own.

He bases his rejection on the fact that the properties these philosophers lift up as foundational for moral human rights are in Buchanan's terms "scalar ones." Keeping in mind that Buchanan often leaves out the adjective "moral," I cite him to the effect that "the success of an argument for the Principle of Equal Status depends not only on being able to show that all people possess some characteristic or capacity that confers high moral standing. It is also necessary to explain why those who have that characteristic to a higher degree do not have a higher moral status" (Buchanan 2013, 136). If rational agency is what yields moral status, then is it not reasonable to assume that someone who has a greater degree of agency does not on that account also have a higher moral status than someone who has very little of that capacity or, as in some cases, none at all? These scalar, or degree, properties cannot explain, so argues Buchanan, why people with different degrees of the property have *equal* moral status or standing. Too many human beings with all sorts of disabilities do not have enough of the required property and so cannot be said to have the full status. "In other words, it is necessary to make a convincing case that basic status is a threshold (not scalar) concept *and* to give a cogent account of the location of the threshold that yields the intutively [*sic*] right result that is the conclusion that all humans, at least all humans who are not seriously deficient in the characteristic or capacity in question, lie at or above the threshold" (136).

I agree that any property selected to ground EB*MS* must explain why those who have that characteristic have the status and have it equally, never mind the degree to which they have the property. I agree with Buchanan's worries and have faced this charge myself in a discussion with Nicholas Wolterstorff, who thinks that the property that is needed for the equal moral status of all is that everyone is loved by God. That for Wolterstorff is the "threshold property" that Buchanan is looking for and that he says his opponents have not provided. My response to Wolterstorff was twofold. I argued that the capabilities approach of someone like Nussbaum is not based on a single property but on a set of capabilities that range over the whole of human development (Morsink 2017, chap. 6). To have the shared moral status, someone needs to have any one or several of the set of capabilities that humans typically share. But I admit that that still does not pull in all the members of the human family, even if we say that some have these capabilities potentially, as in children, and that some used to have them, as in Alzheimer patients. The problem with most of his philosophical opponents, says Buchanan, is that they hold that "what is true about moral human rights constraints what sorts of legal human rights there ought to be" (Buchanan 2013, 138). For instance, this made Beitz doubt that women in some places have human rights as he defines them, and Griffin came to doubt that children have human rights as he defines them.

Buchanan then asks the crucial question: "But what are we to make of the fact that the international legal human rights system ascribes robustly egalitarian status to all individuals?" (Buchanan 2013, 138). There are outliers who have multiple and severe disabilities at birth and never develop any capacity for any kind of agency or personally controlled capacity. That is why for me the threshold for moral status ultimately is that someone is born into the human family, as is noted in Article 1 of the Universal Declaration. Being born into the human family is the threshold property that the UDHR drafters used to claim that all members of the human family have moral rights that are inalienable and inherent in all human beings. In 2017 Eva Kittay defended this view in her presidential address to the Eastern Division of the American Philosophical Society. She titled her talk "The Moral Significance of Being Human" and argued against the idea that human rights are based on intrinsic properties that all humans share. Instead, she defended, as do the UDHR drafters, their being grounded in being born into the human family.

The Holocaust and EBS Grounding

In what follows I continue to insert the *M* into Buchanan's EB*M*S feature, even though at times he might disallow this. I appeal to his belief "that the Principle of Equal Status is a genuine moral principle and an extremely basic one, not merely a parochial preference" (Buchanan 2013, 135). This insertion of the *M* highlights what I see as Buchanan's ambivalence between equal legal and equal moral status, pushing him to explain the relationship between these two statuses. It also enables us to see more clearly why Buchanan calls in the Holocaust to help him justify this key feature of the system as he sees it. We have arrived at the postwar philosophic moment of human rights that is defined by the meeting of the Holocaust and the justification of the present international legal human rights system. In the first three chapters, I defended the view that the Holocaust is the primary cause of the UDHR. I then showed at the start of this chapter that this meeting of the Holocaust and the legal human rights system is facilitated by the preambular references to the UDHR in many of the treaties that make up the system. This is what the second arrow of our flowchart (idea → Holocaust + UDHR text → system ↔ movement) indicates. The "+" between *Holocaust* and *UDHR text* is what creates the EBS feature and is the reason I insert the *M* of morality into it. From there we get the preambular references that lie behind the EB*M*S feature of the system.

Buchanan thinks that "the Principle of Equal Basic [Moral] Status is correct" but admits that he is "not sure how to provide an argument to support it" (Buchanan 2013, 135). Any moral principle invoked to support the EB*M*S would, he thinks, be "no more intuitively plausible and possibly less so" than the EB*M*S itself. The principle is so basic that "every legal system, whether domestic, regional, or international should affirm it" (135). There is a difference between the claim that "every system" should affirm EB*M*S and that the international legal human rights system does support it. Buchanan begins his explanation of how the international legal human rights system came to support EB*M*S with a negative entry in the domain of human rights, noting that "the weight of historical experience" shows that when people are not treated as having equal basic moral status, that fact is "sufficient to create a presumption in favor" of EB*M*S. This is the argument for human rights given by Alan Dershowitz in his book *Rights from Wrongs* (2005) and by me in a previous publication (Morsink 2009). Each of us made the "wrongs" of the Holocaust the epistemic door to the rights in the Universal Declaration. Buchanan holds that this approach shifts the burden of proof, for it can be pointed out that when justifications are given for discriminatory treatment of women or of people of color "they always seem to rest either on factually false assumptions about the natural characteristics of the group in question . . . or on implausible assumptions about which characteristics are determinative of" EB*M*S. Such defective information shifts the burden to those who oppose a presumption in favor of EB*M*S, but as I pointed out earlier, it does so only after it has been made clear what rights are at stake. For nondiscrimination does not work in a legal vacuum. If it is the right to maternity leave, it may be acceptable to favor pregnant women before others.

Buchanan's vacillation between equal moral and legal status is evident in his drawing a line between those statuses domestically, where constitutions often proclaim all citizens equal before the law, and international equal moral status, which is wholly dependent on what treaties states have ratified. I inserted "moral" to draw attention to this fact. Buchanan admits, "There is a profound ambiguity in the assertion that the international legal human rights system is designed in part to affirm and protect equal basic status for all. This assertion admits of an intrasocietal or a global interpretation" (Buchanan 2013, 144). The domestic designation pertains to equal status within any given society, while the second, global EB*M*S "aims to affirm and protect the equal [moral] status of each human being vis-à-vis all other human beings" (144). Then comes this puzzling addition: "My surmise is that the current international legal system, with its primary emphasis on setting standards for how each state should treat those under its jurisdiction, focuses on intrasocietal" EBS and not on the global kind of EB*M*S (144–45). We are not told how the system, despite this narrow jurisdictional focus, nevertheless ascribes "international legal rights *to all human beings*, and *in so far as* they all have these legal rights, they have an equal [moral?] status under international law" (145; italics added). The "in so far as" clause points to my earlier point that this international legal EBS depends on whether the state where the person is domiciled has or has not ratified certain treaties that spell out what rights are involved. This is the one respect in which Buchanan admits that "the system does not affirm equal basic status in a global sense" (145). In my view it is also the Achilles' heel of Buchanan's defense of a global EBS without a clear insertion of the *M* factor that I trace back to preambular references to the UDHR. Buchanan seems to agree, for he tells us that there "are no analogs, at the level of global governance institutions, of the rights of citizenship that the system confers at the domestic level" (145). I argue in the conclusion that Hannah Arendt's theory of human rights runs aground for the same reason. Other than the nondiscrimination articles that we find in most international treaties—which I argued cannot do the EB*M*S job by themselves—the global EB*M*S feature is basically left without support.

To strengthen this global sense of EB*M*S, Buchanan finally admits halfway through his book that "any attempt to justify an existing international legal human rights system like the one we have . . . is greatly strengthened by four aspects of the historical context" in which it arose (Buchanan 2013, 150). Here he links part 1 and part 2 of this book. The first aspect of the historical context is that the idea of "universal individual rights" was not new in the 1940s and had roots in the eighteenth and nineteenth centuries. I agree. Second, in some of the extant constitutions, individual legal rights were justified on "universalistic grounds." No examples are given, but thinking of the US, I agree. Third, "the group rights" experiment of the League of Nations was a failure. I agree that Hitler trashed it by waging aggressive wars under the pretext of protecting German minorities in other countries. I return to this point in the next chapter, in which I use it to raise doubts about the status of third-generation human rights.

The fourth reason for drawing attention to the context in which international law developed in the 1940s and beyond is that "the notion of individual rights understandably seemed to be a powerful tool for repudiating the racial fascist ideology that had, in the eyes of many people, been responsible for the horrific destruction of World War II and the Holocaust, because it aptly expressed a rejection of two core elements of that ideology, the belief that the individual had value only so far as he contributed to the nation and the rejection of equal basic status for all human beings" (Buchanan 2013, 150–51). In other words, the EB*M*S feature of the system is a response to the denial of that same feature by the Nazis, a denial clearly evidenced by the camps and the ovens. By merging the Holocaust into other historical considerations, Buchanan has weakened the presumption in favor of a global EB*M*S, for these other considerations push the Holocaust into the background instead of keeping it front and center. I showed in chapters 1 and 2 that the Holocaust was not just one aspect of the historical context. As far as the resulting global EB*M*S is concerned, it was *the* context. The other factors mentioned by Buchanan absolutely pale in comparison. The home that Buchanan seeks for the global EB*M*S is none other than the UDHR text that came straight out of the experience of the Holocaust. The Holocaust was the main factor in the adoption of the UDHR, and more than any other postwar text, this document harbors the concept of global EB*M*S for which Buchanan seeks a home. This home is both part of and outside the system he seeks to explain and justify, just as the mouse gave rise to the elephant and over time became part of it, all the while remaining different because it spelled out the equal *moral* status that was translated by the treaties in the system into equal *legal* status.

The moral and legal are brought together by the already discussed acts of translation that states engage in when they ratify treaties. While the UDHR spells out a global EB*M*S, treaties are limited to a jurisdictional kind of legal EBS (without the *M*), for the rights involved belong only to those under the ratifying states' jurisdiction. What best explains the global EB*M*S feature of the international legal system is the repeated invocation in the system of the rights in the UDHR as stimulants to the drawing up of those other international legal human rights texts. The UDHR gives to all human beings equal moral standing when it says that all and every human being is "born free and equal in dignity and rights." In various places, including chapter 3 of this book, I have cited comments by the UDHR drafters that clearly show that the rights in their document reflect a moral consensus among nations from around the world about the concept of equal basic moral status of all human beings. They kept this view even or especially after the Cold War intervened and they ran out of time and could not draft a legally binding convention. Because of these time pressures, they were stuck with proclaiming equal moral status for all human beings, hopefully to be followed by an equal legal status in later texts and documents. That is for the most part what happened, with the already noted proviso that there "are no analogs, at the level of global governance institutions, of the rights of citizenship that the system confers at the domestic level" (Buchanan 2013, 145).

We saw that Buchanan links his EB*M*S feature to the Holocaust and offers resounding support for the second arrow in this now familiar flowchart: idea → Holocaust + UDHR text → [global] system ↔ [1970s] movement. The passage I cite later in this paragraph uses the Holocaust to offer a historical explanation for the second link in this chart and for its influence on the later global legal system. But unfortunately, these connections are watered down. The system being one that was created by and still is maintained by states clearly aims to inculcate and instill values that benefit whole societies, states, and communities as the *collectivities* that they are. The surprise is that it aims to do this by way of an emphasis on the *individual* rights of the equal basic moral status, a contrast in ontologies I explore more fully in the next chapter. The reason for this surprising mix, Buchanan tells us, is that "the documents were developed as a reaction to the horrors wrought by Fascism during the Second World War, including prominently, the Holocaust, and therefore understandably proceeded on the assumption that two essential features of fascist ideology were largely responsible for these great evils, namely radical collectivism and radical basic status inegalitarianism" (Buchanan 2013, 268–89). Emphasizing key phrases, I quote more of this explanation:

> Radical basic status inegalitarianism is a denial of the principle that all human beings have an equal basic moral status. The idea that there are certain fundamental moral rights that all individuals possess simply because they are human beings, that are unearned and not dependent upon social contribution or social or legal recognition, was quite reasonably thought to be an apt way of repudiating both radical collectivism and radical basic status inegalitarianism. In other words the founders of the international legal human rights regime apparently believed that the best justification for the system of law they were creating would include an emphatic repudiation of what they considered to be the worst abuses of state power and they employed the language of the inherent dignity of the individual to accomplish this. In taking this path the founders may have unwittingly suggested that the justification of the international legal human rights regime was *exclusively* individualistic, despite repeated references in the major documents to the essentially social nature of human beings and the fact that many international human rights clearly provide valuable protections for groups and relationships. (269; original italics)

I do not think the UDHR drafters thought, even unwittingly, of their list as exclusively individualistic if by that is meant that they saw human beings as atomistic and separated from each other. There were in 1948 not many major human rights documents, but the one that is the subject of this book clearly affirms (and Buchanan opposes this to exclusive individualism) "the social nature of human beings" in several places: in its first recital, which says that the possessors of these human rights are "all members of the human family"; in Article 1, which bids us act "towards one another in a spirit of brotherhood"; in Article 22, which speaks of "everyone, as a member of society, [having] the right to social security"; and in Article 29, which mentions "the community in which alone the free and full development set forth in this Declaration can be fully realized." When Buchanan points out that the drafters of the declaration "went out of their way to repudiate any notion that humans are atomistic individuals" (27n30), he is right on. Thus, his speculation that "the founders may have unwittingly suggested that the justification of the international legal human rights regime was exclusively individualistic" has no foundation in the text or its history. The previous quotation supports my contention that at bottom the EBS feature of the international legal human rights system is best explained by the mouse that gave international lawyers and diplomats a list of moral rights to guide them in their work, turning what would have been a positivist EBS feature into an EB*M*S feature. And the mouse is best explained, as I did in chapter 3, by the influence of the Holocaust when the UDHR was created by visionaries in the late 1940s. In the cited passage, Buchanan acknowledges linkages that he plays down in his book generally.

The cited passage also hints at a split in the international legal system between an emphasis on individual rights and the duties of states that seek to instill collectivist values of the kind not easily correlated with a narrow or philosophically pure understanding of moral human rights, which are also supposedly correlated with the directed duties that Buchanan finds in the theories of his opponents. On this point I agree with Buchanan. I follow the UDHR drafters who put all the correlated duties in Article 29 and at the end. But I am not a purist and do not think of the relationship between the declaration's rights and duties as a one-to-one relationship in which some scalar property functions as mediator between the two. I believe that people indeed have moral duties that come with the inherent moral rights listed in the declaration and that these duties are not necessarily directed ones, as they clearly also were not for the authors of the declaration. All that matters from this point of view is that the right is fulfilled, never mind by whom. If you promise to pick me up at the airport tomorrow, I have a moral right to expect that to happen. And if you delegate that moral obligation to a friend or send a bus to fetch others and me, that is no damage to me. If I am picked up, consider your promise fulfilled. If parents cannot feed their child, it is not an abrogation of their moral duty if they seek help from the Red Cross or, if the parents are criminally negligent, the child's right is fulfilled by local neighbors calling in the authorities.

Buchanan rightly does not see the UDHR as simply a list of moral human rights with built-in, directed duties. The document contains plenty of what he calls "nonrights norms" for which he says his opponents' theories have no room because they (as he reads them) pay little attention to the international system as it is. At the end of his book, Buchanan has an appendix that lists the "Nonrights Norms in Major Human Rights Documents," the first section of which lists nine duties in the UDHR that are not correlated with single right holders in the text. Most of them start with the phrase "No one shall be . . . " and then list what may not be done to anyone. For example, Article 4 tells us, "No one shall be held in slavery or servitude; slavery and the slave trade shall be prohibited in all their forms." Article 9 says, "No one shall be subjected to arbitrary arrest, detention or exile." Article 11(2) says, "No one shall be guilty of any penal offence on account of any act or omission that did not constitute a penal offence . . . at the time when it was committed." Article 15(2) tells us, "No one shall be arbitrarily deprived of his nationality nor denied to change his nationality." In Article 16(2) we read, "Marriage shall be entered into only with the free and full consent of the intending spouses." In Article 17(2), we read, "No one shall be arbitrarily deprived of his property." Article 20(2) says, "No one may be compelled to belong to an organization." And in Article 21(3) we read, "The will of the people shall be the basis of the authority of government."

Many of these so-called nonrights norms have rights hidden in them in that they take a negative approach to the rights in question but in that way are just as universal as are the positively stated articles that start out with the word "everyone." The fact that "no one shall be held in slavery" gives everyone the right not to be owned by another person or organization. And when "no one shall be arbitrarily deprived of his nationality," everyone has a right to citizenship in a nation-state. Many of these nonrights norms turn out to be universal rights in disguise. Be that as it may, I grant that a certain number of nonrights duties in the declaration clearly go beyond the idea of stating an individual human right. Those norms have larger social and collective goals in mind than more narrowly focused individual rights, even of a large number of people. I do not think there are many of these, but the idea in Article 21(3) that "the will of the people shall be the basis of the authority of government" might be one such norm, as might be the instruction in Article 30 that "no State, group or person [has] any right to engage in any activity or to perform any act aimed at the destruction of any of the rights or freedoms set forth herein." This article explicitly states that no one has the right to violate any of the human rights in the declaration. That clearly is a nonright duty aimed at collectivities as well as individuals.

The declaration is a hybrid document of mostly individual rights and some crucial nonrights duties that aim at collective social values, though by doing so they also say that the members of the collectives have the right that these things be or not be done to or for them as individuals. These nonrights norms show that in spite of first of all drawing up a list of individual rights, the declaration's drafters did also and at the same time think of modern states as duty bearers correlated with these rights. But Buchanan is right to think that since they did their work against the background of the Holocaust, they foremost wanted to cast their text as one of individual rights and in that way safeguard equal global moral status for all members of the human family. This hybrid character of the UDHR does not mean that the UDHR blends into the international legal human rights system without remainder. The legal elephant cannot swallow the moral mouse, because—other than the link with the UN Charter—the mouse has no translational connectors that make for global equal legal standing. Each international legal human rights treaty carves out a section of the global moral human rights territory mapped out by the 1948 discoverers and stipulators. That treaty then translates the moral rights so stipulated into legal rights that ratifying states are obligated to make real for those under their jurisdiction. Until all the moral human rights of the UDHR become part of customary international law—which is not likely to happen any day soon—the declaration will always stand apart from the rest of the system as a separate and distinct Holocaust-created moral beacon.

For Buchanan the absence of this one-to-one relationship between right holders and duty bearers in the international legal system is a major stumbling block to the mirroring view offered by his philosophical opponents. I see two ways such a mirroring view can work. The view can be constructed in the abstract *before* one takes a look at the UDHR and then used to judge that document as good or as deficient, as the case may be. In that case the philosopher who constructed the theory stipulates beforehand what moral human rights people have. This approach often leads philosophers to reject or even make fun of Article 14 of the declaration, which talks about the human right to rest and leisure. There are numerous ways in which philosophers can find discrepancies between what their theories tell us a human right is and what we find listed in the UDHR or some other international text. These offers of help are very useful, especially when it comes to juridical interpretations of specific rights that judges from time to time need to make. I believe that this kind of philosophical help should be used only *after* it has been stipulated in the abstract or universally what human rights people have. The system has been around long enough that it is not likely to be redone from the philosophical ground up, which is what some of Buchanan's philosophical opponents seem to want to do. Buchanan believes that philosophers should contribute to "the development or maintenance of morally defensible social practices of assessing legitimacy for various types of important [human rights] institutions. It is not [up to the philosopher] to *discover*, through a priori reasoning, a timeless set of necessary and sufficient criteria of legitimacy for all institutions" (Buchanan 2013, 180; original italics).

I agree but submit that this kind of discovery—while not of a timeless set of criteria—was indeed made by those who drafted the Universal Declaration in light of the Holocaust experience and proposed it to the Third General Assembly in 1948. The link between the declaration and the Holocaust, backed by a list of extant constitutional practices and philosophical and legal argumentation, makes the social practices of writing and then monitoring the later human rights treaties "morally acceptable." To me the mirroring view is most useful *after* we have studied the list we find in the UDHR, which is what I did in a previous study (Morsink 2009), in which I offered the capabilities approach to help flesh out the ideas of inherence and inalienability that the UDHR drafters used in their first recital, as well as the idea of "born with" in their first article. Looked at this way, the stipulation of what moral human rights people have is done by the UDHR, or more precisely by those who drafted and adopted that text. Simply put, I hold that the 1948 Third UN General Assembly stipulated for the modern world what moral human rights people have.

Buchanan titled his fifth chapter "An Ecological View of the Legitimacy of International Human Rights Institutions." The basic idea of ecological justification is that "the legitimacy of a particular [human rights] institution cannot be judged in isolation and, more specifically, is not determined solely by the relationship between it and those to whom its rules are addressed, but also depends upon its relationship with other institutions" (Buchanan 2013, 47). Translated, this means that the legitimacy of the 1940s Human Rights Commission and the Third Committee that wrote and then proposed the declaration to the Third General Assembly of 1948 must be assessed in the context of other human rights institutions. That sounds plausible, but it does not obviate the mistake Buchanan makes when he does not include these two crucial institutions in his ecological system of justification. In a section titled "The Legitimacy of Key International Human Rights Institutions," the main institutions he evaluates are the UN Social Security Council, the treaty-drafting groups, and the treaty bodies that monitor states' adherence to the human rights treaties. I understand that for the most part the institutions that created the international legal system need to be what they are and that on the whole they have legitimacy commensurate with their results. But nowhere does Buchanan discuss the legitimacy of the Human Rights Commission and the Third Committee that together drafted the UDHR and proposed it to the 1948 Third General Assembly for adoption. He does not vet these institutions, even though they produced the moral engine of the system he seeks to justify. The UDHR is part of the system, and Buchanan refers to it occasionally as "the founding text," but he does not single it out as produced by unique historical and motivational factors that tie the document directly to the Holocaust. He pretty much lets the legal elephant swallow up the moral mouse. But that mouse is itself also embedded in and created by institutions that need to be assessed for their legitimacy. I did some of that in the first chapter of my 1999 *Origins* book. The result is that Buchanan does not give the preambular references to the UDHR in the system the special attention they deserve.

The reader can well imagine that Buchanan's title *The Heart of Human Rights*—when read from his perspective of international *legal* human rights—started my alarm bells ringing. For, as I argued in this chapter, this view of international human rights sells short the moral impact of the Universal Declaration and its preambular offspring on international human rights treaties. According to Buchanan, the heart of human rights is their legality and not the morality that feeds them. Fortunately, by holding up EBS as a special principle in the system, Buchanan's theory of human rights stops short of being a positivist one, for that principle is not simply grounded in legal procedures. I reported on how unsure Buchanan is of any argument that would protect "everyone's equal basic status . . . that does not begin with a presumption of equality" (Buchanan 2013, 136). This inability to prove the EBS principle is not unique to the international legal human rights system. "It is simply an expression of the increasing salience of an idea that is arguably one of the most momentous improvements in human morality, the abandonment of various forms of tribalism in favor of a genuinely cosmopolitan outlook" (137). Right here I want to inject the influence of the Holocaust on the Universal Declaration and of these two events on the rest of the international legal human rights system, giving that system the cosmopolitan outlook Buchanan rightly praises. By not clearly and consistently enough linking EBS to its moral engine or locomotive, Buchanan has opened up the international human rights system to the challenge and threat of international legal positivism. I discuss and combat that threat in the next chapter.

5

PORTABLE, NOT TERRITORIAL

Prevailing opinion has it that there are three more or less equal generations in the human rights family. All three have a history that precedes what in chapter 3 I defended as the 1940s moment of modern human rights. The first generation is made up of civil and political human rights that we inherited mostly from the eighteenth century and that, after the UDHR, are enumerated primarily in the International Covenant on Civil and Political Rights and other texts. The second generation consists of economic, social, and cultural human rights that we inherited mostly from the nineteenth and early twentieth centuries and that, also after the UDHR, are primarily encoded in the International Covenant on Economic, Social, and Cultural Rights and other texts. The third generation of human rights comprises various kinds of group-differentiated rights, both of whole peoples or nations and of minority groups in majoritarian settings. The whole people's part is based on the Westphalian system—in which a people is said to have sovereign rights over its nation's territory—that has more or less successfully governed our planet since 1648. The minorities' rights part made its debut at the end of the First World War when it played a large role in the Minority Rights Treaties, which defeated and newly created nations were asked to sign at the 1919 Versailles Peace Conference. The natural supposition scholars have operated with is to consider these generations of human rights as having equal status within the human rights family.

In this chapter I dissent from this prevailing opinion. I split the human rights family into just two large groups. Into one group I put the human rights of the first two generations and also the human rights of members of minority groups that are often separately considered part of the third generation. I do this because I consider all these human rights portable. People carry these rights, which are inherent in human beings, like knapsacks wherever they are or go. As birthrights these rights are portable, but because of their inherence in people, they can't be put down or given away. But many other third-generation human rights are collectivist because they belong to whole groups of people or nations. These collectivist kinds of third-generation rights are often tethered to a territory or a chunk of planet Earth, and for that reason they are not portable. Of course, under international law whole peoples and groups of them can and do have rights simpliciter, and some of these rights are territorial rights. But because of their collectivist character, these rights are not *human* rights and therefore are not portable. I see the connection with the Holocaust as twofold. First, in the camps only flesh and blood human beings died. Second, the Universal Declaration written in the shadow of the Holocaust gives human rights only to flesh and blood human beings and not to groups as such.

I present my objections to complete generational equality in three steps. First, in the next section, "Questioning Third-Generation Human Rights," I raise questions of status resulting from the weak legal standing that third-generation human rights have in the United Nations system. Second, in "Amending the Universal Declaration," I make an exception and work to pull members of minority groups into the human rights family. Third, in "*Appellation Contrôlée* and Common Article 1," I discuss the inflation that has taken place in the human rights domain, ending with a case study in which I seek to demote third-generation collectivist rights because they are not properly vetted and have territorial aspirations. Last, as it now stands in human rights literature, we are presented with two options for the modern meaning of the phrase "human rights": a UN-based one and a UDHR-based one. By way of conclusion, I defend my choice of the Universal Declaration as central to our modern notion of human rights.

Questioning Third-Generation Human Rights

In his book *The Sovereignty of Human Rights*, Patrick Macklem (2015) has constructed a theory of international law that makes human rights sovereign over the whole province of that type of law. In Macklem's account, "human rights require the international legal order to attend to pathologies of its own making. They monitor the distribution and exercise of sovereign power to which international law extends legal validity" (Macklem 2015, 1). This is a most intriguing definition of human rights. It gives human rights sovereignty over world affairs the way God is thought to have sovereign power over the universe, and the queen of England over the United Kingdom. The field of international law has, of course, many branches: the law of the sea, international labor law, diplomatic law, private international law, aviation law, economic or trade law, environmental law, international humanitarian law, piracy law, and international criminal law, all of which can be broken up into yet smaller pieces explained by a myriad of bilateral and multilateral treaties between the states of the Westphalian system and by declarations these states from time to time make to underscore their own customary behavior. It is therefore very good news to be told that human rights are sovereign over this entire field of operations. Just like police departments have their own (hopefully civilian) review boards, so international law wants to and knows that it needs to clean up and correct the mistakes it inevitably makes anywhere in this huge system. It has given this oversight authority to international human rights law, which performs its task by way of the three generations that are the subject of this chapter.

This delegated sovereignty of human rights over world affairs fits the aspirations of the human rights movement, but my view is that we have not yet reached Macklem's expansive definition of human rights sovereignty. It is far too early to declare this kind of victory for human rights over world affairs, though I admit that the morality of human rights does have an independent voice in those affairs. It just isn't always a legal one. Macklem's indiscriminate conception of human rights drowns out and endangers the narrower conception of human rights set forth in the UDHR, which this book seeks to make better known. That narrower conception embraces only the first two generations of human rights, plus rights applying to members of minority groups, and not also the rest of the third generation, which plays such a large role in Macklem's sovereignty thesis.

Macklem compares his own views of human rights sovereignty to those of Buchanan, which we discussed in the preceding chapter. "International human rights, for Buchanan," Macklem writes, "constrain sovereignty for the purposes of affirming and protecting the equal basic status of all people . . . and helping to ensure that all have the opportunity to lead a minimally good or decent life" (Macklem 2015, 24). In chapter 4 I interpreted Buchanan's EBS feature as requiring the insertion of an *M* standing for "moral." With that *M* inserted, his equal basic (moral) status feature floats above the Westphalian system maintained by sovereign states. It seeks to constrain those states from above. This feature and by extension the UDHR from which this morality derives have oversight without real control over how these sovereign states treat persons under their jurisdiction. While states themselves created the legal texts in which the EB(M)S feature is embedded, Buchanan had trouble grounding these EB(M)S norms. He admitted that they are at least partly grounded in the historical circumstances that gave rise to the international human rights system. Those circumstances included the events of the Holocaust that then issued forth into a worldwide code of ethics.

By way of contrast, "the conception offered in [Macklem's] book is that human rights in international law aim to ameliorate harms associated with not only the exercise but also the distribution of sovereignty to which international law extends legal validity" (Macklem 2015, 24). Here the very distribution of sovereignty itself and therefore the creation of sovereign states, which traditionally was thought of as the prerogative of international law generally, is seen as being supervised by sovereign human rights. This reverses the order Buchanan sees. Instead of already existing states being asked to adhere to external human rights norms, these norms themselves are present at the very creation of sovereign states—a claim I doubt. In both cases there is a sort of moral transcendence. For Buchanan it comes from the partially external EB(M)S principle and norms. For Macklem the transcendence is internally dispersed throughout the interstices of the system itself. It comes from "legal contestation over the scope and content of the various human rights that collectively constitute the field of international human rights law" (24). According to Macklem, the judgments made in these legal "contestations" or contests "need not be guided by these [Buchanan EB(M)S] norms; they can just as easily be guided by other universal norms, or less universal norms, as well as by text and precedent and the various pragmatic considerations, such as efficiency, utility and prudence, characteristic of legal argumentation" (25). Again: "The purpose or role of international human rights law is not necessarily to protect these [EB(M)S] norms in the face of the exercise of sovereign [state] power. It is instead to ameliorate harms associated with the distribution and exercise of sovereignty to which international law extends legal validity" (25). This is a thoroughgoing legal positivist account of international human rights law. All principled moral transcendence and with it the whole of the second link of our flowchart (idea → Holocaust + UDHR text → system ↔ movement) has been pulled down into the interstices of international legal judgments that may or may not give credence to the norms encapsulated by Buchanan's EB(M)S feature. I question this positivist account of human rights because it plays down the principled moral role of the UDHR in international human rights law. In the citation that follows, I have highlighted the terms that make explicit the contrast with my own (and possibly Buchanan's) position. Recall that Macklem's account seeks to make sense of the

> rich variety of rights and instruments that make up the field of international human rights law in ways that moral accounts cannot. It ascribes a richer mission to the field by placing the legitimacy of the international legal order under its watch. It comprehends human rights in international law as legal sites of moral and political contestation over fundamental questions that relate to the structure and operation of international law, but it does so in distinctively legal terms. The legal existence of international human rights is the product not of moral insight, but of the enactment of the various instruments that place them on *the international register*, and their critical force rests in their capacity to attend to some of the adverse effects of how we organize global politics into an international legal order. (Macklem 2015, 2)

The "moral" part of the contestation derives from the influence the Universal Declaration has had and still has on numerous human rights conventions but generally not on other parts of the system. At the birth of the legal human rights system, "moral insight" did play a role when ratifying states translated moral rights into legal duties. Macklem's definition casts its net too widely. His "rich variety" of international law does not merely include but stresses the third generation of human rights that, as I argue later, has weakened in its fourth phase (1950–89) and should not now be used in the handover of human rights sovereignty from the 1948 UDHR meaning of "human rights" to the much later developed UN meaning of that concept. International law at present gives the third generation of human rights, which is mostly sponsored by the UN General Assembly, a status it has not yet earned and in my view should not have as long as it gives human rights with a collectivist ontology the same status as those with the individualist ontology found in the Universal Declaration.

For Macklem, human rights law is the cleanup crew for mistakes that are made in international law generally. These rights have been given oversight authority for the entire domain of international law, from whence the book's title, *The Sovereignty of Human Rights*, derives. Accordingly, Macklem's third chapter includes two sections on human rights "as monitors of sovereignty's exercise": one for the first generation of civil and political rights and one for the second generation of economic, social, and cultural ones. The other chapters of Macklem's book discuss the same monitoring of sovereignty's exercise done by the third generation of group-differentiated human rights. I submit that the legal pedigree of many of these third-generation legal texts is not as solid as that of the other two generations' texts.

But first I want to register some puzzlement about the monitoring of the first two generations. Macklem makes it look like the treaties that make up the elephant of chapter 4 have somehow received delegated authority from some central authority of or in international law. But he never explains when or where that delegation of authority took place. Most of the treaties included in chapter 4's elephant have their own built-in monitoring committees. It therefore makes no sense to speak of civil and political rights as in themselves being monitors. They are not monitors; they are the real thing, assertions of human rights that have no authority above them. These rights have committees that monitor and oversee the treaties that embody them and see them codified. These separate committees, and not some other unrelated area or organ of international law, monitor violations by states that have ratified these human rights treaties. The same is true of economic, social, and cultural rights; the UN Committee on Economic, Social, and Cultural Rights monitors just the violations of the ICESCR and not of other texts, and just in the states that have ratified this convention and not in others. Thus, the violations brought to the attention of these committees are not violations of international law generally; they are violations of specific treaties that deal with the rights there listed. Since the elephant is not all inclusive, where no human rights treaty applies to a particular area of life, human rights are not sovereign over that area of international relations and law. However, the morality of human rights might raise its voice and intrude to push for a new treaty to cover that area too. Aside from this puzzlement, I do accept Macklem's idea of the central role that the first two generations play in the human rights enterprise. The monitoring of the third generation is a different story.

Macklem tells us, "Minority rights, indigenous rights, and, more broadly, the right to self-determination typically vest in some communities and not others for reasons that appear to be steeped in contingencies of history and geography" (Macklem 2015, 2). That is the point I made in chapter 3 when I showed that owing to assimilationist headwinds in the late 1940s, the Human Rights Commission adopted a Haitian motion that made the same point we see Macklem making about local "contingencies" that give rise to third-generation collectivist rights. These types of human rights are based on a different ontology that refers to collectivities and to territorial human rights. To make his case for the sovereignty of human rights in this sphere of collectivity, Macklem crucially, and I think mistakenly, shifts the emphasis of his discussion from the requirement of states' *consent* to the ICCPR, the ICESCR, and other legally binding human rights conventions that implement the moral norms of the UDHR to the much looser requirement of a *consensus*, which is the basis for UN adoption of various third-generation collective rights. This latter kind of adoption through consensus is typically reserved for aspirational General

Assembly resolutions and declarations that in Richard Falk's words have only "quasi-legislative" status (Falk 1966, 782). This difference in manner of adoption (through consensus instead of consent) has in effect created two kinds of meaning for our modern conception of "human rights": a UDHR meaning, which is given legal teeth through consent ratifications of conventions, and a UN meaning, which is given legal teeth through consensus UN resolutions and declarations. Macklem's sovereignty thesis relies on this broader UN meaning of human rights instead of the narrower and more secure—because more deeply grounded—UDHR one that I defend in this chapter.

Instead of working with three generations, as most scholars do, Macklem proposes that we accept just one generation, all the rights of which are covered by his definition of international human rights as "seeking to rectify an array of adverse consequences" (Macklem 2015, 30) produced in the normal operations of international law. Since there are so many different adverse consequences, a wide definition of human rights is called for, and Macklem is happy to provide it. For the third generation, the connections between these diverse adverse consequences and Macklem's definition are made first by the role the International Labor Organization plays in international labor law (Macklem's chap. 4) and then by the "Ambiguous Appeal of Minority Rights" (chap. 5), by "International Indigenous Recognition" (chap. 6), by the "Right of Peoples to Self-Determination" (chap. 7), and finally, by "Peoples' Right to Development" (chap. 8). My objection to this dominance of third-generation collective human rights in the conception of what ties the human rights family together is not just the idea that the role of the UDHR and its connection with the Holocaust has been ignored. That is indeed my main objection, and I return to it later. Here I focus on the fact that the international legal instruments used to create these third-generation collectivist human rights are primarily resolutions and declarations of the United Nations General Assembly. As such, these instruments have a lesser legal status than the more strongly binding conventions that were the subject of Macklem's chapter 3 and that became legally binding on the nations that ratified the ICCPR and the ICESCR, which provide legal teeth to the UDHR.

No such strong legal ties bind nations that voted for the General Assembly resolutions that dominate chapters 4–8. The reader can see from the tallies I give that all these declarations were adopted either with an overwhelming majority of votes or by acclamation and without votes. I list seven of the main ones Macklem uses:

1. Resolution 1803, containing a declaration on Permanent Sovereignty over Natural Resources, adopted December 14, 1962, with 87 votes for, 2 against (France and South Africa), and 12 abstentions (Bulgaria, Burma, the BSSR, Cuba, Czechoslovakia, Ghana, Hungary, Mongolia, Poland, the UKSSR, the USSR, and Romania) (A/RES/1803[XVII]; http://bit.ly/2CIP8ms);
2. Resolution 1514, containing the Declaration on the Granting of Independence to Colonial Peoples and Countries, adopted December 14, 1960, with 89 votes for, 0 against, 9 abstentions (Australia, Belgium, the Dominican Republic, France, Portugal, Spain, South Africa, the UK, and the US), and 1 nonvoting (Dahomey) (A/RES/1514[XV]; http://bit.ly/2lWix24);
3. Resolution 2625, containing the Declaration on Principles of International Law concerning Friendly Relations and Cooperation among States in Accordance with the Charter of the United Nations, adopted without vote October 24, 1970 (A/RES/2625[XXV]; http://bit.ly/2CoeJwD);
4. Resolution 3201, containing the Declaration on the Establishment of a New International Economic Order, adopted without vote May 1, 1974 (A/RES/3201[S-VI]; http://bit.ly/2CoeJw);
5. Resolution 47/135, containing the Declaration on the Rights of Persons Belonging to National or Ethnic, Religious, and Linguistic Minorities, adopted without vote December 18, 1992 (A/RES/47/135; http://bit.ly/2CH8yqQ);
6. Resolution 41/128, containing the Declaration on the Right to Development, adopted December 4, 1986, with 146 votes for, 1 against (the US), and 8 abstentions (Denmark, Finland, Federal Republic of Germany, Iceland, Israel, Japan, Sweden, and the UK) (A/RES/41/128; http://bit.ly/2lVxZvk); and

7. Resolution 61/295, containing the Declaration on the Rights of Indigenous Peoples, adopted September 13, 2007, with 143 votes for, 4 against (Australia, Canada, New Zealand, the US), and 11 abstentions (Azerbaijan, Bangladesh, Bhutan, Burundi, Colombia, Georgia, Kenya, Nigeria, Russian Federation, Samoa, and Ukraine) (A/RES/61/295; http://bit.ly/2Ar8OoP).

Clearly, these are more aspirational and agenda-setting texts that, if anything, have only quasi-legislative force for UN member states. The reader may have noted that the only one of these resolutions that works with an overt individualist ontology is the 1992 Declaration on the Rights of Persons Belonging to National or Ethnic, Religious, and Linguistic Minorities. In the next section, I take these rights of members of minority groups and classify them under the individualist umbrella of the UDHR. Here I prepare the ground for the demotion of these other alleged human rights—to be completed in the section after the next—by making a case for their lesser legal efficacy.

I need to admit that the Universal Declaration of Human Rights is itself just such a "soft" declaration contained in General Assembly Resolution 217 (III), adopted on December 10, 1948, with forty-eight votes for, none against, and eight abstentions (the USSR, the BSSR, the UKSSR, Poland, Yugoslavia, Czechoslovakia, Saudi Arabia, and South Africa). When the UDHR drafters first considered how they would implement the mandate the commission received from ECOSOC to write an "international bill of rights," Humphrey, the first human rights commissioner in the Secretariat, told the delegates about the "essential difference" between a declaration or manifesto and an international convention. "Whereas the resolution of the Assembly would [have] the force of a recommendation only, a convention would be part of international law and legally binding on the states which signed and ratified it" (E/CN.4/Sub.2/SR1/3). So, the UDHR drafters knew what they were doing when they went ahead and refused the United Kingdom's proposal to take its version of a convention (which had no social and economic rights in it) as the basis for their discussions. Instead, when the Cold War started to have an impact in the late summer of 1948, they chose to focus all their remaining energy on a declaration of moral rights that at that time would have no binding legal force but that over time might, and did, develop it. The difference between this particular UN declaration and the ones that play such a large role in Macklem's sovereignty thesis is my argument of chapter 4 that the UDHR became the moral engine of a large legally enforceable human rights system made up of many conventions tailored on the last of the UDHR. None of that kind of legal follow-up was created for the resolutions on which Macklem relies for his third-generation collectivist rights, to which he assigns equal status in the human rights family.

Writing in 1981, Christopher Joyner wanted to see if the "legal status" of these UN resolutions had "undergone any salient transformation over the past three decades" (Joyner 1981, 446). At that time the UN had at least a hundred more members than it had had in 1948, and the loosely affiliated Group of 77 (G77) wanted to achieve a more equitable distribution of "transnational political, economic and natural resources" among the UN member states (446). The G77 chose UN General Assembly resolutions to achieve their goal. According to Joyner, the key stumbling block for the group—which counts against Macklem's generational equality thesis—was that "within the United Nations system there exists no international law–creating organ, per se" (452). Samuel Bleicher also notes that "the United Nations Charter makes no allocation of formal prescriptive authority to the General Assembly" (Bleicher 1969, 446). Article 13 of the UN Charter gives the General Assembly competence to engage in studies and make recommendations, including on human rights, that can "enhance the norm-creation process of international law," but it cannot create these norms de novo. These powers are only "recommendatory" (Joyner 1981, 449). Other organs involved in UN norm creation are the General Assembly's Sixth Committee and the International Law Commission, both of which can help prepare convention texts to be presented under UN auspices to member states for ratification. The second of these is especially slow and ponderous in its goal of codifying new developments in international law.

Another possibility is for General Assembly resolutions to be linked to different sources of international law mentioned in Article 38 of the Statute of the International Court of Justice. After having surveyed these options, Joyner believes that "the most prevalent perspective regarding the legal station of General Assembly resolutions places them within the context of customary international law" (Joyner 1981, 458). It has, however, been notoriously difficult to show when state practice makes the customary behavior of states obligatory and binding on them. States cannot be bound by a stance they take in General Assembly debates and votes. According to Joyner, "the fact persists that General Assembly resolutions are not binding and that a state's vote in favor of any resolution-embodied practice does but little to insure that resolution's future acceptance and implementation by that state as a customary norm in the international community" (459).

Writing a good ten years earlier, Samuel Bleicher also noted that "a vote for a particular General Assembly resolution by itself creates little more basis for a fixed expectation than does a unilateral declaration of intended future behavior by a representative of that state, which in the absence of special circumstances can be altered at will" (Bleicher 1969, 447). Bleicher went on to argue that the "repeated subsequent citation of a particular resolution by the General Assembly" can give that resolution some legal efficacy (453). That states can change their General Assembly positions "at will" weakens Bleicher's wanting to hold on to "the increased reasonableness of the expectation that principles which have been often reiterated will be followed" (454). It is evident that the binding character of the General Assembly's quasi-legislative aspirational practices depends very much on treaties that await ratification by states.

Both Bleicher and Joyner support my contention that Macklem's shift from consent to consensus should not be used to equalize the generations of human rights. Bleicher found little promise in linking General Assembly resolutions to the UN Charter Article 38's "'general principles of law,' especially as it relates to morality and justice" (Bleicher 1969, 460), which is what Macklem does when he envelops the "Declarative Statements of Law" found in General Assembly resolutions with exegeses of *opinio juris*. According to Bleicher, the dividing line between the principles enunciated by these juridical scholars and the bindingness of customary law is "scarcely discernable" (Bleicher 1969, 460). Joyner also rejects the idea of interpreting General Assembly resolutions as "Declarative Statements of Law" because "coalition politics in that organ [the General Assembly] can and often do obscure the real reasons motivating votes for and against resolutions. . . . Moreover, attaining a unanimous vote on a resolution, or for that matter, even having the recommendation redundantly recited in subsequent resolutions, cannot obviate the fact that such recourses fail to alter its legal station; the resolution remains a nonbinding recommendation" (Joyner 1981, 461).

I conclude that a good case can be made for the thesis that the resolutions and declarations in which the collectivist human rights of the third generation are proclaimed to the world have nowhere near the legal validity that bone fide human rights conventions have.

Amending the Universal Declaration

My main objection to this dominance of third-generation collectivist human rights in the conception of what ties the human rights family together is the idea that the role of the UDHR and its connection with the Holocaust has been ignored. To bolster this main objection, I show how in 1966 the international community amended the UDHR with an article in the ICCPR that acknowledges the human rights of members of minority groups that had been "set aside" in 1948.

UDHR Article 27 and the Cultural Defense of Nations

I begin my discussion of amending the Universal Declaration with the widely held belief—including at one time by myself—that the Universal Declaration has a more obvious cultural blind spot than the omission of the Humphrey-Lauterpacht minority rights article discussed in chapter 3. I have in mind the clear assimilationist wording of UDHR Article 27(1): "Everyone has the right freely to participate in the cultural life of the community." The reference to "the" cultural life of "the" community argues against any acknowledgment here that a person's life as a citizen of a nation need not have an attachment or identification with the national culture of his or her nation. This article was crafted with the same assimilationist mind-set that blocked a minority rights article from being adopted in 1948, making for two UDHR cultural blind spots: one hidden because "set aside" and one openly displayed in the text of Article 27. As I defend the inclusion of this article in the declaration and then also want to see the declaration amended with ICCPR Article 27, it is crucial that my reader keep in mind that UDHR Article 27 is part of a set of articles and should not be lifted out of the context that the entire set supplies. Doing so might lead to a "majoritarian nationalism" that, according to Mukul Kesavan (2018), has led to genocidal consequences in Myanmar and to other "Murderous Majorities" in South Asian states. So, UDHR Article 27 requires the restraining influence of all other UDHR rights—especially of Article 18 about freedom of religion—and the amendment I plead for in the next section.

UDHR Article 27 is a good example of what Will Kymlicka in 1989 described as "the current liberal hostility to minority rights" (Kymlicka 1989, 214). Bhikhu Parekh (2000, 110) and Charles Taylor (1994, 26–28) have made similar criticisms of this liberal assimilationist stance toward minority participation in culture. Before I discuss the need to amend this liberal stance of the declaration with ICCPR Article 27, I briefly defend UDHR Article 27 on participation in culture as it stands. It is not as far off the mark as might seem at first. Both philosophically and practically, Article 27 can be seen as a much-needed element for the cultural defense of nations, which puts a question mark behind the multiculturalist criticisms of a text like the Universal Declaration.

I glean my defense of UDHR Article 27 from the first three steps of a four-step argument constructed by Alan Patten in his 2014 book, *Equal Recognition: The Moral Foundations of Minority Rights*. These three steps are as follows:

1. "The state has strong reason to embrace policies that secure conditions of individual freedom."
2. "To be free, individuals must have access to an adequate range of options."
3. "Culture plays a role in making available an adequate range of options." (Patten 2014, 74–75; I add and discuss Patten's fourth step at the start of the next section.)

Culture for Patten (and those he criticizes) matters because it gives people a range of options to live meaningful lives. He calls this the "social lineage account of culture" (sec. 2.4) and spends two whole chapters explaining what that entails. It basically means that cultures give their participants a range of choices in speaking, living, working, and playing from which they can choose to build meaningful lives for themselves. A century ago the Dutch in western Michigan did this in one way, and today the Cuban expatriates in Miami do it in another way; French speakers in Quebec make their choices, while Flemish speakers in Belgium make others. All these participants had and have a sufficient range of choices within what both Patten and his critics call "societal cultures." That kind of culture is the subject of step 3 of the argument, in which Patten tells us that "culture plays a role in making available an adequate range of options" to its members.

As his subtitle indicates, Patten focuses on what he calls an "options disadvantage" that often plagues members of minorities. His language "consciously echoes not only Margalit and Raz but also Will Kymlicka's proposal that culture is valuable to its members as a context of choice" (Patten 2014, 70). Culture provides a context of choice for someone who lives in a minority culture in Quebec or in the Turkish region of Iraq or in any of the much smaller ethnic enclaves in modern cosmopolitan cities like London, New York, Vancouver, or Miami; in these places, he or she has close to enough choices for a full life.

But I see step 3 as also applicable to the majoritarian cultures of any one of our Westphalian nation-states. This broader application of the argument yields the cultural defense of nations that the drafters of UDHR Article 27 created when they spoke about the right of participation in *the* culture of *the* community. Patten devotes many pages to showing how majoritarian cultures can in various ways accommodate and pay special attention to members of minority groups. One important way is through the adoption of a package of basic civil or human rights. In a section called "The Access Account," he gives us a good summary of the thinking behind UDHR Article 2(1). He describes three mechanisms through which a state's minority citizens are excluded from having a wide enough range of options in the majority culture: "control," in which members of the majority culture control the options available for members of minority cultures; "prejudice," in which "many members of the majority culture have negative attitudes about the minority culture"; and "identifiability," in which "members of the minority culture have certain conspicuous characteristics based on appearance, or accent, or surname, or some other trait" (Patten 2014, 79–80). These mechanisms explain why a loss of cultural access may "bring about an options disadvantage for members of a disappearing minority culture" (80), in which case the government should intervene with new policies.

These mechanisms informed the UDHR drafters' thinking when they expanded the short UN Charter's list of "race, sex, language, and religion" to their own much longer list in Article 2(1): "race, color, sex, language, religion, political or other opinion, national or social origin, property, birth or other status." Also, the majority of the UDHR drafters might not have balked at our own later additions of "disability" and "sexual preference." So, UDHR Article 27 cannot stand alone. It must be supplemented by the nondiscrimination list of Article 2(1). Patten also discusses how education systems and curricula can throw up impediments to accessing the majority culture, depending on what "generic capacities of literacy, numeracy, social skills, technological skill, and, above all, competence in the language in which institutions and practices operate" they teach. By requiring that "everyone" be given these generic capacities, UDHR Article 26 also wants to avoid saddling a child with an "options disadvantage." Also, Article 16 of the declaration, which deals with marriage rights, says that "men and women of full age, without any limitation due to race, nationality or religion, have the right to marry and found a family" and that these vows must be undertaken "only with the free and full consent of the intending spouses."

It would seem then that UDHR Article 27 paired with a strong enforcement of Articles 2(1), 16, and 26 is the correct fallback position to take when it comes to the right to participate in culture. But not all these generic capacities operate at the same level of abstraction. Writes Patten: "Whereas numeracy implies mastery of a convention that is universal or near-universal in scope, competence in a language means mastery . . . of a convention that is local to some culture, so that language proficiency is typically a *locally* generic capacity" (Patten 2014, 81; original italics). He continues, "Mostly obviously, if minority language speakers are not also competent in the majority language, then they will not be able to participate in the practices and institutions that operate in the majority-language medium" (81), and so they may suffer an options disadvantage when, for example, it comes to gaining access to social services provided by the state, as called for in UDHR Article 25.

It turns out that the model today, as it was in 1948, is still that of a voluntary assimilation or integration into the main cultural tradition of a nation. What has changed is the fact that far more than in the past, this assimilation must be primarily and mostly voluntary. The state must not be too forceful when it nudges its citizens to integrate into the mainstream to gain an adequate range of options for living what to them are meaningful lives. Patten devotes the whole of chapter 6 to how a country like the United States can do that by offering different kinds of ESL courses up and down the educational ladder. The notion of a "societal culture" that supplies ample choices to its members, which Kymlicka uses primarily to refer to substate national units—like those of Quebec, Catalonia, Scotland, Wales, and Kurdistan—applies equally well to the nation-states that make up our Westphalian system. It is only when we assume that there is a dominant national culture that we can and should worry about any kind of loss for the cultural rights of minorities. UDHR Article 27 articulates this background vision and possibly, but not obviously, incorrectly assumes that members of minority groups will assimilate or, in Patten's term, "integrate."

Not just philosophically but practically speaking, the time may also have come for theorists to call for protection of majoritarian cultural traditions. The tables Liav Orgad presents in his book *A Cultural Defense of Nations* (2015) indicate that in the last fifty years, we have seen significant changes in the percentages of "international migrant stock" between "more developed regions," where the percentage of migrant stock rose from 3.6 in 1960 to 10.1 in 2010, and "less developed regions," where it dropped from 2.1 to 1.4. As expected, in Africa (from 3.2 to 1.9), Asia (from 1.7 to 1.4), and Latin America and the Caribbean (from 2.8 to 1.3), the percentage of migrant stock went down, while in Europe (from 3.4 to 9.5), North America (from 6.7 to 14.2), and Oceania (from 13.5 to 16.8), it rose significantly (Orgad 2015, 22). Naturally, these migration figures are reflected in the percentages for individual countries. Italy's migrant figure rose in fifty years from 0.9 to 19.6, Norway's figure went from 1.7 to 10.0, and the US figure rose from 5.8 in 1960 to 13.5 in 2010 (23). Orgad points out that in Austria, Belgium, Canada, Greece, Italy, Luxembourg, Spain, Sweden, and Switzerland, "the net migration to national population growth [between 2005 and 2010] was slightly higher than the contribution of natural increase (births minus deaths)" (23). If these trends continue, we can readily grasp why Orgad's table 1.3 shows that the percentages of "persons with a foreign background" will rise in the European Union from 10.4 in 2011 to 24.0 in 2051. This means that in Austria, Belgium, Cyprus, Germany, and Spain, "the current majority becomes a minority" (25). Extending these projections to the United States, Orgad's table 1.4 shows that the non-Hispanic white percentage of the population will decrease between 2010 and 2050 from 64.7 to 46.3, making it also a minority (28). All other racial and ethnic groups—Hispanics, American Indians and Alaska natives (AIAN), blacks, and Native Hawaiian and other Pacific Islanders (NHPIs), and those of two or more races—will all rise, the most dramatic increase being that of people of Hispanic origin (which can be of any race), rising from 16.0 to 30.2 (28).

These figures and trends explain why Orgad's book has the title it has: *The Cultural Defense of Nations*. As he notes in his introduction, "Trans-cultural diffusion is greater today than in any other period in human history. The 'other' is present in the national boundaries not just physically, but also spiritually" (Orgad 2015, 2). As a result, these democracies have set out to tighten their immigration laws to ensure the continuation of the majority's cultural autonomy and identity. This new threat complicates but does not negate the thesis of this chapter: that not all generations of human rights should be given equal status in the human rights family. The lesson is that today the right to participate in culture is no longer just a question for members of minority groups. It is and will very much be a human right that endangered majorities also want and need to claim. Orgad names and discusses four such groups:

1. The diminishing majority, in which the majority feels that significant immigration will greatly affect its majority culture;
2. The regional-minority majority, in which the majority in a nation feels like a minority when it is viewed regionally;

3. The victimized majority, in which "the majority has a rich history of being persecuted" (193);
4. The minoritized majority, in which "the national majority displays a state of mind of a minority" (194).

The new threats to majority cultures do not take away the need to amend the Universal Declaration with ICCPR Article 27; they give the needed amendment its proper context.

Amending the Universal Declaration with ICCPR Article 27

We are now ready for step 4 of Patten's argument cited earlier. The first three of the steps were (1) the state must be interested in the freedom of its people, (2) its people must therefore have an ample range of choices, and (3) those choices must include an ample range of cultural options. Add to this step 4: "When a culture is lost, its members are left without one of the necessary conditions of freedom," and we reach the multiculturalist conclusion that "the state has strong reason to embrace policies intended to prevent cultures from being lost" (Patten 2015, 74–75).

The 1966 ICCPR Article 27 that I am proposing we look at as an amendment to the Universal Declaration—to complete the UDHR's philosophical framework—is the international community's response to the loss suffered by members of minority cultures under, for instance, conditions of discrimination. For Patten's terminology of "choice" and "loss" to make practical sense, we must understand it against the background of a dominant and probably majoritarian cultural tradition, such as what I laid out as the basis of UDHR Article 27. When cultures threaten to go extinct or become weaker—say, because of dwindling numbers—that leads to what Patten calls an "options disadvantage" (70) for members of these disappearing or struggling cultures. That is what step 4 of Patten's argument and its conclusion tell us. The loss of cultural options and the conclusion that the state needs to prevent that sort of loss fit precisely what ICCPR Article 27 asks ratifying nations to do. I now ask my reader to recall from our chapter 2 discussion of the Humphrey-Lauterpacht minority rights article that the proposed article was not included, not

1966 ICCPR Article 27	1948 Minority Rights Proposal
In those States, in which ethnic, religious or linguistic *persons* belonging to such minorities shall not be denied the right, in community with other members of their group, to enjoy their own culture, to profess and practice their own religion, or to use their own language.	In States inhabited by a substantial number of *persons* of a race, language or religion other than those of the majority of the population, persons belonging to such ethnic, linguistic or religious minorities shall have the right, as far as compatible with public order and security to establish and maintain schools and cultural or religious institutions and to use their own language in the Press, in public assembly and before the courts and other authorities of the State.

FIGURE 5.1: 1966 ICCPR Article 27 and proposed 1948 UDHR article

because its proponents did not have the vote but because they were not well-enough organized. For comparison, I have placed these two texts side by side.

Given how similar these two articles are, it makes a good deal of sense to consider the 1966 version as an amendment to the Universal Declaration, *as if* the Humphrey-Lauterpacht minority rights proposal had been adopted in 1948, which it was not. The reader will notice that in each article I italicized the word "persons." I want to draw attention to the fact that each of these versions is crafted with an individualist ontology, as was the UDHR as a whole. The rights involved belong in the first instance to the members of minority groups and not to the groups as such. This section will focus on the question of whether human rights belong in first instance only to individual persons or can also and in the same manner belong to the groups they join, are born into, or are subsumed under. I discuss the proposed amendment in two steps. First, I place this ICCPR Article 27 in the company of other human rights texts of that time, all of which operate with this same individualist ontology. They all follow the UDHR paradigm of ascribing human rights only to flesh and blood human beings. Second, I consider the question of what then to do with "national minorities." The relevant UN debates show that these kinds of minorities are not covered by this amendment. The problem is that national minority rights more often than not involve collective claims to land or territory. Since groups as such are not flesh and blood human beings, it is my view that they therefore cannot possess human rights.

The Early Reign of Individualist Ontology

There are, I argue, no such things as territorial *human* rights. Though its reasoning was different, the international community in my view was correct when it excluded these collectivities from being covered by ICCPR Article 27. Just as UDHR Article 27 applies only to individuals, so only *members* of national minorities can be said to have human rights. While groups may well be special from an economic or security perspective, only group members, and not the groups as such, count from a human rights perspective. This outcome conflicts with what Will Kymlicka (for a long time) and Alan Patten (2014, sec. 7.3) have maintained. This difference in ontology might be the reason these theorists often speak of collectivist rights *simpliciter* and not of collectivist *human* rights.

Allen Buchanan—whom I criticized in the preceding chapter for selling short the declaration's moral significance—also reserves the phrase "human rights" for individuals because in the international legal system "ultimately" (his word) only individuals count morally. Legal rights can and constantly are being ascribed to nations, to groups, and to corporations, but none of these entities can be said to have moral rights. The reason is that collectivities like nations and groups *as such* are not moral entities. For instance, according to Buchanan, the "ascription of group rights to indigenous peoples could only challenge the conceptual framework of an individualistic moral theory of international law [such as his own] if group rights in the sense of (2)—[i.e.] if groups are understood to be the *possessors* of the rights in question, where the reference to groups is not simply shorthand for saying that the right is a right of each member of the group" (Buchanan 2004, 413; original emphasis). He explains, "To understand why this is so, it is important to emphasize the so-called individualist framework is only individualist in a *justificatory* sense: According to moral individualism in the justificatory sense, all justifications for moral and legal rights (and duties) must be grounded ultimately on consideration of the well-being and freedom of individuals" (413; original emphasis). The question Buchanan is left with, he writes, "is whether individualism in the justificatory sense is compatible with group rights in the sense of (2), rights whose possessors are groups. It clearly *is*, if the sense (2) group rights are *legal* rights; but not if they are *moral* rights" (413; original emphasis). That is my own view as well. It means that the international community can ascribe all the legal rights it wants, but if it wants to be true to the mother text of moral human rights, that is, the UDHR, and make its international legal ascriptions reflect the moral human rights standard set forth in that text, then no group rights can enter the domain of human rights proper. That is indeed the picture we get from much—but as the next section shows, not all—of human rights legal history.

The international community has certainly moved far beyond the simple assimilationism reflected in the unamended UDHR Article 27. Elsa Stamatopoulou's 2007 book, *Cultural Rights in International Law: Article 27 of the Universal Declaration of Human Rights and Beyond*, is mostly about the *Beyond*. Her book shows us that the international community has moved far beyond the assimilationism of the 1940s. Many central legal human rights instruments (like the ICCPR, the ICESCR, CEDAW, CRC, ICERD, and UN-affiliated organizations, like the UN International Children's Emergency Fund [UNICEF]) have corrected the alleged cultural myopia of the 1948 Universal Declaration. Stamatopoulou's fourth chapter is devoted to the cultural rights of indigenous peoples and minorities as well as of women, children, youth, persons with disabilities, migrant workers, refugees, other noncitizens, and the poor. As to my ontology question, while human rights, for example, to association, to education, and even to food are possessed by individuals, they are practiced in common with others (Stamatopoulou 2007, 53). To say then that a group has this right is, in Buchanan's words, "shorthand" for saying that in the first instance its individual members have this right. Stamatopoulou admits that throughout her book she has "focused mostly on the right [of individuals] to participate in cultural life, which is the most comprehensive of cultural rights" (243). Contrast this with her admission that collective rights present special problems. She writes, "Although cultural rights have not always been called collective rights in international instruments, it is logically and morally impossible not to recognize the collective elements of cultural rights when speaking about [national] minorities and indigenous peoples" (248). While there are the collective aspects to cultural rights—especially to those of national minorities and indigenous peoples (discussed later)—generally internationally recognized human rights follow the individualist paradigm of the UDHR, even in Stamatopoulou's updated account of participation in culture.

The four paragraphs of ICESCR Article 15 stick to this individualist ontology but change the nationalist impulse of UDHR Article 27 discussed earlier. The first paragraph of ICESCR Article 15 states, "The States Parties to the present Covenant recognize the right of everyone: (a) To take part in cultural life"; the rest of the article expands on this. This wording leaves the choice of which cultural life or lives to participate in totally up to the individual. Stamatopoulou reports that in 1952 UN discussions of this 1(a) segment of ICESCR Article 15, an amendment was offered to "include in 1(a) some notion of restriction," the idea being that "everyone has the right to participate in the cultural life 'of the communities to which he belongs'" (Stamatopoulou 2007, 17). The same attempt was made in the Third Committee in November 1954 (Saul 2016, 2143/par. 75). Each time the more restrictive idea was rejected. This restrictive notion is not as assimilationist as the original wording of UDHR Article 27, which speaks of *the* cultural life of *the* community, but it still restricts an individual's right to participate in the culture of just those communities "to which he belongs." It takes the fluidity and some of the choice out of the stated right "to take part in cultural life," whether newly endangered or not. My italicizing the word "persons" in figure 5.1 above highlights this individualist mold. We see the same thing in other main human rights texts—and I have again highlighted the relevant terms—the Convention on the Elimination of Discrimination against *Women* speaks of the rights of women (plural) as individuals; the Convention on the Rights of the *Child* throughout speaks of the rights of the child (singular); the International Convention on the Elimination of All Forms of Racial Discrimination says that "*everyone*" has the right to be free from discrimination. The titles of both the Declaration on the Rights of *Persons* Belonging to National or Ethnic, Religious, and Linguistic Minorities and the International Convention on the Protection of All Migrant *Workers* and *Members* of Their Families also have their individualist ontologies written on their faces.

As happened in discussions of the UDHR, in these covenantal discussions the individualist ontology was intimately linked to the principle of nondiscrimination as the best way to safeguard the rights that ontology yielded, which is why Buchanan based his EBS feature on the presence of so many nondiscrimination articles in the system. Stamatopoulou also hints at this emphasis on nondiscrimination when she reports on the program of action of the 2001 World Conference against Racism, Racial Discrimination, Xenophobia, and Related Intolerance: "Above all the World Conference projected the vision of multiracial and multi-cultural societies living together in harmony, the vision of societies that would reshape their modern identities in light of the new international realities, with a commitment to non-discrimination and human rights" (Stamatopoulou 2007, 28). The cement holding multicultural societies together is the principle of nondiscrimination that lies at the root of Buchanan's equal basic status feature (discussed in chapter 4), and nondiscrimination is the chief tool Patten suggests states use to combat the three mechanisms of exclusion we discussed in the preceding section. This principle was carried over to the question of minority cultural rights.

National Minorities Not Covered in ICCPR Article 27

From the start it was laid down that the main purpose of ICCPR Article 27 was "a general prohibition of discrimination [and that] differential treatment might be granted to minorities in order to ensure them real equality of status with the other elements of the population" (Bossuyt 1987, 491). That is what Patten has in mind with his "equal recognition" approach to participation in culture. The main way for nations to protect members of minority groups is through strict adherence to the principle of nondiscrimination; this is what most UDHR drafters thought and why they had so little interest in a specific minority rights article. In the early 1950s, phrases like "long established," "distinct," "well defined," "national," and "stable" were all rejected in favor of the broader and more generic "persons belonging to ethnic, linguistic or religious minorities." There was not much support for and a lot of ambivalence about accepting other words and phrases that could possibly lead to demands for special protection of "national minorities." This ambivalence is reflected in the ten abstentions (five votes for and one against) on a 1953 vote to not use the phrases "well defined" and "have long been established" in the text of ICCPR Article 27 (494). The 1953 decision not to cover national minorities echoes a 1948 Belgian proposal that the words "historically constituted" be added to the minority rights article then being considered for the declaration. Owing to a lack of support, the Belgian proposal was not even voted on. Similarly, in 1953 the question of how to deal with national minorities and indigenous peoples was quickly dismissed. Indigenous peoples as such were dismissed when the Third Committee "stressed that the autochthonous population in Latin American countries could not be regarded as a minority. It should be treated as a vital part of the nation and should be assisted in attaining the same levels of development as the remainder of the population" (496).

As to national minorities, we read in the report of the ninth session of the Human Rights Commission to the Third Committee: "Provisions concerning the rights of minorities . . . should not be applied in such a manner as to encourage the creation of new minorities or to obstruct the process of assimilation" (E/CN.4/SR.368/10). This ninth session rejected a text that specifically applied minority rights to national minorities. During the UN debates on ICCPR Article 27, the question was raised whether Article 18(3)'s right to manifest one's religion, "subject only to such limitations" as are described in UDHR Article 29, needed to be repeated in the planned ICCPR Article 27. The delegations from China, India, and Turkey, among others, thought there "was no need to do so, since article 18 was of a general nature and applied to 'everyone', therefore to minorities and majorities alike" (Bossuyt 1987, 497; A/5000, para. 124). The covenant's drafters understood the difference between religion and culture. Whereas the state can for the most part be neutral and respect everyone's right to practice his or her religion in his or her own way, subject to the limitations of UDHR Article 29 (Morsink 2017, chap. 2), neutrality is not so easy when it comes to participation in culture. In the case of culture, Patten is right to argue that a state's supposed neutrality by itself does not really work. Symbols, flags, holidays, language policies, and finances get in the way of a strict hands-off culture policy. Some cultural traditions, most likely those of the majority, are bound to come out ahead and thrive, while others, probably minority ones, might be at an "options disadvantage." Hence the declaration needs a minority rights amendment like ICCPR Article 27. However, for security reasons national minorities were not included in the scope of ICCPR Article 27 unless seen from an individualist and therefore basic nondiscrimination perspective.

In the 1953 ninth session of the Human Rights Commission, the Soviet Union proposed that "the State shall ensure to national minorities the right to use their native tongue and to possess their national schools, libraries, museums and other cultural and educational institutions" (Bossuyt 1987, 496; E/CN.4/L222). Note the collectivist ontology here. Probably because it has the land factor attached to it, the phrase "national minorities" was rejected by eight votes to four, with four abstentions (Bossuyt 1987, 496; E/CN.4/SR.371/6). The worry expressed in the 1948 Haitian motion (with which we ended chapter 3)—that these kinds of rights might endanger the unity and security of member states—also dominated these UN debates some three years later. A Yugoslav-proposed second paragraph to the Soviet proposal makes this clear: "Such rights may not be interpreted as entitling any group settled in the territory of a State, under specific terms of its immigration laws to request special privileges or to form within that state separate communities which might impair its national unity or security" (Bossuyt 1987, 496; E/CN.4/L225). This paragraph was rejected by seven votes to five, with four abstentions (Bossuyt 1987, 496; E/CN.4/SR.371/6). Implicit in these negative votes is a rejection of a collectivist ontology with which to define minority rights, leaving ICCPR Article 27 with just an individualist ontology. Because they were worried about their national security, delegates representing their nations were reluctant to extend human rights to whole groups instead of to individuals within groups.

This ontology question did not go unnoticed. Delegates from the United Kingdom and India wanted to know "whether protection should be accorded to individual members of a minority group or to the group as such" (Bossuyt 1987, 497; A/5000, para. 122). While opinions differed, the majority seems to have had national unity and security uppermost in mind. And the overall context was still assimilation into the majority culture, which should be achieved voluntarily in such a way "that members of minority groups should not be deprived of the rights enjoyed by other citizens of the same state, so as to enable them to integrate should they so desire" (Bossuyt 1987, 497). Clearly, ontological limitations are placed on the practice of "minority rights," even in this locus classicus. The majority of the covenant drafters sought to protect their nations against threats that "might impair its national unity or security" (Bossuyt 1987, 495; A/2929, chap. IV, para. 186), which is why they opted for an individualist ontology similar to the Humphrey-Lauterpacht article left aside in 1948.

Liav Orgad, whose tables I used at the end of the preceding section to show that some cultural majorities also worry about their cultural attachments and identifications, gives five reasons why it is not appropriate for these majorities, whether "newly endangered" or not, to make use of ICCPR Article 27. His first reason supports my argument for not letting land claims into the domain of the human rights family. Land claims would involve, as he puts it, a "shift *from individual to collective rights*" (Orgad 2015, 173; original italics). Orgad correctly notes that ICCPR "Article 27 was not designed to create or protect collective rights. The ICCPR and the Universal Declaration of Human Rights do not focus on group rights, but on the principle of non-discrimination" (173). He is right. The UDHR blind spot I explored in chapter 3 is diminished by the fact that the list of nondiscrimination items in Article 2 of the 1966 ICESCR—according to which some 150 "States parties to the present Covenant undertake to guarantee that the rights enunciated in the present Covenant will be exercised without discrimination of any kind as to race, colour, sex, language, religion, political or other opinion, national or social origin, birth or other status"—was taken from Article 2(1) of the 1948 Universal Declaration. If Orgad's figures of immigrant stock hold up, that nondiscrimination fix may no longer be enough. This could place an extra burden on the realization of UDHR Article 27, probably making it less voluntary.

Second, Orgad rightly notes that ICCPR Article 27 is phrased in the negative (rights are not to be denied) but that now other kinds of positive measures are called for. Third and very important, the ICCPR Committee has widened the scope of Article 27 to extend protection to "migrant workers" and "visitors in a state" (Orgad 2015, 174). The committee did this in its General Comment 23, when it noted that "it is not relevant to determine the degree of permanence that the term 'exists' connotes" (Fiftieth Session 1994, para. 5.2). The relevance here is to the article's opening sentence: "In those States in which ethnic, religious or linguistic minorities exist, persons belonging to these minorities shall not be denied the right, in community with the other members of their group, to enjoy their own culture, to profess and practice their own religion, or to use their own language" (para. 5.2) If there is no permanence built into the "exist" here, then the groups involved can be of any minority, including those of immigrant stock mentioned in Orgad's (2015) tables and discussed in Patten's (2014) chapter 8. The members of a minority group, the committee noted, "need not be nationals or citizens, they need not be permanent residents. Thus migrants workers, or even visitors, in a State Party, constituting such minorities are entitled not to be denied the exercise of those rights" (Fiftieth Session 1994, para. 5.3). This very much accentuates an individualist ontology for the right to participate in the culture or religion of one's group, whatever the language used.

Fourth, Orgad points out that "in the mid-1980s global interest in indigenous rights increased" and that these groups no longer want to be classified as minority groups (Orgad 2015, 174). He notes that the 2007 declaration adopted by the General Assembly recognizes indigenous peoples' claims to "ancestral lands, cultural preservation, self-governance, and the like" (174). Paragraph 7 of the ICCPR Committee's General Comment 23 sets aside how culture manifests itself differently in indigenous peoples, whose "way of life [is] associated with the use of land resources" in the way of "fishing or hunting and the right to live in reserves protected by law" (Fiftieth Committee 1994, paras. 7, 3.2). Fifth, Orgad points us to "an *expansion of national minority rights*" (Orgad 2015, 176; original italics). Rights for these groups were left out of earlier texts, like the 1948 UDHR, the 1950 European Convention, and the two 1966 international covenants, but are now demanded "by groups of all kinds" (176). The committee's denial that there is any permanence to the word "exist" in ICCPR Article 27 supports the earlier cited *travaux* of the article in which coverage was denied to national minorities with land claims.

These individualist readings of ICCPR Article 27 stand in tension with what Will Kymlicka, the dean of multicultural studies, has been arguing for decades. They conflict with the collectivist tone that Kymlicka often uses when defending multiculturalism. But he does not explicitly draw out the land factor embedded in the thesis that "national minorities are [to be] allowed to engage in their own nation-building, to enable them to maintain themselves as distinct societal cultures" (Kymlicka and Opalski 2001, 48). Even in cases of multinational federalism when a minority cultural tradition overlaps with a unit of a federation, the land question is overshadowed by other tools of nation building, like language laws, education policy, and public service employment, as they also are in Patten's discussion. In a drawing called "The Dialectic of Nation-Building and Minority Rights," Kymlicka and Opalski's list of "Tools of State Nation-Building" includes citizenship policy, an item not repeated in the list of "Minority Rights Claims" (49). The matter of statecraft and citizenship policy is left ambiguous between the clear right "to state nation-building" of a sovereign Westphalian state and a minority with similar, often unspoken ambitions.

In a 2010 contribution ("Minority Rights in Political Philosophy and International Law") to a volume on the philosophy of international law, Kymlicka made his views more explicit. He explored the gap that has developed between international law and his own philosophy of liberal multiculturalism. Both areas have, he said, been "seeking alternatives to earlier models of the unitary, homogeneous 'nation-state'" (Kymlicka 2010, 379) that I identified with the adoption of UDHR Article 27. However, developments in international law have not kept up with developments in political philosophy that seek to do justice to minority rights claims. Kymlicka believes that the adoption of ICCPR Article 27 has been of no help because it "does not articulate rights that are tied to the fact that a group is living on (what it views as) its historic homeland. Yet it is precisely claims related to residence on a historic homeland that are at stake in most violent ethnic conflicts around the world, whether in post-communist Europe (Bosnia, Kosovo, Chechnya), or the West (Basque Country, Cyprus, Northern Ireland), or Asia, Africa, and the Middle East (for example Pakistan, Sri Lanka, Indonesia, Turkey, Iraq, Israel, Sudan, Ethiopia)" (381).

A proposed article for a future convention on the rights of minorities in Europe promised to bring the two sides together. It read, "In the regions where they are a majority, the persons belonging to a national minority shall have the right to have at their disposal appropriate local or autonomous authorities or to have special status, matching this specific *historical and territorial situation* and in accordance with the domestic legislation of the state" (Kymlicka 2010, 383n3; italics added). If adopted, this would have been the first international legally binding convention to honor the idea of "homelands" claimed by certain national minorities. Its collectivist ontology with territorial claims for national minorities would have supplemented the portable claims of individuals laid out in ICCPR Article 27. Kymlicka does not think that the yielding of "territorial authority" to these minorities amounts to giving them the right to (external) self-determination that under international law only already existing nation-states can claim. While he saw the difference here as a "semantic disagreement," the upshot of the European discussions was that the Framework Convention for the Protection of National Minorities adopted in Strasbourg in February 1995 does *not* include this proposed minorities' "homeland" article.

The convention shuns and stays away from defining the human rights involved with a collectivist ontology. Kymlicka's conclusion—which he states at the start of his essay—is that "There are some aspects of the theory and practice of liberal multiculturalism that have proven impossible to codify in the form of international norms" (Kymlicka 2010, 381). The European framework convention does indeed create such a gap. Section 1, Article 1 states that "the protection of national minorities and of the rights and freedoms of persons belonging to those minorities forms an integral part of the international protection of human rights." But then paragraph 31 of the "Commentary on the Provisions of the Framework Convention" tells us that this article "refers to the protection of national minorities as such and of the rights and freedoms of persons belonging to such minorities. This distinction and the difference in wording [between the group as such and its members] make it clear that no collective rights of national minorities are envisioned." I conclude from this that the convention does not envision any collectivist *human* rights. Article 5(1) spells out more clearly than could have been done in either of the 1966 international covenants what conditions states must create to help members of minority cultures "maintain and develop their culture," to which Article 5(2) adds that they should refrain from "policies or practices aimed at assimilation of persons belonging to national minorities against their will and shall protect these persons from any action aimed at such assimilation." Throughout, the framework convention stresses the free activity of the members of minority cultures and puts the survival and thriving of these cultural traditions in the hands of their members, much like Patten also argued in his philosophical analogue to this legal text. However, at the end he seems to backtrack from this individualist ontological stand when he asserts that a state not federally constituted still must draw boundaries and assign powers "in such a way as to acknowledge the group as a group and give it space [read "territory"] in which to enjoy self-government" (Patten 2014, 241). This requirement of constitutional recognition seems very much in line with the preservationist approach Patten rejected earlier in the same book.

In this dispute between, on the one hand, theorists of multiculturalism that in extremis allow a collectivist right to land into the human rights family and, on the other, the UN and European debates that curtailed the scope of ICCPR Article 27, I take the side of the latter. In the volume on the philosophy of international law, Kymlicka's chapter "Minority Rights in Political Philosophy and International Law" is paired with Jeremy Waldron's "Two Conceptions of Self-Determination." Waldron criticizes what he calls Kymlicka's and Raz's identity-based approach to minority rights. He takes the same kaleidoscopic approach to minority rights as (for the most part) Patten does. Waldron writes, "People pick and choose among options furnished by a variety of cultures, individual cultures that are not their own. They may locate their religious practice and their family ties in the culture to which they take themselves to 'belong', while looking elsewhere for their politics, their career, and their recreation" (Waldron 2010,

403). Waldron believes that "the 'menus' from which people make their autonomous choices have exactly this disorderly character." Children, for example, "often tolerate or relish a certain tension between" their own more modern ways and their parents' more traditional ways (403). This criticism of the identity-based approach to minority rights is the negative side of Waldron's ledger.

On the positive side, he places his own territorial-based approach to these rights, which I discuss in some detail at the end of the next section. It leads him to defend a Westphalian realist approach to international law and world affairs, one within which human rights law must perform its mission. We see this larger domain of peoples' (external and internal) self-determination reflected in the common Article 1 of the two international covenants that are the subject of our next section. In my discussion of that article, I make use of Waldron's Westphalian arguments, not because the collectivities involved do not have any international rights (they obviously do) but to make the point that they cannot have international *human* rights, which is also Waldron's underlying theme. Politically and legally, states and their subnational units must work out their disagreements as peacefully as they can and whenever possible constitutionally, all the while protecting the portable human rights of all the individuals involved.

Appellation Contrôlée and Common Article 1

Appellation Contrôlée is the method that Philip Alston recommends be used to inject "substantive requirements" into whatever procedures the United Nations uses to adopt new human rights. In various essays (Alston 1982, 1984, 2001), he has bemoaned the sloppy way in which those UN adoptions, starting in the 1950s, have taken place. It is, he believes (and I agree), a question of quality control. The French use the *Appellation Contrôlée* designation for their wines to indicate that a certain wine "was made in the prescribed manner, taking account of the conditions and traditions prevailing in the relevant region. It also attests that the proper ingredients were used and that quality was not sacrificed to quantity" (Alston 1984, 618–19). Two years before he had asked whether the introduction of "solidarity rights" was a "progressive development or obfuscation of international human rights law," clearly opting for the second choice. In this essay he criticized the very concept of "generations" of human rights, as Macklem has also done, but with opposite results. Alston's fifth objection to this kind of terminology is its suggestion that "the resort to generational terminology in order to develop new rights implies that the best human rights response to new needs or changing circumstances is the formulation of additional rights as part of a new generation, rather than the progressive development of the content of existing rights" (Alston 1982, 317). Both essays turn the screws on these developments and hint at my own thesis that the International Bill of Human Rights, comprising the UDHR and the two covenants, is good enough as it is. Writes Alston: "In a field where understanding of existing international norms is poor, the further 'sophistication' introduced by the concept of third generation solidarity rights seems more likely to confuse and complicate than to enlighten and clarify" (319). Alston wants to apply the *Appellation Contrôlée* method to the way the UN General Assembly vets proposals for new human rights, leading him to suggest a seven-step method for quality control. My interest in preserving the connection between the Holocaust and the declaration makes me sympathetic to this proposal. I think all new human rights proposals should be measured against the "common standard of achievement" announced in the UDHR and its most legitimate—meaning individualist—offspring.

To make Alston's case in my own way, I first exhibit the tremendous human rights inflation that has taken place since the 1948 UDHR adoption and that has upset and possibly ended the early reign of the individualist ontology. I want to show that applying the *Appellation Contrôlée* method mostly threatens the human rights of the third generation of human rights. The rights in the first two generations are safe because they are part of the International Bill of Human Rights, which comprises the UDHR and the two international covenants adopted in 1966. After I have shown in a table the inflation that has taken place and reported on Alston's *Contrôlée* of seven steps, I discuss the common Article 1 as an exhibit of how I think we can use Alston's idea of quality control to curtail this inflation.

Alston is more of a proceduralist than I am. He countenances a few collectively held rights as genuinely human because the General Assembly said they were. We part ways when I draw a line between the first two generations and the third generation on the basis of the ontology of the rights involved and not just on the fiat of the General Assembly, no matter how carefully considered. Accordingly, I have indicated in the last column of table 5.1 the ontology of certain UN-sponsored texts. It is wholly individualist and thus fits with the (amended) UDHR, or it is mostly or wholly collectivist and does not fit the UDHR model, or it is both because it has individualist as well as collectivist ontology clauses. The best example of this mixed approach is the 1981 African Charter of Human and Peoples' Rights. To cover the wide range of peoples' human rights, I allowed the table to grow to over twenty items, omitting numerous others. I mark the peoples' rights texts that I want to demote with the label "collectivist ontology," meaning that in that text human rights are ascribed to collectivities as such and not in first instance to the members.

I based my list of UN documents that grant peoples' rights on three sources. I used the list of seven from Macklem's discussion of third-generation rights, documents that I argued earlier have only quasi-legislative status instead of the full-fledged status of the two international covenants. For these seven I have included the vote tallies in the second to the last column. These seven are included in the list of twenty "Selected Documents on Peoples' Rights" that James Crawford included at the end of his *The Rights of Peoples* (1988) and that makes up the bulk of my table. I supplemented the Crawford list with a few items from Philip Alston's "The Rise and Fall of Peoples' Rights," the concluding essay to his volume *Peoples' Rights* (2001). These two volumes of essays contain the views of fourteen international law scholars on the topic of third-generation peoples' rights. What Crawford and Alston say about recent developments of peoples' rights carries great weight and supports my proposal to split up the third generation of human rights into first-order human rights inherent in individual human beings and second-order helpmates of third-generation peoples' human rights ascribed to collectivities by the UN General Assembly. My main objection to raising up these helpmates to an equal status with the first two generations is that they almost always involve a land or territorial factor, against which I also argued in the preceding section. This land factor is anathema to the very concept of modern Holocaust-inspired human rights.

Crawford begins his 1988 concluding reflections, "The excessive generality and the disregard for content demonstrated in some of the elaborations of new [human] rights not only raise questions about individual proposals, but reflect badly on the notion of a 'third generation' of [human] rights as such. Their relation to existing human rights is also problematic" (Crawford 1988, 159). Alston concluded his 2001 volume with the observation that "the best way to get a sense of the greatly diminished significance of peoples' rights during this fourth phase, and of their failure to live up to any of the more ambitious expectations that their proponents harbored in the preceding phases," is to take a quick view of how peoples' rights have fared in various policy areas. Alston then shows us "the fall" of peoples' rights in the areas of self-determination, minority rights, and indigenous peoples' rights and of the rights to peace, to environment, and to development. The only possible exception he allows has to do with the rights of indigenous peoples.

In his 2001 essay "Peoples' Rights: Their Rise and Fall," Alston divides his version of table 5.1 into four phases. The first one (1940–49) includes the United Nations Charter and the adoptions of the UDHR and the Genocide Convention. As I also point out in my case study, the UN Charter does not refer to the self-determination of peoples as a right, let alone as a *human* right. The charter instead makes it operate as a political principle. I put the UDHR in this table because I believe it gives us the standard of what a real human right is. It does not acknowledge the self-determination of peoples either as a principle or as any kind of right, except that in Articles 16, 22, and 29, it speaks of every individual person's right to the full development of his or her personality. Like Alston, I somewhat question the Genocide Convention as a bone fide collectivist document. It clearly has the outward appearance, but (in his words) "the Convention proceeds primarily by emphasizing the obligations of potential offenders . . . and the need to punish offenders rather than by proclaiming the rights of the groups who are thereby protected. Nevertheless, the Convention represents a significant step in the direction of recognizing certain rights as belonging to certain groups ('national, ethnical, racial or religious'), including peoples" (Alston 2001, 262).

In the second phase (1950–71), peoples' rights rose to prominence. Alston places four "landmark documents" in this phase. First,

TABLE 5.1: Ontology of UN human rights documents

Number	*Year*	*Document*	*Notes*	*Ontology*
1	1945	United Nations Charter	Uses the self-determination of peoples as a political principle	Individualist
2	1948	Universal Declaration of Human Rights (UDHR)	The Holocaust connection	Individualist
3	1948	UN Convention for the Prevention and Punishment of the Crime of Genocide	Has an individualist subtext	Collectivist
4	1957	International Labour Organization, Indigenous and Tribal Populations Convention (No. 107)	Ignored because of its assimilationism	Mostly individualist
5	1960	UN Declaration on the Granting of Independence to Colonial Countries and Peoples (A/RES/1514[XV])	Anti-colonialism in full swing Vote: 89-0-9	Collectivist
6	1962	UN Permanent Sovereignty over Natural Resources (A/RES/1803[XVII])	Rights of peoples and nations Vote: 87-2-12	Collectivist
7	1965	UN International Convention on the Elimination of All Forms of Racial Discrimination (A/RES/71/180)		Individualist
8	1966	UN International Covenant on Economic, Social, and Cultural Rights (ICESCR) (A/RES/2200[XXI])	Common Article 1 collectivist ontology	Overall individualist
9	1966	UN International Covenant on Civil and Political Rights (ICCPR) (A/RES/2200[XXI])	Common Article 1 collectivist ontology	Overall individualist
10	1966	UNESCO Declaration of Principles on International Cultural Cooperation		Collectivist
11	1970	Declaration on Principles of International Law concerning Friendly Relations and Cooperation among States in accordance with the Charter of the United Nations (A/RES/2625[XXV])	Adopted without a vote	Collectivist

TABLE 5.1: *continued*

Number	*Year*	*Document*	*Notes*	*Ontology*
12	1970	UN Declaration on the Establishment of a New International Economic Order (A/RES/3201[S-VI])	Adopted without a vote	Collectivist
13	1972	UN Convention concerning the Protection of the World Cultural and Natural Heritage		Collectivist
14	1974	UN International Convention on the Crime of Apartheid	Refers back to document 3	Collectivist
15	1976	Universal Declaration of the Rights of Peoples		Collectivist
16	1977	UN General Assembly Resolution on Alternate Approaches and Ways and Means within the United Nations System for Improving the Effective Enjoyment of Human Rights and Fundamental Freedoms (A/RES/32/130)	Peoples' rights as inalienable human rights	Collectivist
17	1978	UNESCO Declaration on Race and Racial Prejudice	Right to be different for individuals and groups	Primarily individualist
18	1979	UN General Assembly Resolution on Alternative Approaches and Ways and Means within the United Nations System for the Improvement of the Effective Enjoyment of Human Rights and Fundamental Freedoms (A/RES/34/48)	Emphasis on a nation's right to development	Mostly collectivist
19	1981	African Charter on Human and Peoples' Rights		Mixed
20	1981	UNESCO and the Struggle against Ethnocide, Declaration of San Jose		Mixed
21	1986	UN Declaration on the Right to Development (A/RES/41/128)	Vote: 146-1-8	Mixed

TABLE 5.1: *continued*

Number	*Year*	*Document*	*Notes*	*Ontology*
22	1992	UN Declaration on the Rights of Persons Belonging to National or Ethnic, Religious, and Linguistic Minority Cultures (A/RES/47/135)	Adopted without a vote	Individualist
23	2007	UN Declaration on the Rights of Indigenous Peoples (A/RES/61/295)	Vote: 143-4-11	Collectivist

Note: All the documents can be found online.

he includes the two international covenants (docs. 8 and 9) with their common Article 1, which I discuss in my case study. Also included is the Declaration on Granting Independence to Colonial Countries and Peoples (doc. 5), which obviously has collectivist ontology. This declaration does not even say that the real goal of independence is the enjoyment of first- and second-generation rights of the individuals who make up the peoples or inhabit the nations. The last landmark document is the 1970 Declaration on Principles of International Law concerning Friendly Relations and Cooperation among States in accordance with the Charter of the United Nations (doc. 11), which brings out a key feature that underlies many of peoples' rights texts. This feature is the claim of a people to sovereignty over its own territory (discussed more fully later). From control over its own land follows the right to mine its resources, to set up the kind of government it wants, and to set up the economic and cultural relations a people want to maintain with other peoples and their governments. Alston points out that in both the South West Africa and Namibia cases, the International Court of Justice upheld this principle of self-determination for peoples.

Alston tells us that during its third phase (1972–80), "the concept of peoples' rights, broadly defined, blossomed and reached its high-point" (Alston 2001, 264). The reader can see that during this phase UNESCO was quite active in enunciating peoples' rights (docs. 17

and 20). Regarding the Universal Declaration of the Rights of Peoples (doc. 15), Alston observes that General Assembly Resolution 32/130, on which it is based, "was widely seen as a turning point by many observers. Its assertion that 'all human rights . . . of the human person and of peoples are inalienable' and that the UN should give 'priority to the search for solutions to the mass and flagrant violations of human rights of peoples and persons'" (265). As I see it, this referring to both persons and peoples as having *human* rights conflicts with the idea that only flesh and blood human beings can have first-order human rights. Peoples' rights are not members of the human rights family in the way inherent moral rights of persons are, because peoples as such are not flesh and blood persons. My case study will elaborate on this point. The African Charter of Peoples and Human Rights makes the same mistake. It does not subordinate the rights of peoples to the goal of protecting individuals' human rights. It puts them both, in Alston's words, in the title and "on the same footing," which he thinks is a mistake. He points out that it is not clear how "the innovative peoples' rights provisions" of the Banjul Charter will affect the supervisory work done by the African Commission of Human Rights as compared to similar bodies in other regions" (266). Other high points in this phase were the adoption of peoples' rights to development (doc. 22) in 1986 and to peace in 1984. According to Alston, neither of these new rights was properly vetted.

Before we leave this third phase of peoples' rights, I need mention that document 21, the Declaration on the Rights of Indigenous Peoples, which came out of the 1984 World Conference of Indigenous Peoples held in Panama, clearly makes the connection between peoples' rights and the already mentioned land factor. Not only do "all indigenous peoples have the right of self-determination" (principle 1); the states within which they live "shall recognize the population, territory and institutions of the indigenous people" (principle 2). Also, "indigenous people shall have exclusive rights to their traditional lands and its resources. Where the lands and resources of the indigenous peoples have been taken away without their free and informed consent such lands and resources shall be returned" (principle 9).

The Declaration on the Rights of Indigenous Peoples leads us to the heart of a territoriality question much discussed in international law:

Do a people have a right to their territory? Jeremy Waldron thinks that they do, but more because of the political and legal arrangements they have made than because of any cultural heritage they share, a point I'll come back to shortly. According to the Charter of the United Nations, the answer also is a clear yes. In Article 2(4) it states, "All Members shall refrain in their international relations from the threat or use of force against the territorial integrity or political independence of any State." But note the shift here from "peoples" to "states." This holds for all the close to 250 peoples (the French, Belgian, South African, Ethiopian, Peruvian, Vietnamese, etc., peoples) who formed and now control the member states of the United Nations and send their government representatives to participate in its affairs. The Westphalian system that underlies the UN Charter gives to all peoples that have evolved into full-fledged member states the benefit to have their land or "territorial integrity" recognized by all the other member states. The mention in Articles 1 and 55 of the principle of self-determination raises political and international jurisprudential, but not human rights, questions.

The only possible exception to this international territorial sovereignty principle is indigenous peoples, none of which are themselves UN member states, although they reside within UN member states and nevertheless have a right to their own territorial integrity, as can be seen in document 21 of table 5.1. However, of late the international community has had second thoughts on this territorial right of indigenous peoples. An ECOSOC forum set up in July 2000 to deal with what used to be called the right of indigenous peoples to self-determination was given the low-key name "permanent forum on indigenous issues," indicating, according to Alston, "a longstanding governmental reticence to embrace the terminology of 'peoples'" (Alston 2001, 279). The third contribution to the 2001 Alston collection is one by Benedict Kingsbury titled "Reconciling Five Competing Conceptual Structures of Indigenous Peoples' Claims in International and Comparative Law." Kingsbury did not succeed at reconciling these structures and at the end concludes that there is in international law "an absence of a singly unifying structure," which leaves the possible exception unresolved (Kingsbury 2001, 109). Kingsbury also concluded, "Within liberal societies, the multiplicity of concepts offers a way beyond the limits that liberalism repeatedly confronts in coping with issues raised by indigenous peoples" (109).

Whatever the eventual resolution, I think that these developments take the land factor out of the human rights equation, leaving all human rights to be portable ones. The landmasses of planet Earth are cut up into national domains held by peoples who through war and negotiations have gained state sovereignty over that chunk of the planet and its adjacent space. Unless he or she is an absolute dictator in one of those domains and therefore embodies its government, as Hitler did Nazi Germany, no human being can as an individual lay legal claim to a piece of the planet's territory. Macklem is right to argue that international law governs the relations between these UN member states, but no flesh and blood human being as such has a *human* right to any part of that landmass. The closest an individual can come to having a *human* right to a piece of planet Earth is if he or she lives in a nation that honors the much-neglected UDHR Article 17, the right to property "alone or in common with others." Since the territorial factor is central to many of the third-generation human rights listed in our table, such as the rights to natural resources, to development, and to peace, these rights should not be counted as genuine *human* rights. If we look at land rights as human rights, it should only be because they are ascribed to a people or its government to help implement the human rights listed in or derived from the amended Universal Declaration. This brings us to Alston's seven steps to control the quality of newly proposed human rights and thus to our case study of the common Article 1.

But first a word about the last and final phase of peoples' rights. During that fourth phase (1990–present), "many of the principal liberation movements, whose struggles had been an important background factor encouraging the focus on peoples during the previous phases, were transformed either into governments (as in Namibia, South Africa and Eritrea) or into a different 'state in-waiting' status (as in Palestine and East Timor)" (Alston 2001, 268–69; Catalonia and Kurdistan may now also join the state-in-waiting list). The Cold War eclipsed the liberation movements of the Polisario in Western Sahara. The breakups of the Soviet Union and Yugoslavia into their various "constituent parts" also has made governments leery of "excessive fragmentation as more and more groups within existing state borders were tempted to think that secession might suddenly be a viable option" (269). Alston records the "fall" of peoples' rights, such as self-determination, in which case the annual resolution by the General Assembly has become "little more than a sad relic of a bygone golden era" (272); minority rights, which have seen an ontological shift to the rights of individual members; and indigenous peoples' rights, which I mentioned previously in connection with document 21. He argues that the draft Declaration on the Human Right to Peace as the Foundation for the Culture of Peace, which was presented to UNESCO experts in 1997, was "platitudinous," "vacuous," and "eloquent in its hollowness" (280). Similarly demoted as a peoples' right was document 22, the Declaration on the Right to Development; according to Alston, the economist Arjun Sengupta, in his 2000 report to the General Assembly, went "to some lengths in his analysis to avoid using the term 'peoples' and instead refers to the 'people of the developing countries' and even 'indigenous people', always in the singular" (285–86).

Alston writes, "The General Assembly appears to have dropped the terminology altogether in its 1999 resolution in which it reaffirmed 'the importance of the right to development for every person and *all people* in all countries, in particular the developing countries" (Alston 2001, 286). His overall conclusion is that "while the discourse of peoples' rights continues to thrive in a few settings, the situation in both law and practice today is characterized by a systematic reluctance on the part of governments to attach any significance to this [collectivist] dimension of human rights" (289). He sees in international law "a general trend towards the downgrading of the right to self-determination" away from "conceptions of group autonomy" toward "a concern with democratic legitimacy and more limited forms of autonomy" (273). I offer the help of UDHR Article 21 in creating legitimacy and limited autonomy. Together with the nondiscrimination item "political opinion" in UDHR Article 2(1), this article calls for multiparty elections in UN member states.

So much then for the "fall" of peoples' rights around the turn of our century. Against this background of demotion after an initial burst of interest, I present my case study of peoples' *human* rights.

Case Study: Human Rights and Common Article 1

1. *All peoples have the right to self-determination. By virtue of that right they freely determine their political status and freely pursue their economic, social and cultural development.*
2. *All peoples may, for their own ends, freely dispose of their natural wealth and resources without prejudice to any obligations arising out of international economic co-operation, based upon the principle of mutual benefit, and international law. In no case may a people be deprived of its own means of subsistence.*
3. *The States Parties to the present Covenant, including those having responsibility for the administration of Non-Self-Governing and Trust Territories, shall promote the realization of the right to self-determination, and shall respect that right, in conformity with provisions of the Charter of the United Nations.*

I begin with a cautionary note: the right to self-determination of various peoples is the fulcrum of the collectivist third-generation rights that belong to peoples as such, and not in the first instance to the individuals that constitute a people. Because of their collectivist ontology, I propose that we assign a lower status to collectivist rights such as those found in Article 1 of the two covenants. That will split the human rights family into two parts: individuals' human rights and collectivist ones. The former will be found in the first two generations and the latter mostly in the third. In addition to the self-determination right of flesh and blood human beings—asserted in UDHR Articles 22, 26, 29—there are two kinds of collectivist self-determination rights: internal and external. *Internal* self-determination results when a state gives a group great leeway to arrange its *internal* affairs, for example, by setting up schools, houses of worship, and ethno-cultural centers and using its own language in public places like courtrooms. As we saw in the preceding section, that type of self-determination need not have a collectivist ontology and can result from a careful implementation of ICCPR Article 27. *External* self-determination allows a group by the rules of international law (often helped by a group flexing its own muscle) to constitute itself into a state and thereby receive independence from domination and exploitation by other states that make up the Westphalian system. While internal self-determination can—but need not—involve a group's claim to land or territory, in cases of external self-determination that claim is almost always part of the group's goal and strategy. When given to the same group of people, these two types of self-determination (internal and external) create the sovereign states that make up the UN system. If every cohesive group were given this kind of complete (both internal and external) self-determination, the world map would have thousands of sovereign states on it instead of the roughly two hundred it now has. It is therefore important to keep these two types of collectivist self-determination rights separated from each other and not go too quickly from the internality discussed in the previous section to the externality discussed in this one.

Just before he gives us the seven steps of his *Appellation Contrôlée* method, Alston lists seven substantive requirements for any new human right. A new human right must be

1. a "fundamentally important social value";
2. "relevant . . . throughout a world of diverse social values";
3. "eligible for recognition" under various sources of international law;
4. "consistent with, but not merely repetitive of, the existing body of international human rights law";
5. "capable of achieving a very high degree of international consensus";
6. "compatible . . . with the general practice of states"; and
7. "sufficiently precise as to give rise to identifiable rights and obligations." (Alston 1984, 615)

My focus will be on the fourth requirement: that any new human right must fit with or be derived from the "existing body of international human rights law." That requirement depends, of course, on the date the norm is proposed. The common Article 1 was proposed in the 1950s, during discussions about whether or not there should be one or two covenants to translate the moral rights of the UDHR into international legalese. It was proposed during the early reign of the individualist ontology.

The problem with the common Article 1 was that it did not derive from any moral rights in the UDHR but instead went straight back to the political principle of self-determination enunciated in the 1945 UN charter. Delegates were quick to point out that the article bypassed the 1948 UDHR, which was drawn up under UN auspices to flesh out the seven human rights references found in the charter. All of Alston's substantive requirements make sense, but when it comes to third-generation solidarity or collectivist rights, I put even more stress than he does on the requirement that any new right be consistent with "the existing body of international human rights law." Alston in fact allows the common Article 1 into the fold. My departure from Altson comes in step 2 as follows.

The seven steps of Alston's *Appellation Contrôlée* are not difficult to fathom. Step 1 says that the process of adopting a new human right should be initiated by a UN organ, be it the Human Rights Commission or the General Assembly. That step was met when on February 5, 1952, the General Assembly accepted Resolution III of the Third Committee, which then became General Assembly Resolution 545(VI). In that resolution the General Assembly "decided that the covenant or covenants on human rights should include an article on the right of all peoples and nations to self-determination in reaffirmation of the principle enunciated in the Charter of the United Nations." I discuss the lead-up to and the aftermath of Resolution 545(VI) later in this chapter.

Step 2 says that the secretary general should prepare a preliminary study "identifying the major qualitative issues raised by the proposal, such as the content and definition of the proposed norm, the basis on which it may be considered part of international law, *its relationship to the existing range of human rights norms,* and the extent to which it reflects existing (or proposed) state practice" (Alston 1984, 620; added italics). This step was completed with document A/2929 of July 1955, chapter 4 of which deals specifically with the rights of peoples and nations to self-determination. The italicized clause is where, for objectors to the expansion, the shoe pinches most; thus, the linkage of the common Article 1 with existing human rights norms is the subject of this case study. In the early 1950s, the only extant international human rights norms were those of the UDHR and the Genocide Convention, the text of which was not phrased in the terminology of human rights. During the common Article 1 debates of the 1950s, the Genocide Convention was not seen as a precursor for the rights of collectivities. At the time the only close competitor to the UDHR was the European Convention for the Protection of Human Rights and Fundamental Freedoms, which was signed in Rome on November 4, 1950. This European convention was cast in the individualist mold and was a regional and not a universal norm. Naturally, the participants and later interpreters of common Article 1 see the adoption of the article as a revolutionary step for the General Assembly to have taken.

Step 3 requires the Secretariat to collect reactions from governments and NGOs on the proposed new human rights norm. Reactions were collected for the common Article 1, and some of the earlier responses can be found in documents like E/CN.4/694/Add.2, which contains the United Kingdom's response to the proposed inclusion of the article. Under the same designation, varied responses by Poland, Canada, Norway, the US, the BSSR, Sweden, and the UKSSR can be found. Responses and amendments by other governments and by organizations like UNESCO, the ILO, and the World Health Organization can be found in *The International Covenant on Economic, Social and Cultural Rights*, vol. 1, *1946–1948 Travaux Préparatoires* (Saul 2016). Step 4 says that on the basis of that government and NGO input, the secretary general will prepare a comprehensive study reflecting all the aspects of the proposal. This step was completed with the Secretariat's help when the Third Committee issued the already mentioned Document A/2929 of July 1955. Step 5 requires that an ad hoc committee set up by the Human Rights Commission give a report on the proposal to the commission within three months. That report too is included in A/2929. Step 6 calls for the commission to come up with a recommendation for the General Assembly. In the case of the common Article 1, the commission gave its recommendation more than once. In 1952 the eighth session of the Human Rights Commission adopted the article as a whole in a vote of thirteen to four, with one abstention (E/CN.4/SR.260/4; Bossuyt 1987, 47), and in 1955 the tenth session of the Third Committee voted thirty-three to twelve, with thirteen abstentions (A/C.3/SR.676/para. 27; Bossuyt 1987, 47). Finally, step 7 suggests that this whole process should "culminate in a proclamation of a new human right or in a decision to defer action on the proposal for a certain period of time (either indefinitely or for a given period of time)" (Alston 1984, 620). On December 16, 1966, both covenants (with their common Article 1) were adopted, and these new alleged human rights were proclaimed in General Assembly Resolution 2200 A(XXI) (A/6316 [1966]). After they had been offered to the member states for ratification, the ICESCR entered into force on January 3, 1976, and the ICCPR on March 23, 1976. Each covenant has been ratified by more than 150 UN member states.

In the case of common Article 1, the *Appellation Contrôlée* process was more or less followed, giving us some brand new human rights that are not mentioned in the Universal Declaration. While for most scholars, including Alston, Buchanan, Macklem, and Moyn, a new human right can be proclaimed by fiat of the UN General Assembly, I believe that the General Assembly made a conceptual human rights error when it expanded the field of human rights to collectivities as such. This conceptual or philosophical question was contested during Article 1's adoption debates in the early 1950s. General Assembly Resolution 545(VI), demanding that the covenant include "nations' and peoples' right to self-determination," went on to say, "This article shall be drafted in the following terms: 'All peoples shall have the right of self-determination', and shall stipulate that all States, including those having responsibility for the administration of Non-Self-Governing Territories should promote the realization of that right, in conformity with the purposes and principles of the United Nations, and States having responsibility for the administration of Non-Self-Governing Territories should promote the realization of that right in relation to the peoples of such territories" (A/2929, 13). The adoption of this February 1952 General Assembly resolution greatly strengthens the second phase (1950–71) of the rise of peoples' rights, which diminished enormously in later years, supporting my contention that they should not have been added in the first place. The assembly was clearly focused on the liberation of colonial peoples living in territories controlled by metropolitan powers.

As early as November 1950, in the 309th Meeting of the Third Committee, the delegations of Afghanistan and Saudi Arabia had started the ball rolling with a proposal that later mushroomed into a thirteen-nation proposal. Abdul Rahman Pazhwak, the Afghan delegate, "asked the Committee quite objectively whether or not the right of nations to self-determination was indeed a basic *human* right. If it was, the amendment should be adopted and the article dealing with the rights should be included in the covenant. Such an article would be of great benefit to all nations, especially those which had not yet won their independence" (GAOR, 3rd Comm., 309th Mtg., para. 53; added italics). I added the emphasis on the term "human" here because, in the ensuing debates, delegations were careful to avoid that term while nevertheless insisting that the covenant was the right place for stipulating this right of nations. Pazhwak's colleague from Saudi Arabia, Jamil M. Baroody, glossed over this ontological difference when he said, "The first eighteen articles of the draft covenant defined the rights not of individual man but of man as a member of society. The right to self-determination, however, appeared nowhere in the covenant. . . . Unless the covenant contained an article ensuring the [human?] right of nations to self-determination, it would merely encourage colonial and mandatory Powers to postpone indefinitely the establishment of equal [human?] rights among all nations" (paras. 55, 57). Between them these two delegates stirred up two sides to a long debate. They got the majority to go along with their proposal that the time had come for the United Nations to reiterate the principle of self-determination of all nations. At the same time, their phraseology and my brackets planted the seeds of opposition doubts to the effect that national self-determination was not really a *human* right and therefore, whatever its merits, the planned human rights covenant was not a good place to declare any rights of peoples.

The debates reveal interesting exchanges of amendments piled on amendments. For instance, at one point the US had proposed, "All states, including those . . . controlling in whatsoever manner the exercise of that right [to self-determination] by another people, shall promote . . . the realization of that right in all their territories" (E/CN.4//L28/Rev.2). The guide to the *travaux* tells us, "The Belgian oral amendment to replace 'another' by 'a' in the US amendment was rejected by 6 votes to 5 with 7 abstentions" (Bossuyt 1987, 43). Just one word tells a big story. As I noted in my *Origins* book, even in 1948 during the UDHR debates in the Third Committee, the application of human rights to the colonies became an issue (Morsink 1999b, sec. 3.2). The key difference between the 1948 debates and this 1966 repeat is that the former—in addition to favoring the metropolitan powers—was cast in the individualist mold and the latter in a collectivist mold. The entire common Article 1 reflects this shift in ontology, which is why some scholars see the adoption of this common article as a "conceptual revolution" in our modern notion of human rights. They see this UN ascription of human rights to collectivities as basic to the entire human rights enterprise. I contest this view and argue instead that the international community made a mistake when it allowed the General Assembly to expand the definition of what a human right is beyond its Holocaust origins.

The vote in the General Assembly for Resolution 545(VI) took place in the 375th meeting on February 5, 1952. The phrase "all peoples shall have the right to self-determination" was adopted by thirty-six to eleven votes, with twelve abstentions (GAOR, 6th Sess. [1952], 375th Mtg., para. 78). Moyn is right when he says, "In an astonishing short space of time the UN could move from seriously considering a proposal to exempt colonial (trust and non-self-governing) territories from coverage by the draft 'Covenants on Human Rights' to naming the right to self-determination of peoples as the very first of all human rights in those drafts" (Moyn 2010, 96). He adds that these debates "fundamentally transformed the whole meaning of UN human rights" (96). After two pages of anti-colonialist citations, to which I take no exception, Moyn tells us what he thinks is involved in this transformation of "the meaning of UN human rights." It is, he says, that "the restoration of human rights to the principle of self-determination emphasized *their necessary basis in collectivity and sovereignty* as the first and most important threshold rights" (98; emphasis added). In his talk of "restoration," Moyn reaches back to the 1941 Atlantic Charter and to the principle of self-determination articulated in Articles 1 and 55 of the UN Charter. This high esteem for the right to self-determination conflicts with the story Philip Alston tells us in his already discussed "Rise and Fall" essay. Alston rightly points out that the UDHR "contains no reference at all to self-determination, which seems an odd omission if we are to take at face value the assertion originally put forward in the early post-War years by the Soviet

Union, but [think of Moyn] commonly made even today, that in the absence of the achievement of self-determination other human rights have little meaning" (Alston 2001, 261). I agree that it is indeed "odd" for the UDHR not to include any reference to self-determination of peoples *if* that is the foundation of all "other" human rights. I think it is not, and so it is not odd.

This collectivist self-determination right inclusion in the identical first article of the two international covenants cannot bear the weight that Moyn and others put on it. It is the main culprit of the inflationary trend reflected in table 5.1. The human rights debates in the United Nations were indeed transformed by the infusion of postcolonial states into the UN membership. This infusion obviously informed the reported February 1952 vote tally. However, the poor philosophical fit between the common Article 1 and the rest of the International Bill of Human Rights shows up clearly during the debates for its adoption. I found at least three prolonged discussions of this lack of fit: first in November 1950, with the submission of the revised Afghanistan and Saudi Arabia amendment to the draft covenant (A/C.3/L88/Rev.1); then again in January and February 1952, with the discussion of the thirteen-powers proposal (A/C.3/L 204) that fed into General Assembly Resolution 545(VI); and after that in the fall of 1954, before and after the report of a working party that was to finalize the text. This working party proposed a radical change when it deleted the term "nations" from the text, simply saying, "All peoples have the right to self-determination" (A/C.3/L489 and Corr. 1 and 2). This contravened an earlier discussion in the eighth session of the commission that had led to the insertion of the term "nations" into the text, making it say that all "peoples and nations" have a right to self-determination.

In its 1952 report (A/2112) to the General Assembly, the Third Committee summarized both sides of this debate. It correctly noted that "a very great number of delegations" had voted for the inclusion of the common article in the February meeting. They included Liberia, Mexico, Nicaragua, Pakistan, Paraguay, Peru, Philippines, Poland, Saudi Arabia, Syria, Thailand, the UKSSR, the USSR, Yemen, Yugoslavia, Afghanistan, Bolivia, Burma, the BSSR, Chile, Cuba, Czechoslovakia, the Dominican Republic, Ecuador, Egypt, El Salvador, Ethiopia, Greece, Guatemala, Haiti, India, Indonesia, Iran, Iraq, and Lebanon

(GAOR, 6th Sess., 375th Mtg., para. 78). The report tells us this majority thought that since the Human Rights Commission had not produced an article on self-determination

> the General Assembly should take action on the matter in its sixth session. . . . They emphasized that the right of self-determination was set forth in the Charter of the United Nation as a principle, and that it was necessary and useful to start its implementation by inserting a provision thereon in the draft covenant. They said that the Universal Declaration of Human Rights has proclaimed it by providing that the will of the peoples shall be the basis of the authority of government. (Annex/Agenda item 29/Doc. A/2112/41)

The *s* of "peoples" raises issues in the philosophical literature about plebiscitary votes on unification and secession that I briefly explored at the end of the last section on minority rights and that at the time of this writing in the fall of 2017 have again come up in the votes taken by "the" Turkish and "the" Catalonian peoples, as if these independence votes themselves are not highly problematic when seen from a democratic perspective either in the regions themselves or in the nations within which these peoples are domiciled.

The *travaux* of the meeting leading up to the February vote indicate that the Third Committee accurately reported in Document A/2112 to the General Assembly what had happened. I therefore cite the views at length. The majority that voted for the inclusion of the common article had thought

> that world public opinion required such an action by the United Nations and it would not be understood why that right was not included in the covenant. Its inclusion would give moral and legal support to peoples aspiring to political and social independence and would be a valuable contribution to the maintenance of international peace and security. The respect for the self-determination of peoples would affect the respect for and the observance of individual human rights; no basic human rights could be ensured unless the right of peoples to self-determination were ensured at the same time. (UNOR A/212/para. 26)

The minority, according to the report, had "stressed the necessity of solving a great number of technical problems" (para. 27). For example,

> the definition of the notions of "people" and "nation" involved great difficulties. It was necessary to distinguish between majority and minority, and to examine when a majority ceased to be a people and became a minority. . . . It was also necessary to establish an organ or machinery which would decide upon the granting of the right. . . . In any case the covenant on human rights was not the document in which the right to self-determination [of peoples] should be stated, since the purpose of that instrument was to define the relations between the State and the individual. . . . Others stressed that the article would only be declaratory without means of enforcement, and would also encourage separatist movements, [leading to] a multiplication of frontiers. (para. 27)

Opposition views like this support the idea of "a people" as a political construction and therefore not a matter of moral rights inherent in the human person that were to be spelled out in the covenants being drawn up. While many of the points made in these citations fit the pure proceduralist approach to the addition of new human rights to the corpus, this last point about constructivism versus inherence does not and is still a bone of contention today.

I am not suggesting that we let a sole philosopher—Alston was right to dismiss Cranston—or even the mirroring group dismissed by Buchanan in chapter 4 tell us what our modern conception of human rights should be. I believe we can resolve this standoff by staying within the confines of the United Nations if we take our cue for what human rights are from the Universal Declaration and let that historic UN document with its individualist ontology set the standard for our modern conception. Doing so does not require us to "escape" into the academy. We simply need to clarify what the objectors to common Article 1 were saying, which amounts to proceduralism "light" instead of "heavy." It means that instead of going with the General Assembly's fiat reflected in the majority vote, we take the side of the minority because we believe it had the better case. Alston's "fall" of peoples' rights and contemporary caution regarding plebiscitary independence votes support these early UN objectors.

The main point of the thirteen objecting delegations was that common Article 1 conflicted with the purpose of the covenants, which "was to define the relations between the State and the individual" (A/2112/ para. 27). For instance, during the General Assembly debate just before that February 1952 vote was taken, René Cassin, the delegate from France, said that he had no objection to a repeat from the charter of the principle of self-determination. But he went on to say that what

> we should like to warn our fellow delegations against is the insertion in a covenant on human rights of a provision which includes purely collective rights. The provisions of the Charter and the Universal Declaration of Human Rights emerged from the revolt of free peoples against the totalitarian massacres and atrocities of the last war; there was a desire to restore to the human person his dignity and prestige and to defend them in practice. That was the goal of the Universal Declaration of Human Rights. Human rights are, moreover, purely individual rights, or such collective rights as the rights to vote, trade union rights and the right of association; but the right of peoples is necessarily and exclusively a collective right and is connected with the totality of human freedoms the Charter was intended to proclaim. The Charter has balanced parts, and it is natural to study the rights of peoples to self-determination in its own place and human rights in their place. Let us avoid downward trends that upset the balance of the Charter. (GAOR, 6th Sess., 375th Plenary Mtg., para. 26)

Cassin is separating the right to self-determination, with its attendant rights, as a purely collectivist right of a people seeking to create or maintain a nation-state from the UDHR rights inherent in the human person. He did acknowledge the collective rights in the declaration that are possessed by individuals but practiced in common with others, such as "the right to vote, trade union rights or the right of association." But those were very different from the rights ascribed in the common Article 1, which were "necessarily and exclusively collective," or in my terminology, collectivist.

The difference between these "collective" rights practiced in common with others and what I call "collectivist" rights is that the latter, as common Article 1 makes clear, contain territorial claims, while the former do not, at least not necessarily. In the Third Committee that later wrote the report (A/2112) I cited previously, the defenders of Article 1 maintained, in the words of Baroody, the Saudi delegate, that the colonial peoples "had reached the end of their tether and could no longer be appeased by arguments for patience. The metropolitan States averred," he said, "that, if they were to withdraw from the territories under their control, the peoples of those territories would cut one another's throats; the fallacy of that argument had been proved by experience but even if it were true, that risk was preferable to subjection" (GAOR, 6th Sess., 3rd. Comm., 398th Mtg., para. 37). During the 1950s and 1960s, when these covenants were drafted and ratified, many (but not all) colonial peoples got their independence and cast their votes in the UN in favor of "all peoples shall have the right to self-determination," which is reflected in the thirty-six to eleven vote, with twelve abstentions, in the General Assembly on February 5, 1952. We must be careful counting the eleven no votes cast that day by Luxembourg, the Netherlands, New Zealand, the United Kingdom, the United States, Australia, Belgium, Brazil, Canada, Denmark, and France (GAOR, 6th Sess., 375th Mtg., para. 78), for some of them were metropolitan powers tainted by ongoing or recent colonial suppression, and others were equally intent on not giving territorial rights to the indigenous peoples under their jurisdiction.

The no votes of the following nations are suspect. The French were not yet willing to let their Indochina and North African holdings go free. Neither was the British Empire totally finished. The Dutch had only recently let go of Indonesia. In the Third Committee, one month before the previously cited report, L. J. C. Beaufort, the Dutch delegate, had repeated Cassin's theme in these debates: "The chief purpose of the covenant of human rights was to safeguard the rights and dignities of the individual. . . . The rights of groups and nations would have their place in another document, the draft convention on the rights and duties of States. People and groups were entitled, when they had reached a sufficiently high stage of development to claim the right to self-determination, but such rights could be enforced only by governments, which must be placed under a moral obligation to do so" when these colonial peoples were ready (GAOR, 6th Sess., 3rd. Comm., 398th Mtg., para. 40). In the earlier 310th meeting of the committee, the Belgian delegate, Mr. Soudan, briefly retraced for his colleagues the history of the Belgian mandate over the Congo. His country

> had from the start done what it could to promote the welfare and raise the standard of living of the indigenous inhabitants by abolishing slavery, spreading enlightenment and education, and by other measures calculated to lead the people towards self-government, but no country could claim to be blameless in that regard. If the principle of self-determination were to be applied forthwith in such territories as the Congo, and if popular elections were held for that purpose, the people would elect chiefs who would deprive them of many of the human rights accorded by the authorities responsible for their administration. The result would be anarchy, as the populations were not yet sufficiently advanced to decide their own fate. (GAOR, 6th Sess., 3rd Comm., 310th Mtg., para. 24)

Over top of these not-so-hidden imperial ambitions, the objecting metropolitan nations openly raised a more philosophical point, which I cited Cassin as making. They did not want the territorial claims involved in common Article 1 recognized as *human* rights, which was in danger of happening if such territorial claims were listed in the very first article of the new international covenants meant to implement moral rights inherent in individual human beings. Cassin's suggestion to mention the charter principle of self-determination in the covenant's preamble instead of its body was not taken (GAOR, 6th Sess., 3rd. Comm., 399th Mtg, para. 33). The main debating episodes in the *travaux préparatoires* (late 1950, January–February 1953, and November 1954) are replete with this mixture of reasons. But once we strip this imperial lingering away, the philosophical question still stands: Are there or are there not territorial *human* rights? Are there or are there not collectivist *human* rights to a portion of planet earth? Might it not be the case, as John Locke argued, that God gave the earth to mankind in common and that the parceling up of the planet is foremost a political process governed by moral natural laws that call for the protection of human beings during that process? Could it be that it took the event of the Holocaust to make clear what that protection entails? While the objecting delegations were all along in the minority, that itself does not necessarily put them in the wrong. The dissenting, objecting, and abstaining nations had more than one reason for their negative view of the common article. My view is that a key philosophical point was lost in a cloud of anti-colonialism. As an artist with a "clouded" personal life can produce works of great beauty, so UN delegations from nations under "suspicion" can score well in a philosophical debate over human rights, which I think is what happened here.

Although pretty much every nation has an independence story to tell that involves political struggles and often wars, particularly interesting in these UN debates on the common article are the views of delegations that cannot easily be accused of having sheltered lingering imperial ambitions. While none of them are as pure as we would like, we can distill Cassin's point about limiting the covenant(s) to "purely individual rights" from the votes of some of the twelve abstaining delegations: Norway, Sweden, Turkey, Uruguay, Venezuela, Argentina, China, Colombia, Costa Rica, Honduras, Iceland, and Israel (GAOR, 6th Sess., 375th Mtg., para. 78). Several of them shared Cassin's philosophy of what a human right is. I cite two of them and add a third one from the no votes because it made the connection with World War II explicit. The Turkish delegate, Ilhan Savut, said he thought "there were three categories of human rights." In the third category, he placed "the rights of nations, peoples or sovereign groups" (GAOR, 6th Sess., 3rd Comm., 310th Mtg., para. 48). He was right to argue that "the draft covenant, like the Declaration, dealt with individual rights" and that "the right to self-determination clearly fell outside that category" (para. 49). He added that "the Commission of Human Rights was not competent to deal with that particular right" (para. 49), a point that Eleanor Roosevelt had made earlier when she noted "the promotion of that principle [of self-determination] was the responsibility of the Trusteeship Council and the Fourth Committee" (para. 28).

Savut's colleague, Turgut Menemencioğlu, repeated many of these points in a later meeting. Having alluded to "the Turkish people's long struggle for their very existence," he noted that his delegation had come to the conclusion that the Third Committee was not the right organ to take up this matter of self-determination of peoples. The Turkish delegation thought

> that the covenant on human rights was not the document in which the right to self-determination should be stated. The purpose of the covenant was to define the relations between the State and the individual. It had been claimed that the concept of human rights extended to the family which was a collective unit, but the concept of the family in connexion with human rights concerned the rights and duties of individuals who constituted families, rather than the family as a collective legal unit. (GAOR, 6th Sess., 400th Mtg., para. 30)

Alfonzo Ravard of Venezuela, who spoke right after Menemencioğlu, made the very telling point that in Resolution 421(V), which called for a covenant article on the right to self-determination, "the General Assembly had not in fact recognized the right of peoples and nations to self-determination as a fundamental *human* right, but had merely requested the Commission on Human Rights to study ways and means which would ensure that right" (GAOR, 6th Sess., 400th Mtg., para. 33; added italics). That is precisely the point most of the objecting delegations also made in their repeated observations that the covenants were the wrong place for the articulation of this principle. T. P. Davin of New Zealand said his delegation would vote against the first paragraph of the common article. He argued, "The covenant was concerned with the individual within a given political setting and with the individual's equality of treatment with the rest of humanity. It was intended to secure to individuals the great fundamental rights and freedoms which transcended all political boundaries" (para. 24). He noted that the principle of self-determination, which was to be the basis of "friendly relations" among nations, had been violated "for their own ends by Germany and Italy" (para. 23). He was worried about the principle of self-determination being used by minority peoples and political secession movements in quests for their own "area or territory." "Such problems concerned, not individuals as such, but groups or entities identifiable with a particular area or territory, and would normally fall within the purview of United Nations organs other than the Third Committee" (para. 23). Under international law, nations have collectivist rights to territory and individuals have human rights, but there are no such things as *territorial human* rights. That oxymoron flouts the connection between the Holocaust and the Universal Declaration.

When asked for feedback on the draft covenants, the United Kingdom made the point that the common Article 1

> has no place in the present covenant because it is not concerned with an individual human right, because self-determination is not an absolute, but a political principle whose application in practice may have to be subordinate to other principles (e.g. the maintenance of peace), and because the assertion of a general right to self-determination for "all peoples" and "all nations" without any definition of "peoples" and "nations" would have the most far-reaching consequences for many States, and not merely for those administering non-self-governing territories. (E/CN.4/694/Add.2/9)

Self-serving as it is, this statement fits Jeremy Waldron's argument "that a people's right to determine what happens in a given territory is not predicated on their having an immemorial ancestral relation to the land nor on its being an integral part of their shared culture or way of life," but only and simply on what political and legal arrangements the inhabitants of that land happen to have made, a relationship that does not go "deeper than ordinary habitation" (Waldron 2010, 407–8). It also finds support in a 2016 collection of essays by a group of six philosophers (Alain Badiou, Pierre Bourdieu, Judith Butler, Georges Didi-Huberman, Sadri Khiari, and Jacques Rancière) titled *What Is a People?* In his introduction to this volume, Bruno Bosteels notes that all of them, except possibly Bourdieu, "could be said to fall in line with the observation of the late Ernesto Laclau when in *On Populist Reason* he posits that 'the political operation par excellence is always going to be the construction of a 'people'" (Bosteels 2016, 4). That is also the point of the just-cited Waldron argument.

Waldron defends what he calls a "territorial approach" to self-determination against Kymlicka's identity-based approach, lifting territory in its Westphalian dress far above culture as the determining factor in the process of the self-determination of peoples. Waldron writes, "Because it does not assume that the entitlement to self-determination is vested in a people with a distinct identity of its own, the territorial approach will see it more in light of an individual right, albeit necessarily exercised in common with similar rights of millions of other persons" (Waldron 2010, 408). That is also what the defenders of the common Article 1 claimed when they sought to anchor it in UDHR Article 21. The difference is that Waldron removes any "memorial ancestral relation to the land" from the democratic political equation. For him, "the phrase 'the people of a territory' simply refers to all the individual men and women who happen to inhabit the territory in question. It is not assumed that they have any relation to the land that is much stronger than habitation: they live there, they are making a life there, maybe they were born there and are raising a family there" (407). To the question as to who should form a state, Waldron answers that it is people "who happen to live side by side" (408). "Among those who live unavoidably side by side in a particular territory, the potential for conflict is dense and entangled because of frequent and faceted dealings among the same class of persons" (411). This raises the question as to why a despot should not come in and settle matters rather than having the people or peoples that share the territory create certain "political and legal arrangements . . . to deal with conflict that arises from our proximity to one another in a given territory" (411). And "since conflict is at its most intense in particular localities, political and legal arrangements have, in first instance, on this model, a necessary territorial dimension" (411). In this way a "people" becomes a political construction.

Waldron has steered us into the thicket of international law and politics in which persons and peoples that find themselves "side by side" must work out their political arrangements as best they can. None of them, either as individuals or collectivities, have an inherent human right to a slice of planet Earth, which, if Locke is right, God gave to mankind in common. But, says Waldron, Locke certainly was not right in thinking that when it comes to creating a state, "this any number of people may do because it injures not the freedom of the rest" (Waldron 2010, 409–10). He rightly points out that a view like Locke's "has made it very difficult to map liberal contractarian concerns onto determinate principles of territory and self-determination" (409).

This dismissal of the Lockean contract theory of the state brings Waldron to his Kantian talk of "side-by-side" people making legal and political arrangements and the realism that that entails. So when it comes to General Assembly resolutions for either ICCPR Article 27 or the common Article 1, two views or interpretations face off: the first one is that of Kymlicka and Patten (in a stretch), and the second is Waldron's, citing Kant, that "when you cannot avoid living side-by-side with others . . . 'you ought to leave the state of nature and proceed with them into a rightful condition, that is a condition of positive law'" (411). That means these side-by-side persons or peoples must create a constitution that lays the groundwork for positive law, one—this being Kant's view—that respects the inherent dignity of all human beings involved. According to Waldron, "One view wishes that each people with a culture were in charge of its own affairs, and looks for an acceptable version of that; the other wishes that inhabitants of each territory could be left alone to fulfill their common duty of making provision for the resolution of disputes and it looks for a pragmatic version of that" (412–13). The latter is Waldron's Westphalian realism in a nutshell. The application of the territorial approach to peoples' rights, both for minorities and majorities, "in the modern world will be pragmatic in relation to existing boundaries rather than foundational in setting them *de novo*" (412). By way of example, Waldron notes that "everyone pays lip service to the principle [of self-determination] laid down in ICCPR" Article 1 and in the identical ICESCR Article 1, adding the comment that "a number of the countries just mentioned [Turkey, Iraq, Iran, and Syria] would go to war to prevent the redrawing of boundaries to accommodate self-determination for the Kurds" (398). It does not mean that the Kurds and many other regional peoples seeking self-determination do not have any rights at all. To find out what these rights are, we must investigate the constitutional arrangements of the countries mentioned and any agreements these countries have made between them. But whatever those collectivist rights to land are and whatever political and legal arrangements come out of any plebiscites held, these rights are not *human* rights. As a collective entity, the Kurds are not a human person of flesh and blood.

I share Waldron's Westphalian realism because I do not think that human rights have a territorial dimension. Even the human right to private property, as spelled out in UDHR Articles 13 and 17, must be regulated as to its shape by the national legislation of the state where the person or persons reside. Waldron puts it this way: "Of course, inasmuch as they live *here*, the land will be part of the subject matter of their [constitutional] self-determination. As inhabitants they claim the right to determination, for example, on the basis of which property rights are established or the basis on which disputes about resource use or distributive justice are resolved" (Waldron 2010, 407). He continues, "But the territorial conception does not predicate that right on any relation of people to land that is deeper than ordinary habitation" (407–8). The human right of individuals to self-determination or the free and full development of their personalities is stated in UDHR Articles 22, 26, and 29. Article 17's right to property, "alone or in common with others," is part of that right to self-development. So are all the other rights listed in the UDHR. But the territoriality that plays such a huge role in international law is not part of this *human* rights equation. It is the background against which in the 1940s the birth of modern human rights took place. I have argued that the attempt to fit this collectivist right to territory under this same individualist umbrella of the UDHR must be rejected. As the 1948 Haitian motion already indicated, such rights are contingent on local and regional circumstances and therefore not appropriate for inclusion in either the UDHR or its later instruments of implementation. All UDHR human rights are portable, which is why almost every article of the declaration starts with the word "everyone," but these collectivist self-determination rights—tied to land as they are—mentioned in common Article 1 are not portable.

Conclusion: The Holocaust Meaning of "Human Rights"

When deciding on the modern meaning of the phrase "human rights," the reader has a choice of two perspectives. She can take an international legal positivist stand and accept that international law—including the part derived from UN resolutions—is the sovereign of the human rights domain. That means the phrase "human rights" means whatever the United Nations General Assembly says it means, common Article 1 being a case in point. This gives the three generations equal status. Or she can, for Holocaust-related reasons, hold, as I do, that the Universal Declaration of Human Rights is sovereign in the domain of moral human rights translated into international legalese. In that case not all the generations have equal status. The alleged human rights of collectivities—either as national groupings or as whole nations—do not reflect UDHR moral norms. They accrue to these collectivities or groups as such not by reflection on the Holocaust or similar atrocities but by ascription on account of UN votes or by acclamation in the General Assembly. These rights are not inherent and not inalienable in flesh and blood human beings. They are not really *human* rights, which is why the UDHR drafters did not include them. The 1940s moral visionaries were not interested in the land factor and saw themselves as doing work that transcended the Westphalian system, hoping to influence that system from the outside by adopting a mouse that then to our great fortune gave birth to the elephant described in chapter 4 of this book.

The Romanian Iron Guard who became a well-known French nihilist, E. M. Cioran, has noted that "a discourse approaches universality when it frees itself from its origins, leaves them behind, disavows them: having reached this point, if it would reinvigorate itself, avoid unreality or sclerosis, it must renounce its own exigencies, break its forms and its models, it must condescend to *bad taste*" (Cioran 2012, 22; original italics). This may be what has happened to the language of human rights inside legal international and United Nations' politics, in which, as Macklem's sovereignty thesis also suggests, it is seen as bad philosophical taste to base the meaning of "human rights" primarily on the UDHR and its link to the Holocaust. I have urged letting go of this positivist sclerosis and retaining the original UDHR moral insight that at bottom human rights belong as birthrights to individual human beings first and only secondarily (by later UN-sponsored adoptions) to groups of persons. We need to draw a line between the individualist ontology of the first two generations (including members of minority groups) and the collectivist ontology of some of the third-generation human rights that involve the land factor. When a language loses connection with its origin, Cioran thinks, it tends to lose its openness and creativity. It becomes overly formalized, as in Cioran's view the French language did in the second half of the eighteenth century. This may well be happening to the language of human rights as it becomes formalized in UN declarations that have lost their connection with the original individualist ontology of the Universal Declaration born out of Holocaust horrors. The preambular references to the UDHR that I stressed in chapter 4 derive from the "moral insight" gained in the 1940s. The Holocaust connection with the UDHR is also why in the present chapter I raised doubts about the equal status of the collectivist segment of the third generation in the human rights family. The third generation should not without qualification be welcomed into the human rights family. It should be split into two parts: the part noted in ICCPR Article 27 and the part noted in the common Article 1 of both covenants. The third generation before the split should not be allowed to set the tone for the modern meaning of "human rights." But that is what will happen if we do not stop the UN inflationary trend discussed earlier in the chapter.

In ordinary life, some of us use terms like "water," "gold," "aluminum," or "elm" somewhat loosely. We don't think of them as scientific terms; they are just part of our daily language. Hilary Putnam (1973) confesses not to know how to tell a maple from an elm, and I myself cannot tell the difference between real and fake gold. To help us be more precise in our usage, we rely on "experts" who have methods to sort out the extension of these terms, discarding fake rings and look-alike aluminum pans. Those expert methods also tell us what the "real meaning" of these terms is, so that when necessary I know my ring is not *really* made of gold, and Putnam knows that he is *really* looking at an oak tree. We ourselves, of course, learn these terms from the communities in which we grow up. They teach us the ordinary and often looser meanings of these terms so that anything that looks and tastes like "this" (mother pointing to a glass of water) is water. And "that" is an elm tree, and "that over there" is an aluminum pan. When there is uncertainty about whether an item should have the name we want to give it, we can ask these scientific experts for help. This is a division of labor that helps us be efficient in the use of our language. The people around us teach us the extension of terms, and when needed, experts help settle their intension by spelling out the scientific criteria the thing must possess to be what it is. In the case of water, it must be H_2O. I am proposing that we look at the Holocaust-UDHR connection as we look at the chemical composition of water. Not everyone knows that water is H_2O, but those in the know should know that's what water really is.

The chemical composition of water was discovered sometime between 1750 and 1800. Before that there had, of course, been water that fell out of the sky when it rained, that people drank, and that looked like "this" (mother pointing at a glass of the liquid). When I introduced this flowchart of human rights in chapter 1 (idea → Holocaust + UDHR text → system ↔ movement), the first item in it indicated that there is a history of the idea of human rights that is not unrelated to the connection we defend in this book. Before water was discovered to be H_2O, the term "water" had a useful life. That use became more "rigid" and precise when the chemical composition was discovered so that now issues of vagueness and extension—if and when they arise—can be settled by experts. My complaint in this book has been that too many historians and legal scholars have gone "soft" on what the term "human rights" really means. By going straight from the idea to the system or the movement, they have ignored the human rights equivalent of H_2O. They have ignored or downplayed both the text of the declaration as the moral norm for both system and movement and failed to see that the normativity of that text is grounded in the experience of the Holocaust.

I think that the text of the declaration, which arose out of these horrors, should give the phrase "human rights" more rigidity of reference than it has received in the recent scholarly literature. The expert historians and legal scholars discussed in this book have cut the "extension" of the phrase—as used in world political and United Nations contexts—loose from the modern intension the phrase was given by its Holocaust connection, or so we have argued. I am not objecting to the extension of the phrase in popular usage. Not everyone who wears a gold ring or admires an elm tree or uses an aluminum pan needs to know how to tell real from fake gold or an elm from a maple or aluminum from a metal that looks and acts just like it but isn't the real thing. I am objecting to experts themselves straying off the path by giving the "UN meaning" of human rights too much credence and thereby loosening the real "UDHR meaning" and focus. We should not let other meanings, not even those adopted by the UN General Assembly, eclipse or push aside what the "real" meaning of the phrase "human rights" is. Linked as it is to the experience of the Holocaust, its first but not its only extension is that of the first and second generations of human rights as found in the UDHR, amended by ICCPR Article 27. Those are the ones that inhere in flesh and blood human beings the way we want our water to be H_2O, whatever pitcher or glass it is poured from. The pitchers from which we drink or the groups to which people belong do matter (often a great deal), but these containers are not the real thing. Third-generation human rights accrue to us only after we have honored the connection between the Holocaust and the Universal Declaration. This seems true both historically as I argued in part 1 and philosophically as I argued in part 2 of this book.

CONCLUSION

Enacting the Connection

Implementation as Commemoration

The Holocaust was a case of total *ex*clusion, and the Universal Declaration is one of total *in*clusion. Those in the concentration camps and other hellholes were totally excluded from any society to the point of being killed. Theirs was a biological death called murder. Before that point of totality, there were numerous other exclusionary methods the Nazis used, from the 1933 marriage laws to denial of civil rights and the right of running a business. Many exclusions amounted to legal deaths of being denied participation in civil society and being pushed to the margins in the hope that the victims would disappear from the radar of the German nation-state as well as from that of the world community, which they almost did. When pushing them aside did not work, the Reich killed them, first legally and then also biologically.

The UDHR drafters reacted to these Nazi horrors of *ex*clusion with the total *in*clusion of everyone without exception on the list of those who have inherent in their persons the moral rights listed in the Universal Declaration of Human Rights. These moral rights are inalienable in that they cannot be given or taken away. They are unexceptional because, while they can be and often are violated, there are no exceptions to the having of them. Critics of human rights often neglect the fact that people can have something without being able to enjoy it, like a toy or a car or a marriage. But while these kinds of things can be altered or taken away, having a human right cannot be taken away, because it is part of our moral DNA. All that some person, group, or government can do is violate that right so that one cannot enjoy it any longer, but the right itself cannot be taken away without "taking away" or killing the possessor of that right as well—which is what the Nazis did in and outside the concentration camps. Because human rights accrue to people at their births into the human family, they can be violated but not taken away while the possessor of these rights is still alive. The only way to deny that someone has the birthrights of the UDHR is to deny their births by killing them and thereby totally excluding them from the human family. The UDHR drafters started at the other extreme of inclusivity, which is the point of the inclusion of everyone in the moral community of humankind. After that come the more specific inclusions in particular bodies politic, where these moral rights are to be translated into legal ones, which, as I discussed in chapters 4 and 5, is what the international system of legal human rights is supposed to do and to a large extent actually does do.

This contrast between total Holocaust exclusion and total UDHR inclusion places a huge question mark behind the connection I have defended in this book, for there is no way of restoring to life those that have been killed. While the legality of something or someone that has been declared illegal can be restored and once again made legal, biological death is a total exclusion and it is final. And while someone who has been tortured can be allowed to tell his or her story, be partially healed, and perhaps be given reparation, this cannot be done with the corpses and ashes removed from the ovens in the concentration camps, from the Cambodian killing fields, or from the Rwandan schoolyards or with those who drowned off the shores of the Greek island of Lesbos at the beginning of our century. The absoluteness of the events that constitute the Holocaust and other abominations seems to forestall any real connection with the absolute universality of the rights proclaimed in the Universal Declaration. This gap is unimaginably great. We can only bridge it, and then only partially, by using our moral imaginations.

Let us start by connecting the events of the Holocaust and the adoption of the Universal Declaration in the following way. We can look at the implementation of human rights as a way of commemorating the victims of the Holocaust. I first saw this done when visiting the Jewish History Museum (the Verzetsmuseum) in Amsterdam. After we had seen the exhibit, much of which focused on the treatment of the Jews during the war—with the demand for wearing the star of David, being imprisoned in Westerborg and from there shipped to Auschwitz—visitors were invited to sign petitions drawn up by Amnesty International for the release of prisoners of conscience and asylum seekers in holding centers. This AI request sought to do something about the asylum blind spot in the Universal Declaration, in which Article 14 tells us that "everyone has the right to seek and [once granted] enjoy in other countries asylum from persecution" but does not say that "everyone" in that position also has a human right to enter and be given asylum in another country. The European refugee crisis of 2016–17 shows us how big this blind spot is. In any case, the AI petition drive in this museum sought to do something about this gap by linking commemoration to the implementation of the moral right to asylum. In chapter 4 I argued that most of the legal human rights conventions—in the case of UDHR Article 14, especially the 1967 Refugee Convention—indirectly make this connection between commemoration and implementation. These are commemorative links between the horrors of the Holocaust and the implementation of the Universal Declaration. Far more such commemorative connections would be created if Holocaust museums became even more explicit about advocating human rights and UDHR-related literature.

That is happening, and it is great news for the human rights movement to see that of the thirty-seven Holocaust museums or study centers in the United States and Canada whose mission statements I looked at, about a third link their Holocaust/genocide education and commemoration programs to some form of education about contemporary human rights issues or violations.[1] I looked at fifteen such centers in my home state of New Jersey, which is the only state where Holocaust education is mandated by the state; two in Alabama; three in California; two in Florida; one each in Illinois, Maryland, Massachusetts, Minnesota, and Montana; seven in New York; one in Ohio; and two in Canada. Here are a few of my findings from that list of thirty-seven taken from a total of more than 150 centers. It is a small sample, but it does reveal a trend.

The mission of the Gross Center for Holocaust and Genocide Studies at Ramapo College, New Jersey, is "to promote an understanding of the pernicious consequences of anti-Semitism, racism, ethnic hatred, other forms of bigotry, and violations of human rights."[2] The programs of the Herbert and Leonard Littman Holocaust Resource Center at Rutgers University in New Brunswick, New Jersey, "are designed to enhance public awareness of the Holocaust and promote discussion of racism, genocide, discrimination, and the importance of protecting human rights."[3] The website of the Holocaust Commission of the state of Alabama says, "In a democratic society, human rights must be maintained and discrimination and hatred must be eradicated." Through its education programs, this Alabama commission hopes to cultivate "a sense of individual and collective responsibilities in maintaining human rights."[4] Part of the mission of the Mgrublian Center for the Study of Human Rights (formerly the Mgrublian Center for the Study of the Holocaust, Genocide and Human Rights) at Claremont McKenna College in California is to "advance scholarship in the study of human rights, Holocaust history and genocide studies, including the Armenian genocide."[5] The name of the Center for Holocaust and Human Rights Education at Florida Atlantic University speaks for itself.[6] The Illinois Holocaust Museum and Education Center "fulfills its mission . . . through education programs and initiatives that foster the promotion of human rights and the elimination of genocide."[7] The following names of two centers in New York State also speak for themselves: the Holocaust Education and Human Rights Center and the Monroe Community College Holocaust, Genocide, and Human Rights Project.[8] The Dallas Holocaust Museum / Center for Education and Tolerance is "dedicated to teaching the history of the Holocaust and advancing human rights to combat prejudice, hatred and indifference."[9] Similarly, the mission of the Vancouver Holocaust Education Center is "to promote human rights, social justice and genocide awareness through education and awareness of the Holocaust."[10]

Not all Jewish community centers and museums agree on the expansion of their various missions to educating the world about other genocides. While some centers hold back, others become more explicit.

In the same week that I heard about an artistic director being fired for wanting to expand programming in just this way, I saw an hour-long television program that explained the mission of the Holocaust Memorial and Tolerance Center of Nassau County in Glen Cove, New York. The show was superbly done. It visually encapsulated the center's mission, which is "to teach the history of the Holocaust and its lessons through education and community outreach. We teach about the dangers of antisemitism, racism, bullying and all other manifestations of intolerance. We promote resistance to prejudice and advocate respect for every human being."[11] All aspects of this mission were explained with images ranging from police training to eliminate racial profiling, to the experiences of Japanese comfort women, to the relationship between a teenage girl who lost her immediate family in the 1994 Rwandan genocide and an elderly Holocaust survivor who coached her on how to talk about her experience. Since the center wants to pass on the lessons of the Holocaust to the next generation, it would have been very appropriate if it had handed out copies of the UDHR for the young people to take home as "souvenirs" of their visit.

My hope is that this book helps strengthen and expand these kinds of connections between Holocaust/genocide commemoration and human rights implementation. If the core meaning of modern "human rights" is the sense it received from its connection with the Holocaust, then almost any type of human rights activism is at bottom an act of Holocaust commemoration. This book has sought to bring that commemorative connection to the surface and give it a higher level of awareness. The murdered millions of the Holocaust cannot be resurrected or brought back to life. The past is passed. We can personally and publicly light a candle in memory of horrific events and killed persons. But to these symbolic acts we must add other acts of universal human rights implementation in local times and places. We can turn our human rights activities into Holocaust commemoration acts if—like these museums and genocide study centers—we make awareness of the Holocaust part of our human rights outlook on world affairs. This new kind of commemoration of the Holocaust victims takes aim at those who are culpable of present and ongoing violations of human rights instead of only at atrocities committed long ago. The victims of the Holocaust are for us commemorative anchors because their deaths were the primary cause of the 1948 Universal Declaration of Human Rights.

Once, on a visit back to the Netherlands, my father and I went on a bicycle trip. We passed a spot where the Germans had shot to death a group of hostages they had taken in response to an attack by the Dutch Underground. Since there was no marker, I asked my father how he knew that this corner of the field at the edge of woods was the exact spot where those killings took place. He said he knew because right where he was pointing the grass was lusher and greener than it was in the rest of the field. Just so, we must let our human rights activism be fed by the thousands of mass graves found in the concentration camps. They tell us what the phrase "human rights" really means. As the aforementioned museums and genocide study centers also show, that does not mean that the victims of other past massacres and genocides cannot be commemorated at the same time as we focus our attention on specific new human rights violations. Our consciousness is large enough to take in multiple commemorations in one act of implementation. Many of the centers have in fact changed their names from "Holocaust Study Center" to "Holocaust and Genocide Study Center." Other genocides, mass murders, and human rights violations of all kinds have been brought to live in one commemorative tent, for which the Holocaust provides the central pole. There cannot be allowed in our world any exception to the possession of human rights. I have argued that the Holocaust settled most philosophical questions about who does or does not possess human rights. Everyone does. Our task is to make sure that the protection of these birthrights reaches everyone and stretches into the furthest corners of our world.

No "State of Exception"

The Universal Declaration contains several different types of moral human rights. The right to marry a spouse of one's choice is a social human right, as is the right to an education. The right to have an attorney or to know what crime one is charged with is a legal human right. The right to a job and good conditions of work are mostly economic rights. The right to life obviously is a security and safety human right. The right to travel and come back into one's own country or the right to seek asylum in another country are international types of human rights that more openly than the others require the cooperation of several nations to implement. If we look for a right in the declaration that is basic to most others, one candidate is the right to life. Another might be the right to the development of one's personality, which is stipulated in UDHR Articles 22, 26, and 29. One right that is not mentioned in the text itself but that would also be a candidate for basicality might be the right to speak and be heard. Since the days of Aristotle, the ability to speak and articulate in human language, instead of communicating by the use of mere signs as other animals do, has been the mark of belonging to a political community governed by rules of justice and ideas of right and wrong. This right to speak and the rule of law are intimately connected. Both are built on the dual human capacities for language and justice, in that order.

But as Jean-François Lyotard reminds us, "The very Greeks who invented the *politeia* also excluded *barbaroi*. The right of interlocution is not granted to every human being. The figure of the other is that of a threat weighing on the national community from without, which cannot help but undermine its integrity," especially if those others cross into that national domain (Lyotard 1993, 139). Lyotard takes Aristotle's point about human language capacity and uses it to erase the line Aristotle himself drew between Greeks and barbarians. Says he, "Explicitly or implicitly, every human sentence is destined to someone or something. The polarization is marked in our language by the verbal 'persons' and personal pronouns. Some answer, some response, some link or follow-up is expected. . . . *I* is the one who is speaking now; *you* is the one to whom this communication is currently addressed. *You* are silent when *I* speak, but *you* can speak, has spoken, and will speak" (137; original italics). By locating the polarization or correlation between the right to speak and the duty to listen in the very structure of our languages, Lyotard is able to criticize Aristotle for not expanding the circle of the *politeia* or political existence to include the *barbaroi* outside the border of the *politeia* as Aristotle saw it. Making use of the gap between cosmopolitan rights in a Westphalian world, Lyotard could be saying that everyone, the other included, has the right to speak and thus address those residing in today's nation-states, in effect lifting this civic principle of speaking and being listened to above that of national inclusion. "Let us take it," he says, "that the capacity to speak to others is a human right, and perhaps the most fundamental human right" (140–41). If that is so, then today's 65 million refugees should not be silenced, but their petitions and entreaties should be and must be heard by all the others who enjoy their human rights, either as citizens or aliens, within some legal system or other. No one may be excluded from the human family, which the declaration tells us is constituted by the universal possession (though clearly not by universal enjoyment) of the human rights listed in its text.

Lyotard thinks that the ability to interlocute with someone becomes a real human right to speak—and thus also be heard and listened to by those addressed— only if that interlocution adds some new information and is not just something that has "already been said" (Lyotard 1993, 143). A real interlocution involves a real issue of justice. Any exclusion or "banishment is a harm inflicted on those that undergo it, but this harm necessarily changes to a wrong when the victim is excluded from the speech community. For the wrong is the harm to which the victim cannot testify, since he cannot be heard" (144). This is probably why the minutes of the meetings show that the UDHR drafters included the right to have an attorney and the right to understand the charges and be able to respond to them—all the while being innocent until proven guilty—in the six legal human rights articles (Arts. 6–11) of their document. Since they often do not understand and are not heard when they try to speak up, refugees and migrants end up speaking with their feet by crossing into neighboring nations on the way to secure their lives. "It happens," says Lyotard, "that a speaker is more eloquent dead than alive, and does not therefore die for the community" (144). This was the case with the corpse of a dead child that washed onto shore at the Greek island of Lesbos and became an iconic image for the refugee crisis in 2015. The same thing happened with the photo of a wounded boy in an Aleppo ambulance in October 2016. The wrong of the silence imposed on the refugees before they "spoke" with their feet lies in "the exclusion of the speaker from the speech community. The community will not even speak of this exclusion since the victim will be unable to report it and cannot therefore defend himself or appeal" to—we add—the moral norms in the Universal Declaration (144). The Westphalian rule of national laws was and is used to silence the victims.

In these citations about not being heard, Lyotard was not thinking about the 2015–16 refugee crisis that I took as my example. He was thinking about the concentration camps, asking, "But how can one communicate by means of interlocution the terror of what it means no longer to be destined to anyone or anything? They were not spoken to, they were treated. They were not enemies. The SS or Kapos who called them dogs, pigs, or vermin did not [even] treat them as animals but as refuse. It is the destiny of refuse to be incinerated. The ordeal of being forgotten is unforgettable" (Lyotard 1993, 144). This is why I propose that we think of our human rights activism as acts of commemorating the victims of the Holocaust and other abominations. In our human rights work, including the writing of this book, we exercise our own right to speak, entreat, and be heard by present-day authorities about ongoing violations of human rights. If at the time of our activism we place before the mind's eye names and images of Holocaust victims together with the present-day victims we are trying to help, we are enacting the connection between the Holocaust and the Universal Declaration.

Our activism must be one of commitment and passion. It cannot just be the result of an intellectual assent to the arguments this book has presented, for that would not last. On this one point, we are somewhat (and only somewhat) like Jean Améry during his year in Auschwitz-Monowitz. He saw horrors far worse than we can even imagine. Yet as an intellectual whose "realm of thought is essentially a humanistic one," Améry had great difficulty holding his own (Améry 1980, 2). While plumbers, chemists, and carpenters could make themselves useful and so benefit from the privileges their special talents gave them, Améry could find no social expression for his "well-developed esthetic consciousness" and for his "inclination and ability . . . toward abstract trains of thought" (2). In a "bunk-bed conversation" with another intellectual, he soon discovered that in Auschwitz "the intellect very abruptly lost its basic quality: its transcendence" (7). "The word always dies where the claim of some reality is total" (20) and philosophical argumentation is eclipsed by events. In his essay "At the Mind's Limits," Améry reports that after as an intellectual he had experienced "the collapse of his initial inner resistance" to the horrors based on ideas of right and wrong, he "experienced the logic of the SS as a reality that proved itself by the hour" (11). He asks himself, "Were not those who were preparing to destroy him in the right, owing to the undeniable fact that they were the stronger ones? Thus, absolute intellectual tolerance and the methodical doubting of the intellectual became factors in his autodestruction. Yes, the SS could carry on just as it did; there were no natural rights, and moral categories come and go like fashions" (11).

Amid the horrors around him, Améry came to think that as an intellectual "with all his knowledge and analyses he had less with which to oppose his destroyers than the unintellectual" (Améry 1980, 12). He therefore developed "great admiration for both my religiously and politically committed comrades" (12). It did not matter whether in addition to their commitments they were also intellectuals. What mattered was that "one way or the other, in the decisive moments their political or religious belief was an inestimable help to them, while we sceptical and humanistic intellectuals took recourse, in vain, to our literary, philosophical, and artistic household gods" (12). In the camps abstractions like beauty, knowledge, and death itself went out the window, and all that was left for the inmates to think about was not whether but how they would die. Says Améry, "You do not observe dehumanized man committing his deeds and misdeeds without having all your notions of inherent human dignity placed in doubt" (20).

> A practicing Jew once told him: "You must realize one thing: that here your intelligence and education are worthless. But I have a certainty that our God will avenge us." A leftist radical German prisoner, who had been thrown into the camps already in 1933, put it more pithily: "Now you're sitting here, you bourgeois bullshitters, and tremble in fear of the SS. We don't tremble, and even if we croak miserably here, we still know that after we're gone our comrades are going to line the whole pack of them up against the wall." (14)

Améry aimed his essay about the plight of the intellectual in the camps at younger generations for whom the experiences of the Holocaust were fast fading. He tells the readers of the 1976 reissue of what he wrote in 1964, "Enlightenment can properly fulfill its task only if it sets to work with passion" (Améry 1980, xi). We too must infuse our commitment to human rights with the passion Améry's ideologically oriented friends displayed. For "they were no [Leibnizian] monads; they stood open, wide open onto a world that was not the world of Auschwitz" (14). That commitment helped them transcend the world of Auschwitz and gave them strength to carry on. The Universal Declaration embodies this openness to the world and will help shore up our commitment to that other non-Auschwitz world.

The only human rights book that I have seen with the master plan for the Auschwitz concentration camp on its outside cover is Giorgio Agamben's *Homo Sacer: Sovereign Power and Bare Life*. Published first in Italy in 1995, the book is an intellectual meditation on Carl Schmitt's notion of the state of exception, tracing that state back into Roman law, medieval political theology, and modern contract theories of the state, and forward by way of the Nazi camps to present-day refugee centers and ongoing discussions on dying with dignity. Agamben's book follows through on what Foucault saw as "a kind of bestialization of man achieved through the most sophisticated political techniques. For the first time in history, the possibilities of the social sciences are made known, and at once it becomes possible both to protect life and to authorize a holocaust" (Agamben 1998, 3). Agamben points out how Hitler did that by way of the Führer Principle, which allowed him to be the soul and literally the body of the Third Reich. While he also had a private life,

> what defines [Hitler] as Fuhrer is that his existence as such has an immediate political character. Thus while the office of the chancellor of the Reich is a public *dignitas* received on the basis of procedures foreseen in the Weimar constitution, the office of the Fuhrer is no longer an office in the sense of traditional public law, but rather something that springs forth without mediation from his person insofar as it coincides with the life of the German people. The Fuhrer is the political form of this life: this is why his word is law and why he demands nothing of the German people except what it in truth already is. (184)

Like Lyotard, Agamben also begins with the line Aristotle drew between *zoe* (which refers to just life) and *bios* (which refers to life in a political community), and he locates the führer's body "at the point of coincidence between *zoe* and *bios*, biological body and political body," which two "incessantly pass over into each other" (184). The merger of these two bodies in the person of the führer wipes out any distinction between the fact of bare life and the sovereignty of the modern state. At that point there no longer is a distinction to be made between the normativity of law and the factuality of life, as the "vermin" in the camps experienced when they were selected for extinction, not ever to be heard of or listened to again. It is this line that is at stake in this book's attempt to preserve the connection between the factuality of the Holocaust and the normativity of the Universal Declaration of Human Rights. The norms of the latter arose out of the facts of the former.

As Agamben sees it, "The fundamental categorical pair in Western politics is not that of friend/enemy but that of bare life/political existence, *zoe/bios*, exclusion/inclusion" (Agamben 1998, 8). Originally, bare life was not a political category at all, as can be seen in Roman law in which the paterfamilias had the right of life and death over his own sons. Agamben speculates that this might explain how the "hagiographic epithet 'father of the people,' which is reserved in every age to the leaders invested with sovereign authority . . . acquires its originary, sinister meaning" (89). He traces the sinister character of sovereign power back to a reconstructed fragment of the poet Pindar: "The nomos, sovereign of all, / Of mortals and immortals, / Leads with the strongest hand, / Justifying the most violent. / I judge this from the works of Hercules." At the center of Pindar's fragment, Agamben sees "a scandalous unification of two essentially antithetical principles that the Greeks called *Bia* and *Dike*, violence and justice" (31). The same union of opposites can be found in the Roman idea of *homo sacer*. As the Roman historian of law Pompeius Festus explains it,

> The sacred man is the one whom the [sovereign] people have judged on account of a crime. It is not permitted to sacrifice this man, yet he who kills him will not be condemned for homicide; in the first tribunician law, in fact, it is noted that "if someone who kills the man who is sacred according to the plebiscite, it will not be considered homicide." This is why it is customary for a bad or impure man to be called sacred. (cited in Agamben 1998, 71)

The status of the *homo sacer* is characterized by a double exclusion. "The unsanctionable killing that, in his case, anyone may commit—is classifiable neither as sacrifice nor as homicide, neither as the execution of a condemnation to death nor as sacrilege. Subtracting itself from the sanctioned forms of both human and divine law, this violence opens a sphere of human action that is neither the sphere of *sacrum facere* nor that of profane action" (82–83). From these ancient sources, Agamben draws for us this modern principle: "*The sovereign sphere is the sphere in which it is permitted to kill without committing homicide and without celebrating sacrifice, and sacred life—that is, life that may be killed but not sacrificed—is the life that has been captured in this sphere*" (83; original italics). The bare life of the *homo sacer* is covered by the law and yet totally outside both divine (he may not be sacrificed) and human law (killing him is not homicide).

The point here is not that a killing takes place but that there is no norm that guides or judges it. It explains why in his history of sovereign power Agamben relies a great deal on the contract between Hobbes's sovereign and his subjects who have no norm they can use to judge the legitimacy of their own deaths should their sovereign decide their demise is necessary to uphold national security. Even Rousseau goes against his own deep egalitarian instincts when he lets the General Will decide questions of bare life and death without reference to any external normativity. This modern subjection of bare life to state sovereignty leaves little room for Locke's idea that the state of nature is governed by a law of nature that places normative limits on the uses of sovereign power, limits to which I trace the announcement in the Universal Declaration that human beings as such have inalienable moral rights.

The Western political theorist who most vigorously delineated this "sovereign sphere" of state power to place someone into this legal limbo of being under the law and at the same time outside that law is the Nazi theoretician Carl Schmitt. Even before Hitler came to power, Schmitt wrote in his 1922 book, *Political Theology*, "Sovereign is he who decides on the exception." He repeated this succinct definition in the second edition of 1934, right after Hitler had "won" the election and been appointed chancellor. The test whether an emergency exists and a life or millions of lives must be taken for the sake of the greater national good cannot ever be a "juristic decision." Says

Schmitt, "About an abstract concept there will in general be no argument, least of all in the history of sovereignty. What is argued about is the concrete application, and that means who decides in a situation of conflict what constitutes the public interest or interest of the state, public safety and order, *le salut public*, and so on" (Schmitt 2005, 6). Schmitt would have readily agreed with the general limits (respect for the rights of others, morality, public order, and the general welfare in a democratic society) that UDHR Article 29 places on the practice of human rights. But he also had no objections to Hitler's suspension of the Weimar constitution's civil and political liberties after the German Reichstag was set on fire on February 22, 1933. As führer, Hitler was the physical and legal embodiment of the German people. He personally was the sovereign, and so his will was law. He could decide the exceptions and what was needed to maintain "public order" in times of crisis. He did this hundreds of times, each time with disastrous consequences for millions of people inside and outside Germany. Schmitt never recanted the implications of his theory of the sovereign as "the one who decides on the exception" without being subject to a higher normativity. He pointed out that his way of thinking about state sovereignty was a fairly direct outcome of the modern process of secularization in the intellectual realm in which basic concepts such as sovereignty were transposed from the realm of theology to the realm of politics. The sovereign state had replaced the sovereign God, which suited the Nazis just fine.

Schmitt is probably right that a

> jurisprudence concerned with the ordinary day-to-day questions has practically no interest in the concept of sovereignty. Only the recognizable is its normal concern; everything else is a "disturbance." Such a jurisprudence confronts the extreme case disconcertedly, for not every extraordinary measure, not every police emergency measure or emergency decree, is necessarily an exception. What characterizes an exception is principally unlimited authority, which means the suspension of the entire existing order. . . . The existence of the state is undoubted proof of its superiority over the validity of the legal norm. The decision [of the exception] frees itself from all normative ties and becomes in the true sense absolute. The state suspends the law in the

> exception on the basis of its rights to self-preservation, as one would say. (Schmitt 2005, 12)

Schmitt has put his finger on a very sensitive point in modern jurisprudence, both on the domestic front, as can be seen from the law cases that came out of the Guantánamo Bay detention center, and internationally, as can be seen from discussions about which human rights are and are not subject to derogation by states that have ratified human rights conventions. The conditions of when there is an exception, who has the power to declare one, and what it looks like are constantly under discussion.

Agamben criticizes Schmitt's analysis as understandably too limited. With Schmitt and others writing between the wars,

> the problem of sovereignty was reduced to the question of who within the political order was invested with certain powers, and the very threshold of the political order itself was never called into question. Today, now that the great State structures have entered into a process of dissolution and the emergency has . . . become the rule, the time is ripe to place the problem of the originary structure and limits of the form of the state in a new perspective. (Agamben 1998, 12)

I see this new perspective as one that is informed by the supra-Westphalian normative order of the Universal Declaration of Human Rights. Too many nation-states are failing and either totally crumbling or torn apart by civil strife. If we think of today's juridico-political world order in the context of the roughly 65 million refugees now under the care of the United Nations High Commissioner for Refugees, we run into Agamben's critique of Schmitt and into his point that "*the rule applies to the exception in no longer applying, in withdrawing from it*" (18; original italics). Agamben continues, "Here what is outside is included not simply by means of an interdiction or an internment, but rather by means of suspension of the juridical order's validity—by letting the juridical order, that is, withdraw from the exception and abandon it" (18). Today's millions of refugees and internally displaced persons are feeling abandoned, pure and simple. Agamben concludes,

"The originary relation of law to life is not application but Abandonment" (29). Going beyond and against Schmitt, Agamben presses his case that "in our age the state of exception comes more and more to the foreground as the fundamental political structure and ultimately begins to become the rule. When our age tried to grant the unlocalizable a permanent and visible localization, the result was the concentration camp" (21). He adds, "As the absolute space of exception the camp is topologically different from a simple space of confinement. And it is this space of exception, in which the link between localization and ordering is definitely broken, that has determined the crisis of the old '*nomos* of the earth'" (21).

Agamben titled one of his chapters "The Camp as the '*Nomos*' of the Modern." In it he investigates the juridico-political structure of the concentration camps, the basis of which was "not common law, but *Schutzhaft* (literally, protective custody), a juridical institution of Prussian origin that the Nazi jurors sometimes classified as a preventive police measure insofar as it allowed individuals to be taken into custody independent of any criminal behavior, solely to avoid danger to the security of the state" (Agamben 1998, 167). He traces this concept to Prussian laws and notes that it was widely used

> during the disorder in Germany that followed the signing of the [World War I] peace treaty [and adds that] it is important not to forget that the first concentration camps in Germany were the work not of the Nazi regime but of the Social Democratic governments, which interned thousands of communist militants in 1923 on the basis of *Schutzhaft* and also created the *Konzentrationslager für Ausländer* at Cottbus-Sielow, which housed mainly Eastern European refugees and which may, therefore be considered the first camp for Jews in this century (even if it was, obviously, not an extermination camp). (167)

We must read Hindenburg's suspension of Article 48 of the 1919 Weimar constitution (which Carl Schmitt used a great deal) against this background. That article said, "The President of the Reich may, in the case of grave disturbance or threat to public security and order, make the decisions necessary to re-establish public security, if necessary with the aid of the armed forces. To this end he may provisionally suspend [*auser Kraft setzen*] the fundamental rights contained in articles 114, 115, 117, 118, 123, 124, and 153" of the Weimar constitution (cited in Agamben 1998, 167). This is precisely what Hitler made Hindenburg do the day after the Reichstag fire. This suspension of the Weimar constitution's liberties and rights was an exercise of unbridled sovereignty, which is the unmediated power to decide when there is an exception and what it is to look like. Agamben points out what we all know, that this *state of exception* ceased "*to be referred to as an external and provisional state of factual danger, and comes to be confused with juridical rule itself*" (168; original italics). And again: "*The camp is the space that is opened when the state of exception begins to come the rule*" (168–69; original italics). We should think of this when reading accounts about modern camps like Ben Rawlence's 2016 *City of Thorns: Nine Lives in the World's Largest Refugee Camp*. Fortunately, when the courts in the United States examined President Donald Trump's travel bans, they came to the conclusion that US presidential sovereignty is not and cannot be "unbridled" or be exercised without judicial scrutiny.

The key feature of the modern state of exception is that it is a "willed one." Writes Agamben, "What is excluded in the camp is, according to the etymological sense of the term 'exception' (*ex-capere*), *taken outside*, included through its own exclusion. But what is first of all taken into the juridical order is the state of exception itself" (Agamben 1998, 170). He continues, "Insofar as the state of exception is 'willed,' it inaugurates a new juridico-political paradigm in which the norm becomes indistinguishable from the exception. The camp is thus the structure in which the state of exception—the possibility of deciding on which founds sovereign power—is realized normally" (170). What starts out as a provisional arrangement becomes permanent. Hence the chapter's title: "The Camp as the '*Nomos*' of the Modern." As Agamben sees it, contemporary reports coming out of some of the camps reveal that "whoever entered the camp moved in a zone of indistinction between outside and inside, exception and rule, licit and illicit, in which the very concepts of subjective right and juridical protection no longer made sense" (170). It does not make sense, because these internees live outside or between the cracks of the Westphalian system, which is supposed to be the main delivery vehicle for their human rights. Agamben continues, "Insofar as its inhabitants were stripped of every political status and wholly reduced to bare life, the camp was also the most absolute biopolitical space ever to have been realized, in which power confronts nothing but pure life, *without mediation*" (171; italics added).

I added the italics to "without mediation" because I disagree with it. Like Hannah Arendt, Agamben fails to connect the two events I have consistently linked in this book: the Universal Declaration and the Holocaust. Even someone like John Roth, whose moral reactions to the Holocaust I discussed at the end of chapter 3, follows Agamben by not placing the UDHR at the center of his confrontation with the Holocaust. As I have argued in this and other books, the text of the UDHR is the great mediator between state sovereignty and bare life. Because he does not honor this mediation, Agamben overstates his claim that the camp is the *nomos* of the modern. It is true that more and more people are caught in the state of exception as seen from Agamben's perspective, pulling in, as he does, modern uses of the death penalty and the lack of dying with dignity. He might have added movements, like Black Lives Matter, that point to the aftereffects of the state of exception called slavery. Even so, my response is that the Holocaust connection with the UDHR shows that there cannot be and there never *really* was in the world a state of exception. Every human being—wherever and however situated—had and now has the inherent moral rights stipulated in the Universal Declaration of Human Rights, which was adopted by the international community just as the horrors of the camps became more widely known. To make sure that the power of modern states would not again face nothing but bare life, the UDHR drafters reaffirmed the existence of moral rights in *homo sacer*. Between sovereign power and bare life, the declaration's drafters placed this supranational moral text enunciating rights in nonpoliticized and nondomesticated human beings who live in all of the world's zones and nations but increasingly also in the many cracks that have developed between Westphalian nations. At first these spaces were islands of exception inside the territories controlled by the Nazis, but today we see them springing up all over the world, both inside nation-states and on the borders in no-man's-land at the system's edges.

According to Agamben, the "bare" in "bare life" "corresponds to the Greek *haplos*, the term by which first philosophy defines pure Being" (Agamben 1998, 182), the preoccupation of Western metaphysics. In a previous publication (Morsink 2009), I wrote about "the metaphysics of inherence" and explained how the declaration drafters came to recognize the moral rights that accrue to those who have nothing but bare life. Looking at the Holocaust, they presented their declaration as a mediating path between sovereign power and bare life. The records I cited in chapter 3 of the present book show that these UDHR drafters saw the pure Being of us human beings as the moral core of their modern mediation attempt between sovereign power and bare life. The same is true of our own approach to each other, even in the interstices of the Westphalian system, where we meet each other as persons with moral rights and correlative duties. The inalienable moral rights of the UDHR create an intersection of bare life and *haplos* Being; it is the place where metaphysics and politics meet head on. "And it may be," says Agamben, "that only if we are able to decipher the political meaning of pure Being . . . will we be able to master the bare life that expresses our subjection to political power, just as it may be, inversely, that only if we understand the theoretical implications of bare life will we be able to solve the enigma of ontology" (182).

Emmanuel Levinas too brought bare life and political being together with his arguments that the true nature of Being reveals itself in the face of the Other. Agamben thought that when "brought to the limit of pure Being, metaphysics (thought) passes over into politics (into reality), just as on the threshold of bare life, politics steps beyond itself into theory" (Agamben 1998, 182). This is my translation of this citation: brought face to face with the camps, human thought cannot help but become political, just as when faced with these same camps, politics must become moral. The deep connection between the Holocaust and the declaration shows us that there can be no state of exception. The two "indeterminate concepts" (182) of metaphysics and politics cannot ever really avoid each other. Their inherence in the bare human person gives human rights a transcendence over the Westphalian system, making for supranational norms to which both victims and their advocates can and should appeal. These appeals constitute the politics of human rights. As I said, the Universal Declaration is the great mediator between state sovereignty and bare life. When that mediation is successful, it brings the ancient Greek notions of *zoe* and *bios* back together again. Pace Agamben—who does not link the camps and the declaration—I think we must make that connection and find a return from the camps to classical politics (188). But the return will not be without conflict.

The Politics of Human Rights

Given the size and diversity of the human rights movement, the general subject or type of person pointed to in the so-called politics of human rights would have to be a very basic subject and could not be, for instance, simply the having of citizenship in this or that country, as Hannah Arendt would have it. It might be that there is no single generic subject (or type of person) that is the focus of the politics of human rights. Perhaps there are thousands or millions of different subjects or persons that cannot be grouped together in any sensible way under one conceptual umbrella. That would make the politics of human rights as scattered and fractured in terms of its agenda as "normal" political campaigns and movements. These normal political campaigns differ from one locale, nation, or region to another. However, since we often call these political phenomena by the single name of "the politics of human rights," I want to investigate the elusive single subject of this political phenomenon. What one subject supposedly has the human rights contested in any one of these many different situations?

Hannah Arendt was one of the first theorists to raise this question when she used the expression "the right to have rights." For eighteen years—from 1933, when she fled Germany, to 1951, when she obtained American citizenship—Arendt herself was a stateless person. In 1940, when she was in an internment camp at Gurs in France with other "enemy aliens," she escaped before the others were shipped to German extermination camps. Arendt comments: "We became aware of the existence of a right to have rights (and that means to live in a framework where one is judged by one's actions and opinions) and a right to belong to some kind of organized community, only when millions of people emerged who had lost and could not regain these rights because of the new global political situation" (Arendt 1976, 296–97).

Arendt meant that everyone needs "a place" on the planet where she can locate herself legally as part of a political community, have a domicile, and partake of community life and action. Stateless people lack that connection. Being pushed out of Westphalian-type states and having therefore lost the rights of citizens that come with that kind of connection, the plight of these stateless people raises the question, Who really is "the subject" of the rights of man or of human rights?

When Arendt asked this question in 1940, the declaration had not yet been written, but even if it had been, she would not have drawn comfort from the fact proclaimed in Article 1 that she too had been "born free and equal in dignity and rights" as a member of the human family. Without membership in a political community that shielded her with its protective umbrella, those birthrights had no meaning to her at all. She was caught in a so-called state of exception. As she saw it, there are no rights, human or otherwise, outside the realm of citizenship in a Westphalian state. The French Revolution made a mistake when it in one and the same national declaration avowed the rights of man *and* of citizen as if there was no international or supranational enforcement aspect to these rights of man. Arendt saw correctly that the 1789 declaration encapsulated the rights of man within the legal and physical boundaries of nation-states. According to some of the theorists discussed in part 1 of this book, human rights did not escape from that prison until the 1970s, when, as they see it, the human rights movement acquired a supra-state component. My view is that that supra-state component has been present since the 1940s. Arendt misread both the intent and the effect of the 1948 Universal Declaration. When these 1948 drafters turned the 1789 "rights of man" into "human rights," they freed those rights from their Westphalian prison. The "everyone" who is the subject of most UDHR articles is not simply "a human being in general" (Arendt 1951, 302)—an abstraction that Arendt rejected—but individual human beings in all times and places, including Hannah Arendt (1906–75) herself. The declaration's drafters internationalized, globalized, and, as their title indicates, universalized the 1789 rights of man. They did that especially to help Arendt herself and other victims of the Holocaust. Her plight in 1940, when she escaped to the United States, calls to mind the human rights flowchart of this book (idea → Holocaust + UDHR text → system ↔ movement), for she wrote right after the UDHR text had been adopted and before the system took hold and certainly before the type of international movement we now have. Having that movement and seeing millions of people "housed" in refugee camps makes the question of the general subject of "the politics of human rights" all the more acute.

Alison Kesby explored four possible hosts for this right to have rights and came to the conclusion that each one of them lacked sufficient universality. For reasons similar to the anti-positivist stance I took in chapters 4 and 5, Kesby rightly rejected Arendt's own choice of citizenship in one of our modern nation-states as the proper host for the right to have rights. When Arendt titled chapter nine of her 1951 book, *The Origins of Totalitarianism*, "The Decline of the Nation-State and the Rights of Man," she bought into the idea that "the rights of man" had been imprisoned within the Westphalian state system and that with the decline of the those kinds of states, we would also see "the end" of what we now call human rights. She tells us, "These stateless and minorities [peoples] . . . had no government to represent [them] and to protect them and therefore were forced to live either under the law of exception of the Minority Treaties, or under conditions of absolute lawlessness" (Arendt 1951, 269). The people who at the end of World War I had been pushed out of their own states and were now "wandering" between countries in Europe and elsewhere "had lost those rights which had been thought of and even defined as inalienable, namely, the Rights of Man." After the Second World War, different scenarios, including forced exchanges of populations, were tried, but they did nothing to lighten the plight of the rightless and the stateless. Says Arendt, "The very phrase 'human rights' became for all concerned—victims, persecutors and onlookers alike—the evidence of hopeless idealism or fumbling feeble minded hypocrisy" (269). Seventy years later that kind of hypocrisy is still very much with us.

But things have changed in that we now have both a large international legal human rights system and a huge human rights movement. Even so, with a qualification noted later, I concur when Kesby rejects as hosts for Arendt's meta-right the national, the human of international human rights law, and also whoever engages in dissensual politics. Kesby argues that these options still fall short of the universality that is needed to properly host Arendt's meta-right. It is true that when we look at the details of the international legal system, these options too lack sufficient universality. Too much is delegated to individual states to make this legal system responsive to the moral universality stipulated in the Universal Declaration. There always is an element of transcendence left that cannot be captured by a fractured international legal system. This then makes the politics of human rights a necessity.

Kesby concludes, "What we need is not one final and definitive crossword-filling answer to the problem of the rights to have rights, but quite to the contrary a way of precisely *delegitimating* any hastily given answer when it reaches the limits of its helpfulness. The place-holder does not need to be named. It needs to be *un-named*" (Kesby 2012, 144; original italics). By delegitimating Arendt's idea of a meta-right, Kesby has yielded the floor to Arendt's well-known skepticism about human rights. Like Arendt, Kesby misreads the importance of the Universal Declaration, but unlike Arendt, she does not have an excuse. Arendt had the excuse of writing only a few years after 1948; she had no way of knowing the trajectory that the Genocide Convention and the Universal Declaration would take. Because she had no way of knowing how many millions of people would some seventy years later be involved in the politics of human rights implementation, Arendt misjudged the importance of the Universal Declaration as a text for the movement that has sprung up since her time. We today know the remarkable legacy of that pivotal text and the developments it has brought about in international affairs, politics, and law since the end of World War II. Since to Arendt the abstractions of the then-newly adopted Universal Declaration evidenced "hopeless idealism," she prematurely picked citizenship in Westphalian-type states as the only way to implement that vision.

Pace Kesby, I think that Arendt's search for flesh and blood universality is legitimate. I propose "every human being" as having this right to have rights, no one excluded. For there is no state of exception. Almost every article of the UDHR starts out that way, and there is nothing abstract about that. Just as we might say that every cottage in a certain village is painted white, so the drafters of the Universal Declaration declared some thirty times over that "everyone" has a certain human right. The question is not whether those who have the human rights of the UDHR are flesh and blood human beings—for they clearly are—but whether the politics of human rights can change the lives of the millions of people who for one reason or another do not enjoy one or more of their birthrights. The question of whether there is a single subject in or focus to the politics of human rights clearly is a legitimate one.

Following up on his 1992 book, *On the Shores of Politics*, Jacques Rancière answers our question in a provocative 2004 essay titled "Who Is the Subject of the Rights of Man?" Rancière believes that he can escape what he calls Arendt's "ontological trap" when she claims that the subject of human rights is *either* the citizen of a constitutional state (who therefore has the rights that come with that membership) *or* the rightless person who has been made stateless and now wanders between and outside the borders of those constitutional states where there are no laws that cover those outsiders and where there are no leaders who even want to oppress them. For Arendt these outsiders have the bare life that Agamben spoke of, but—living in the state of exception against which I argued earlier—they do not have rights of any kind. Rancière thinks this is absurd. He thinks there is a third option between being a citizen or being in that weird state of exception in which no law whatsoever applies. Arendt need not have adopted such a "rigid opposition between the realm of politics and the realm of private life," and Agamben should not have stopped short at his observation that in the modern world, we witness a huge increase of the identification of sovereign power with biopower. I agree with Rancière when he looks at "the Holocaust as the hidden truths of the Rights of Man" and also with his astute comparison of the concentration camps with contemporary "camps of refugees, [and] the zones where illegal migrants are parked by national authorities" (Rancière 2004, 301). Agamben and others miss Rancière's point that those very states of exception and people-storage zones give rise to the politics of human rights. According to Rancière, these zones and numerous isolated violations of the rights of man and of citizen (which are not limited to those who seem to have nothing left but their bares lives) invite us to reflect on the use of what Rancière calls "syllogisms of emancipation," which I think must use the Universal Declaration as their first premise (Rancière 1995, 45).

The structure of these syllogisms is what one would expect; they have two premises and a conclusion. "The major premise contains what the law has to say; the minor, what is said or done elsewhere, any word or deed that contradicts the fundamental legal/political affirmation of equality" (Rancière 1995, 46). The conclusion would be the removal of the contradiction, which is the restitution of the violated right. Rancière gives as example the French Charter of 1830. As do the charters of many other nations, that 1830 French one promulgated in its preamble that all French people are equal before the law, as UDHR Article 7 also does. That is the major premise. But in 1933 French workers in the tailoring industry in Paris "went on strike because their master tailors refused to respond to their demands relating to rates of pay, working hours and working conditions" (45–46). The minor premise here comes from the fact that Monsieur Schwartz, the head of the master tailors' association, was not treating these workers as equals, and this discrimination "contradict[ed] the equality inscribed in the Charter" (46). By going on strike, the workers called attention to the subsidiary, "minor" premise case of inequality, appealing to equality promulgated in the major premise. In any of these emancipation syllogisms—which I invite my reader to multiply—the major premise is always some kind of inscribed right, while the minor premise is a local political enactment, calling attention to a conflict with that inscribed equality, thereby bringing that inscribed equality "home" to a local situation in which it is being violated. Hence this chapter's title: "Enacting the Connection." The enactment does this by acting *as if* the equality already exists. The strike in Rancière's example is a minor enactment of the major premise found in the 1830 French Charter. For us that would be vigorously drawing attention to any violation of the rights inscribed in the 1948 Universal Declaration or its international legal offspring. That could be done through protesting by sit-in, crossing borders, or bringing violations to the attention of courts of law or of United Nations organs of oversight. For Rancière, the subject or possessor of human rights is the person who engages in these kinds of enactments. For us it is whoever chooses to enact any article of the Universal Declaration.

Rancière thinks there are two ways of understanding the contradiction between the major premise and the violation that then leads to the minor enacted premise. Either the equality inscribed in the 1830 French Charter is real and the workers' demands are justified, or it is spurious and "illusory," in which case the charter must be rewritten and corrected. For us, either the human rights in the Universal Declaration are real moral rights that everyone has or they are illusory. Either the word "everyone" in UDHR Article 5 on torture covered Giulio Regeni, a twenty-eight-year-old Italian graduate student doing research on Egypt's labor movement, or it is not that inclusive and Regeni is not covered. His body was found on Wednesday, February 3, 2016, on an Egyptian roadside and, according to Egyptian authorities, showed signs of "extensive torture." This despicable deed is a violation of UDHR Article 5 and ICCPR Article 7, as well as of the Convention Against Torture and Other Cruel, Inhuman, or Degrading Treatment or Punishment, which both Italy and Egypt have ratified. With a discovery like this, the domestic and international politics of human rights kick into action. Domestically, Egyptians noted that their own citizens are tortured on a regular basis. Internationally, Italian and Interpol investigators flew to Egypt to "allow for a joint investigation." In the meantime the *New York Times* reported that Egyptian authorities said they had "arrested and were investigating two suspects in Giza" (Walsh 2016). There will never be an end to these and other examples of human rights violations, which is why I call this conclusion "Enacting the Connection." The verb here is a present participle, indicating the action is in progress, because it is up to the human rights movement through its myriad activities to enact the text of the Universal Declaration. A movement needs a text, and ours has one that has stood the test of time, both in its own right and through its multiple offspring. The just-mentioned CAT is only one of the many texts that make up chapter 4's elephant.

Rancière thinks that his syllogisms of emancipation do not merely oppose word and deed but oppose "word to word and deed to deed" (Rancière 1995, 47). Against Monsieur Schwartz's act of dismissal, the striking garment workers placed their own act of the strike. "Against this logic of outright rejection the new practice of the strike strove to transform an alignment of forces into a logical confrontation. This did not simply mean substituting words for action; rather, it meant transforming a power relationship by means of a practice of logical demonstration" (47). Through the act of striking, the workers created the truth of the minor premise that indeed the workers had a dignity equal to that of their masters, which—if they were successful—would then remove the contradiction. Such enactments of inscribed rights take "what is usually thought of as something to be dismissed, as a groundless claim, [and] transforms it into its opposite—into the grounds for a claim, into a space for an open dispute. The evocation of equality is thus not *nothing*. A word has all the power originally given it" (47). This is an interesting observation. From where does a charter get its original power? We know and Rancière admits that people are not readily convinced by words alone and that "other kinds of arguments have always been needed. Thus the reasonable arguments of the strikers of 1833 were audible, their demonstration visible, only because the events of 1830, recalling those of 1789, had torn them from the nether world of inarticulate sounds and ensconced them by a contingent forced-entry in the world of meaning and visibility" (49).

I have argued in this book that the Holocaust brought about the "forced entry" of the Universal Declaration into the world of moral meanings and law. This 1948 declaration too was "torn from the nether world of inarticulate sounds" called the Holocaust. Rancière may well be right when he tells us that "the repetition of egalitarian words is a repetition of that [original] forced-entry, which is why the space of shared meaning it opens up is not a space of consensus" (Rancière 1995, 48) but one of dissensus that comes with hard-fought human rights battles. The politics of human rights is the politics of a movement that knits together a series of these syllogisms of emancipation and liberation. By taking the declaration's text as its major premise and its master text and making use of its original Holocaust power, the movement honors the Holocaust victims while it creates minor premises through litigation (often using the declaration's legal offspring), obstruction, and border crossings.

I think Rancière is wrong to suppose that human rights have just "two forms of existence": one as inscribed in the just-mentioned charters and codes and one as "the rights of those who make something of that inscription" (Rancière 2004, 303) when they cross those borders or litigate before domestic or international courts. He sees the situations of equality as enunciated in these inscriptions and of inequality as portrayed in situations of oppression, persecution, and total neglect as material for these syllogisms of emancipation and liberation. I do too, but, unlike Rancière, I do not look on this possession of human rights as a matter of abstraction and mere inscription that must be acted on by possessors (or passed on to others to act on their behalf) to be made real. Rancière chides Arendt for wanting to think of these "rights as *belong[ing]* to definite or permanent subjects" (306; original italics), which then made her pick the category of citizens as a host for this right to have rights. Instead, Rancière believes that the possessor of these human rights is whoever takes up the mantle of dissensus and disturbs the political equilibrium of liberal consensus politics. For him the subject of human rights is the subject of this dissensus politics that fights the status quo and therefore constantly changes from friction point to friction point, always re-creating the birth of the inscribed rights using the original moral power of the text in the major premise. The subject or possessor of human rights changes from human rights battle to human rights battle. For any subject of human rights to become a real possessor of those rights, that person—that subject—must appropriate and draw to himself or herself those rights by enacting the inscription. Without such enactment, the possession is not real. If she cannot do this herself, others can "inherit" (Rancière's term) the rights she wants to make real. These inheritors can then make those rights real for the violated person. Only the politics of human rights (engaged in by the victims or by those who "inherited" the mantle of dissensus) is what makes these rights real. They are not real rights until, after enactment, they are enjoyed as such. The enactment is what makes them real rights. I disagree for two reasons.

First, Kesby is correct to point out that Rancière stresses the self-emancipation aspect of these enactments too much. Rancière's account of the subject of human rights is still too exclusionary. Citing Watkin, Kesby notes that Rancière "risks excluding from his account those who do not have the capacity to militate for their equal treatment in the manner he prescribes for the *sans-part*" (Kesby 2012, 132), by which Rancière meant those who have no part in the social order. Kesby comments that this incapacity may be internal to the person, as it is for those suffering from "extreme old age" or "congenital disease," or it may be externally imposed, as when the person is confined to an isolated immigration detention center and faces "the enervating predicament of indefinite detention" (133). The person could be housed in one of the many refugee camps scattered around the world, often with no prospect of being able to leave that camp. Incapacity can also result when someone has been locked in solitary confinement by a dictatorial regime and Amnesty International has not yet heard about one's plight. Or it may be that local authorities ignore the fact that the nation, state, or town they represent has ratified a human rights convention that calls for "equality before the law," as almost all of them do. The point is that Rancière ignores the fact that most of the political enactments of inscribed human rights are not done by the victims themselves—though the millions who are fleeing drought or war-torn nations seem to belie this statement—but by those who "inherit" their enactments.

Second, and just as important, is that the idea that to be real a human right must be enacted sells short the influence of the Holocaust on the text of the Universal Declaration. Rancière writes as if those who enact the ensconced rights live in Carl Schmitt's state of exception, but I have argued that there is no such thing or state. The idea that to be real a human right must be enacted belittles the dignity of the victims behind the barbed wire who all along possessed those rights but were prevented from ever enjoying them in the spaces they lived, were incarcerated, were worked to death, or were experimented on. This distinction between possession and enjoyment is crucial. The 65 million internal and external refugees in today's world make human rights violations visible for all to see. The Westphalian system is clearly not delivering what the 1948 visionaries hoped it would. They presciently wrote in their third recital that "*Whereas it is essential, if a man is not to have recourse, as a last resort, to rebellion against tyranny and oppression, that human rights should be protected by the rule of law.*" This rule of law is used to define what a contemporary modern state is and sets the boundary outside which Westphalian nation-states cannot accept or condone protest and dissent, which then leads to millions of people being placed into one of these supposed states of exception. While these people are clearly under the law, they, as Schmitt saw it, just as clearly are totally outside it, as were the millions murdered by the Nazis in and outside the camps. The concentration camp inmates were totally excluded from the human community by decision of the German sovereign state and placed outside any law that would hold culpable those who did the killing, starving, and torturing. But the first recital of the UDHR does not say that this rule of law, as reflected in domestic and international legal systems, should *create* human rights. It says that inherently possessed human rights should be *protected* by this rule of law, meaning that these rights have a pre-political and pre-juridical existence independent of the rule of domestic or international positive law. It means that there is no state of exception anywhere no matter all the attempts to make it look like there is.

Rancière's syllogisms of emancipation and enactment create a clash between this Westphalian system of nation-states that controls most of our planet and the one-world ethical community envisioned by the Universal Declaration of Human Rights. Clashes occur when and wherever millions of members of the human rights movement decide to enact the connection between the Holocaust or any other abomination and the Universal Declaration that this book has sought to uphold and defend. It isn't just that the Holocaust abomination led the international community to draw up a "mere" inscription or to ensconce rights in a text or a document. This is the mistake that the international legal positivists of chapters 4 and 5 make when they allow the elephant to swallow up "the preambular rhetoric" coming from the Universal Declaration. Treaty inscriptions only create these rights as legal mirrors of the moral ones that came out of the Holocaust, where they were seen because they were grossly violated by the Third Reich. Just as the violence of the French Revolution caused the 1789 Declaration of the Rights of Man and of Citizen to be written—unfortunately collapsing these two categories for far too long—so the absolute evil of the Holocaust led to the realization that *every* human being has and possesses these moral rights from the day of his or her birth.

Every human being is the subject of the meta-right to have rights, inherently so. While Hannah Arendt picked the wrong subject (the citizen), she was right about wanting to locate these rights in definite and concrete flesh and blood human beings. The human rights of the Universal Declaration are possessed by every living human being long before violations take place or the ensconced rights are enacted at a later time. The problem is that millions of people do not presently enjoy a great many of these moral birthrights. It is the purpose of the human rights movement to expand and extend that enjoyment. Fortunately, it has a solid text from which to draw the moral energy to go and do battle.

Notes

1. To find these listings, I referred to Remember Us: The Holocaust Bnai Mitzvah Project (n.d.). Names of and URLs for the centers (listed in the following notes) have been updated to those current in June 2018.
2. See Gross Center for Holocaust & Genocide Studies, Ramapo College of New Jersey, https://www.ramapo.edu/holocaust/.
3. See Herbert and Leonard Littman Families Holocaust Resource Center, Rutgers University, https://bildnercenter.rutgers.edu/holocaust-education/about-hrc.
4. See Alabama Holocaust Commission, http://www.alabamaholocaustcommission.org.
5. See the mission statement of the Mgrublian Center for Human Rights, Claremont McKenna College, at https://www.cmc.edu/human-rights/mission-statement.
6. See Center for Holocaust and Human Rights Education, Florida Atlantic University, http://fau.edu/pjhr/chhre/.
7. See Illinois Holocaust Museum & Education Center, https://www.ilholocaustmuseum.org/.
8. See Holocaust & Human Rights Education Center, https://hhrecny.org/; and Holocaust, Genocide, and Human Rights Project, Monroe Community College, http://www.monroecc.edu/organizations/holocaust/.
9. See Dallas Holocaust Museum / Center for Education and Tolerance, http://www.dallasholocaustmuseum.org.
10. See Vancouver Holocaust Education Center, http://www.vhec.org.
11. See Holocaust Memorial and Tolerance Center of Nassau County, https://www.hmtcli.org/.

REFERENCES

Note about References to United Nations Documents

Aside from references to secondary sources throughout this book, the reader will encounter numerous parenthetical references to United Nations minutes of meetings and documents used in those meetings. Most citations from or references to the various meetings use the designation GAOR (General Assembly Official Records) followed by the number of the assembly session, the third session being in 1948, three years after the 1945 birth of the UN. That session number is then followed by the number of a plenary meeting or by the meeting number of a session of one of two committees, the Third Social, Economic, Humanitarian Committee or the Sixth Juridical Committee. For the 1950s references, the number of a meeting is followed by the paragraph number from which the citation was taken. Since in the late 1940s, the page numbering in the official records is continuous and does not give paragraph numbers, for those years I have simply given the page number after the session of either the General Assembly or one of the two committees. All the documents issued for use by the General Assembly start with an *A* and those of the Economic and Social Council begin with an *E*. Since the Commission of Human Rights, which drafted the UDHR, is a creature of the Economic and Social Council, its references also start with an *E*, to which is added "CN.4," which refers to this Commission. "SR" in these references stands for the "Summary Records," which are the minutes of meetings held by the Human Rights Commission or by its drafting subsidiary. The last number always refers to the page number of the meeting or of the document involved. All this material can be found through most general UN search sites such as https://search.un.org (searches the entire UN site); http://www.un.org/en/ga/documents (searches for specific documents); http://research.un.org/en (searches the whole UN Library); http://research.un.org/en/undhr (relates specifically to the UDHR); http://legal.un.org/avl/historicarchives.html (searches the audiovisual library of international law at the UN).

References

Agamben, Giorgio. 1998. *Homo Sacer: Sovereign Power and Bare Life*. Translated by Daniel Heller-Roazen. Stanford, CA: Stanford University Press.

Alston, Philip. 1982. "A Third Generation of Solidarity Rights: Progressive Development or Obfuscation of International Human Rights Law?" *Netherlands International Law Review* 29 (3): 307–22.

———. 1984. "Conjuring Up New Human Rights: A Proposal for Quality Control." *American Journal of International Law* 78 (3): 607–21.

———. 2001. "People's Rights: Their Rise and Fall." In *Peoples' Rights*, edited by Philip Alston, 259–73. Oxford: Oxford University Press.

American Society for International Law. 2011. *International Law: 100 Ways It Shapes Our Lives*. https://www.asil.org/sites/default/files/100%20Ways%20Booklet_2011.pdf.

Améry, Jean. 1980. *At the Mind's Limits: Contemplations by a Survivor on Auschwitz and Its Realities*. Translated by Sidney Rosenfeld and Stella P. Rosenfeld. Bloomington: Indiana University Press.

Arendt, Hannah. 1976. *The Origins of Totalitarianism*. San Diego, New York, London: Harcourt, Brace & Company.

Bauer, Yehuda. 1998. "A Past That Will Not Go Away." In *The Holocaust and History: The Known, the Unknown, the Disputed, and the Reexamined*, edited by Michael Berenbaum and Abraham J. Peck, 12–22. Bloomington: Indiana University Press.

Beitz, Charles R. 2009. *The Idea of Human Rights*. New York: Oxford University Press.

Bell, George. 1949. In *Man's Disorder and God's Design*, by the World Council of Churches, 412. New York: Harper & Brothers.

Bleicher, Samuel A. 1969. "The Legal Significance of Re-citation of General Assembly Resolutions." *American Journal of International Law* 63 (3): 444–78. doi: 10.2307/2198866.

Boerefijn, Ineke. 1999. *The Reporting Procedure under the Covenant on Civil and Political Rights: Practice and Procedures of the Human Rights Committee.* Oxford: Intersentia/Hart.

Borgwardt, Elizabeth. 2005. *A New Deal for the World: America's Vision for Human Rights*. Cambridge, MA: Belknap Press of Harvard University Press.

Bossuyt, Marc. 1987. *Guide to the "Travaux Préparatoires" of the International Covenant on Civil and Political Rights*. Boston: Martinus Nijhoff.

Bosteels, Bruno. 2016. "Introduction: This People Which Is Not One." In *What Is a People?*, edited by Alain Badiou, Pierre Bourdieu, Judith Butler, Georges Didi-Huberman, Sadri Khiari, and Jacques Rancière, 1–20. New York: Columbia University Press.

Brinks, Daniel M., and Varun Gauri. 2014. "The Law's Majestic Equality? The Distributive Impact of Judicializing Social and Economic Rights." *Perspectives on Politics* 12 (2): 375–93. doi: 10.1017/S1537592714000887.

Browning, Christopher. 2016. "The Two Different Ways of Looking at Nazi Murder." *New York Review of Books* 63 (18): 56–58.

Brownlie, Ian, and Guy S. Goodwin-Gill. 2006. *Basic Documents on Human Rights*. 5th ed. New York: Oxford University Press.

Buchanan, Allen E. 2004. *Justice, Legitimacy, and Self-Determination: Moral Foundations for International Law*. New York: Oxford University Press.

———. 2013. *The Heart of Human Rights*. Oxford: Oxford University Press.

Cioran, E. M. 2012. *Drawn and Quartered.* Translated by Richard Howard. New York: Skyhorse Publishing.

Claeys, Gregory. 2015. "Socialism and the Language of Rights: The Origins and Implications of Economic Rights." In *Revisiting the Origins of Human Rights*, edited by Miia Halme-Tuomisaari and Pamela Slotte, 206–38. Cambridge: Cambridge University Press.

Cohen, G. Daniel. 2012. "The Holocaust and the 'Human Rights Revolution': A Reassessment." In *The Human Rights Revolution: An International History*, edited by Akira Iriye, Petra Goedde, and William I. Hitchcock, 53–72. New York: Oxford University Press.

Crawford, James. 1988. "Some Conclusions." In *The Rights of Peoples*, edited by James Crawford, 159–77. New York: Oxford University Press.

Cruft, Rowan. 2015. "Human Rights Law without Natural Moral Rights." *Ethics and International Affairs* 29 (2): 223–32. doi: 10.1017/S0892679415000088.

de Búrca, Gráinne. 2017. "Human Rights Experimentalism." *American Journal of International Law* 111 (2): 277–316. doi: 10.1017/ajil.2016.16.

Dershowitz, Alan M. 2005. *Rights from Wrongs: A Secular Theory of the Origins of Rights*. New York: Basic Books.

Duranti, Marco. 2012. "The Holocaust, the Legacy of 1789 and the Birth of International Human Rights Law: Revisiting the Foundation Myth." *Journal of Genocide Research* 14 (2): 159–86. doi: 10.1080/14623528.2012.677760.

Eckel, Jan. 2014. "The Rebirth of Politics from the Spirit of Morality: Explaining the Human Rights Revolution of the 1970s." In *The Breakthrough: Human Rights in the 1970s*, edited by Jan Eckel and Samuel Moyn, 226–59. Philadelphia: University of Pennsylvania Press.

Falk, Richard A. 1966. "On the Quasi-Legislative Competence of the General Assembly." *American Journal of International Law* 60 (4): 782–91. doi: 10.2307/2196928.

Fariss, Christopher J. 2014. "Respect for Human Rights Has Improved over Time: Modeling the Changing Standard of Accountability." *American Political Science Review* 108 (2): 297–318. doi: 10.1017/S0003055414000070.

Fried, Gregory. 1998. "*Inhalt Unzulässig*: Late Mail from Lodz—A Meditation on Time and Truth." In *Postmodernism and the Holocaust*, edited by Alan Milchman and Alan Rosenberg, 23–52. Amsterdam: Rodopi.

Gardner, Philip. 2010. *Hermeneutics, History and Memory*. London: Routledge.

Gewirth, Alan. 1978. *Reason and Morality*. Chicago: University of Chicago Press.

———. 1982. *Human Rights: Essays on Justification and Applications*. Chicago: University of Chicago Press.

———. 1996. *The Community of Rights*. Chicago: University of Chicago Press.

Glendon, Mary Ann. 2001. *A World Made New: Eleanor Roosevelt and the Universal Declaration of Human Rights*. New York: Random House.

Goodale, Mark. 2009. *Surrendering to Utopia: An Anthropology of Human Rights*. Stanford, CA: Stanford University Press.

Griffin, James. 2008. *On Human Rights*. Oxford: Oxford University Press.

Hart, H. L. A. 1961. *The Concept of Law*. Oxford: Clarendon.

Hochschild, Adam. 2005. *Bury the Chains: Prophets, Slaves, and Rebels in the First Human Rights Crusade*. Boston: Houghton Mifflin.

Hohfeld, Wesley N. 1917. "Fundamental Legal Conceptions as Applied in Judicial Reasoning." Faculty Scholarship Series, Paper 4378. Yale University Law School. http://digitalcommons.law.yale.edu/fss_papers/4378.

Hopgood, Stephen. 2013. *The Endtimes of Human Rights*. Ithaca, NY: Cornell University Press.

Humphrey, John P. 1967. "The Charter of the United Nations and the Declaration." In *The International Protection of Human Rights*, edited by Evan Luard, 39–58. London: Thames and Hudson.

Hunt, Lynn. 2007. *Inventing Human Rights: A History*. New York: W. W. Norton.

Ishay, Micheline R. 2004. *The History of Human Rights from Ancient Times to the Globalization Era*. Berkeley: University of California Press.

Joyner, Christopher C. 1981. "UN General Assembly Resolutions and International Law: Rethinking the Contemporary Dynamics of Norm-Creation." *California Western International Law Journal* 11: 445–78.

Kaiser, Wolfram. 2007. "Hegemony by Default: Christian Democracy in Postwar Europe." In *Christian Democracy and the Origins of European Union*, 163–90. Cambridge University Press.

Kesavan, Mukul. 2018. "Murderous Majorities." *New York Review of Books*, January 18, 2018, 37.

Kesby, Alison. 2012. *The Right to Have Rights: Citizenship, Humanity, and International Law*. Oxford: Oxford University Press.

Kingsbury, Benedict. 2001. "Reconciling Five Competing Conceptual Structures of Indigenous Peoples' Claims in International and Comparative Law." In *People's Rights*, edited by Philip Alston, 69–110. Oxford: Oxford University Press.

Kittay, Eva. 2017. "Moral Significance of Being Human." 113th Eastern Division Meeting of the American Philosophical Association, Baltimore, MD, January 6, 2017. https://www.researchgate.net/publication/321947320_The_Moral_Significance_of_Being_Human.

Korey, William. 1998. *NGOs and the Universal Declaration of Human Rights: A Curious Grapevine*. New York: St. Martin's Press.

Kymlicka, Will. 1989. *Liberalism, Community, and Culture*. Oxford: Clarendon Press.

———. 2002. *Can Liberal Pluralism Be Exported? Western Political Theory and Ethnic Relations in Eastern Europe*. Oxford: Oxford University Press.

———. 2010. "Minority Rights in Political Philosophy and International Law." In *The Philosophy of International Law*, edited by Samantha Besson and John Tasioulas, 377–83. Oxford: Oxford University Press.

Kymlicka, Will, and Magda Opalski, eds. 2002. *Can Liberal Pluralism Be Exported? Western Political Theory and Ethnic Relations in Eastern Europe*. Oxford: Oxford University Press.

La Chapelle, Philippe de. 1967. *La Déclaration Universelle des Droits de l'Homme et le Catholicisme. Lettre liminaire de René Cassin*. Paris: Librairie Générale de Droit et de Jurisprudence, R. Pichon & R. Durand-Auzias.

Lash, Joseph P. 1972. *Eleanor: The Years Alone*. New York: Norton.

Lauren, Paul Gordon. 1998. *The Evolution of International Human Rights: Visions Seen*. Philadelphia: University of Pennsylvania Press.

Lyotard, Jean-François. 1993. "The Other's Rights." In *On Human Rights: The Oxford Amnesty Lectures*, edited by Stephen Shute and Susan L. Hurley, 135–48. New York: Basic Books / HarperCollins.

Macklem, Patrick. 2015. *The Sovereignty of Human Rights*. Oxford: Oxford University Press.

Maritain, Jacques. 1971. *The Rights of Man and Natural Law*. New York: Gordian Press. First published 1943 by Charles Scribner's Sons.

———. 1973. *Human Rights: Comments and Interpretation*. Westport, CT: Greenwood University Press. First published 1949 by Columbia University Press.

Morsink, Johannes. 1999a. "Cultural Genocide, the Universal Declaration, and Minority Rights." *Human Rights Quarterly* 21 (4): 1009–60.

———. 1999b. *The Universal Declaration of Human Rights: Origins, Drafting, and Intent*. Philadelphia: University of Pennsylvania Press.

———. 2009. *Inherent Human Rights: Philosophical Roots of the Universal Declaration*. Philadelphia: University of Pennsylvania Press.

———. 2017. *The Universal Declaration of Human Rights and the Challenge of Religion*. Columbia: University of Missouri Press.

Moskowitz, Moses. 1976. "Whither the United Nations Human Rights Program?" *Israel Yearbook on Human Rights* 6: 81–90.

Mower, Alfred Glenn. 1979. *The United States, the United Nations, and Human Rights: The Eleanor Roosevelt and Jimmy Carter Eras*. Westport, CT: Greenwood Press.

Moyn, Samuel. 2010. *The Last Utopia: Human Rights in History*. Cambridge, MA: Belknap Press of Harvard University Press.

———. 2014. *Human Rights and the Uses of History*. New York: Verso.

———. 2015a. *Christian Human Rights*. Philadelphia: University of Pennsylvania Press.

———. 2015b. "Giuseppe Mazzini in (and Beyond) the History of Human Rights." In *Revisiting the Origins of Human Rights*, edited by Miia Halme-Tuomisaari and Pamela Slotte, 119–39. Cambridge: Cambridge University Press.

Müller, Ingo. 1991. *Hitler's Justice: The Courts of the Third Reich*. Translated by Deborah Lucas Schneider. Cambridge, MA: Harvard University Press.

Neier, Aryeh. 2012. *The International Human Rights Movement: A History*. Princeton, NJ: Princeton University.

Nersessian, David. 2005. “Rethinking Cultural Genocide under International Law.” *Human Rights Dialogue* 2 (12): 7–8. https://www.carnegiecouncil.org/publications/archive/dialogue/2_12/section_1/5139/.

Nicol, Danny. 2005. “Original Intent and the European Convention on Human Rights.” *Public Law*, April: 152–72.

Nolde, O. Frederick. 1948a. “Freedom of Religion and Related Human Rights.” In *Man's Disorder and God's Design*, by the World Council of Churches, 143–210. New York: Harper & Brothers.

———. 1948b. “The United Nations Acts for Human Rights, Release by the American Committee for the World Council of Churches.” *Michigan Christian Advocate*, December 30.

Novic, Elisa. 2017. *The Concept of Cultural Genocide: An International Law Perspective*. Oxford: Oxford University Press.

Nurser, John. 2005. *For All Peoples and All Nations: The Ecumenical Church and Human Rights*. Washington, DC: Georgetown University Press.

Orgad, Liav. 2015. *The Cultural Defense of Nations: A Liberal Theory of Majority Rights*. Oxford: Oxford University Press.

Parekh, Bhikhu C. 2000. *Rethinking Multiculturalism: Cultural Diversity and Political Theory*. Cambridge: Harvard University Press.

Patten, Alan. 2014. *Equal Recognition: The Moral Foundations of Minority Rights*. Princeton, NJ: Princeton University Press.

Pius XI, Pope. 1937a. *Divini Redemptoris: On Atheistic Communism*. Papal Encyclical, March 19, 1937. Papal Encyclicals Online, http://www.papalencyclicals.net/pius11/p11divin.htm.

———. 1937b. *Mit Brennender Sorge: On the Church and the German Reich*. Papal Encyclical, March 19, 1937. Papal Encyclicals Online, http://www.papalencyclicals.net/pius11/p11brenn.htm.

Plesch, Daniel. 2017. *Human Rights after Hitler: The Lost History of Prosecuting Axis War Crimes*. Washington, DC: Georgetown University Press.

Polgreen, Lydia. 2013. “As Extremists Invaded, Timbuktu Hid Artifacts of a Golden Age.” *New York Times*, February 3. https://www.nytimes.com/2013/02/04/world/africa/saving-timbuktus-priceless-artifacts-from-militants-clutches.html.

Posner, Eric A. 2014. *The Twilight of International Human Rights Law*. New York: Oxford University Press.

Putnam, Hilary. 1973. “Meaning and Reference.” *Journal of Philosophy* 70 (19): 699–711.

Rancière, Jacques. 1995. *On the Shores of Politics*. New York: Verso.

———. 2004. “Who Is the Subject of the Rights of Man?” *South Atlantic Quarterly* 103 (2): 297–310. doi: 10.1215/00382876-103-2-3-297.

Rawlence, Ben. 2016. *City of Thorns: Nine Lives in the World's Largest Refugee Camp*. New York: Picador.

Remember Us: The Holocaust Bnai Mitzvah Project. n.d. "Holocaust Centers, Museums and Resources." Accessed June 21, 2018. http://www.remember-us.org/pdfs/holocaust-centers.pdf.

Ritter, Gerhard. 1949. "Ursprung Und Wesen Der Menschenrechte" [The origin and nature of human rights]. *Historische Zeitschrift* 169 (1): 233–63. doi: 10.1515/hzhz-1949-0139.

Robinson, Nehemiah. 1950. *The Universal Declaration of Human Rights: Its Origin, Significance, Application, and Interpretation*. New York: Institute of Jewish Affairs, World Jewish Congress.

Rodick, David W. 2011. "Review of Samuel Moyn, *The Last Utopia: Human Rights in History*." *Review of Metaphysics* 65 (1): 176–77.

Romulo, Carlos P. 1986. *Forty Years: A Third World Soldier at the UN*. With Beth D. Romulo. New York: Greenwood.

Roosevelt, Eleanor. 1999. *Courage in a Dangerous World: The Political Writings of Eleanor Roosevelt*. Edited by Allida M. Black. New York: Columbia University Press.

Roth, John K. 2015. *The Failures of Ethics: Confronting the Holocaust, Genocide, and Other Mass Atrocities*. Oxford: Oxford University Press.

Sands, Philippe. 2016. *East West Street: On the Origins of "Genocide" and "Crimes against Humanity."* London: Weidenfeld & Nicolson.

Saul, Ben, ed. 2016. *The International Covenant on Economic, Social and Cultural Rights*. Vol. 1, *1946–1948 Travaux Préparatoires*. Oxford: Oxford University Press.

Schabas, William, ed. 2013. *The Universal Declaration of Human Rights: The Travaux Préparatoires*. 3 vols. Cambridge: Cambridge University Press. https://books.google.com/books?id=dXPtAgAAQBAJ.

Schmitt, Carl. 2005. *Political Theology: Four Chapters on the Concept of Sovereignty*. Chicago: University of Chicago Press.

Sellars, Kirsten. 2002. *The Rise and Rise of Human Rights*. Stroud: Sutton.

Sepúlveda, M. Magdalena. 2003. *The Nature of the Obligations under the International Covenant on Economic, Social and Cultural Rights*. Oxford: Intersentia/Hart.

Shelton, Dinah. 2015. "Review of *The Twilight of Human Rights Law*." *American Journal of International Law* 109 (1): 228–34.

Sikkink, Kathryn. 2011. *The Justice Cascade: How Human Rights Prosecutions Are Changing World Politics*. New York: W. W. Norton.

———. 2017. *Evidence for Hope: Making Human Rights Work in the 21st Century*. Princeton, NJ: Princeton University Press.

Slotte, Pamela, and Miia Halme-Tuomisaari, eds. 2015. *Revisiting the Origins of Human Rights*. Cambridge: Cambridge University Press.

Snow, David A., and Robert D. Benford. 1992. "Master Frames and Cycles of Protest." In *Frontiers in Social Movement Theory*, edited by Aldon D. Morris and Carol McClurg Mueller, 133–55. New Haven, CT: Yale University Press.

Stamatopoulou, Elsa. 2007. *Cultural Rights in International Law: Article 27 of the Universal Declaration of Human Rights and Beyond*. Leiden: Martinus Nijhoff.

Taylor, Charles. 1994. *Multiculturalism: Examining the Politics of Recognition*. Princeton, NJ: Princeton University Press.

Toebes, Brigit. 1999. *The Right to Health as a Human Right in International Law*. Oxford: Intersentia.

Traer, Robert. 1991. *Faith in Human Rights: Support in Religious Traditions for a Global Struggle*. Washington, DC: Georgetown University Press.

United Nations. n.d. "Drafting of the Universal Declaration of Human Rights." Dag Hammarskjöld Library. Accessed June 8, 2018. http://research.un.org/en/undhr.

Verdoodt, Albert. 1963. *Naissance et signification de la declaration universelle des droits de l'homme, Louvain, Editions Nauwelaerts*. Paris: Societe d'Etudes Morales, Sociales et Juridiques.

Waldron, Jeremy. 2010. "Two Conceptions of Self Determination." In *The Philosophy of International Law*, edited by Samantha Besson and John Tasioulas, 397–413. Oxford: Oxford University Press.

Walsh, Declan. 2016. "Outrage Grows as Italy Investigates Student's Death in Egypt." *New York Times*, February 5. https://www.nytimes.com/2016/02/06/world/middleeast/outrage-grows-as-italy-investigates-students-death-in-egypt.html.

Wellman, Carl. 2011. *The Moral Dimensions of Human Rights*. New York: Oxford University Press.

Wolterstorff, Nicholas. 2008. *Justice: Rights and Wrongs*. Princeton, NJ: Princeton University Press.

Yergin, Daniel. 1977. *Shattered Peace: The Origins of the Cold War and the National Security State*. Boston: Houghton Mifflin.

INDEX

ABOUT THE AUTHOR

JOHANNES MORSINK is professor emeritus of political philosophy at Drew University and the author of three other books on the Universal Declaration, most recently *The Universal Declaration of Human Rights and the Challenge of Religion.*

www.ingramcontent.com/pod-product-compliance
Lightning Source LLC
LaVergne TN
LVHW050148080826
844660LV00002B/114

* 9 7 8 1 6 2 6 1 6 6 2 8 8 *